The Log College

Biographical sketches of William Tennent and his students, together with an account of the revivals under their ministries

Archibald Alexander

The Banner of Truth Trust
78B CHILTERN STREET, LONDON W.1

First published 1851
First Banner of Truth Trust edition 1968

Set in 11 on 12 pt. 'Monotype' Imprint
Printed and bound in Great Britain by
Billing & Sons Limited
Guildford and London

Contents

Dedication

TO THE REVEREND PRESBYTERY
OF NEW BRUNSWICK

DEAR BRETHREN,—There is a propriety in dedicating this book to you, as it owes its existence to your appointment of the author to deliver a centenary discourse on the 8th of August, 1838. A copy of this discourse you were pleased to ask for publication, a compliance with which the preacher respectfully declined, because he found that all the facts and documents relative to the origin of the New Brunswick Presbytery could not be included in a single discourse; but he determined to make use of such materials as he possessed, or could obtain, to form a small volume, and lay it before your reverend body. This purpose he has been enabled imperfectly to carry into effect; and he now solicits your candid and favourable attention to a work, which is intended to give the people of the present age an opportunity of seeing what the state of things in this region was a hundred years ago.

As most of those connected with the New Brunswick Presbytery, in its earliest days, were educated at Mr. Tennent's school, at Neshaminy, commonly called the Log College, to give some appearance of unity to the work, the history contained in it is connected with this humble, but useful Institution.

And as the time when this Presbytery had its origin was a period favoured with remarkable revivals of religion; and the men who then composed this Presbytery, eminent instruments in carrying forward this good work; it was judged to be expedient to give as distinct and full an account of the outpouring of the Spirit of God in those days as could now be obtained. And as narratives were written by those most intimately conversant with this great revival, which were printed in books now rarely to be met with, it was thought best to rescue these documents from oblivion, and give them unaltered in the very words of the original writers.

The editor cannot but think that the biographical sketches here given from authentic authorities will be acceptable to the present members of the Presbytery of New Brunswick; and he is persuaded, that the congregations in which the displays of divine grace were so wonderful a century past, will be benefited by a perusal of the narratives here given. Many pious people among us are not aware that the ground on which they tread has, as it were, been hallowed by the footsteps of the Almighty. And who knows but that prayers then offered in faith remain yet to be answered.

I am with sincere regard,
Your brother in the gospel of Christ,
ARCHIBALD ALEXANDER.

I

The Log College

Association gives interest to places—Log College—Name—Site—Size—
Utter Desolation—Country around—Dr. James P. Wilson—Relic—
Suggestion of a Monument—Importance of the Institution.

By association, objects which have nothing interesting in themselves acquire an importance, by reason of the persons or things
which they constantly suggest to our minds. The rock of Plymouth
has nothing in it which renders it intrinsically superior to thousands
of other rocks in the country; and the site of Jamestown has nothing
but its interesting associations to engage the attention of any one.
But these spots as being the first habitations of the European
settlers in this part of the new world, are invested with an interest
which is felt by all; and this interest, instead of growing weaker
by the lapse of time, gathers new strength every year. Indeed,
it is only a recent thing that the public attention has been particularly called to these objects. And though there may be an
excess in the emotions cherished by some, and an affectation of
lively interest in others; yet, it cannot be doubted that there is a
foundation in human nature for the interest which is excited by
particular objects, places, and scenes. And the more intimately
these associations are related to religion, the deeper and more
permanent the feeling becomes. By the abuse of this principle
much superstition has been generated; but the moderate and
judicious use of it may, undoubtedly, be conducive to piety.
Sacred or holy places figure largely in all false systems of religion:
and under the old dispensation, the people of God were encouraged
to reverence those places where the worship of God was appointed
to be celebrated. Under the gospel dispensation, it is true, we have
no holy places or houses to which the worship of God is confined;
but in every place, whether by sea or land, whether in the grove,
on the mountain top, or in the open field, or the lonely vale, God

may be worshipped. Yet who does not entertain peculiar feelings of interest in relation to those places where Christ was born—where he was brought up—where he preached and wrought miracles—but, especially, where he suffered and died, and where he was buried and arose again—and where he ascended to heaven, in the presence of his disciples. This feeling is natural, and associated with love to Christ, but it readily becomes excessive, and degenerates into superstition. There never was a book in which there is so little to foster superstition as the Bible. We never there read of the apostles, when they came up to Jerusalem, resorting to any of these places, or expressing the smallest degree of veneration for them. The natural tendency of the human mind seems to have been counteracted, for the very purpose of preventing superstition; just as the natural passions of the evangelists seem to have been restrained in writing the gospels.

Of late, considerable curiosity has been manifested to ascertain the place where the first Presbyterian church in this country was formed; and the history of the first Presbyterian preacher who came to America, which had sunk into oblivion, has, of late, been brought prominently into view. Such researches, when un-accompanied with boasting and vainglory, are laudable. And to gratify a similar curiosity, in regard to the first literary institution, above common schools, in the bounds of the Presbyterian church, this small book has been compiled. That institution, we believe, was what has been called the Log College. The reason of the epithet prefixed to the word 'College' might be obscure to a European; but in this country, where log-cabins are so numerous, it will be intelligible to all classes of readers. This edifice, which was made of logs, cut out of the woods, probably, from the very spot where the house was erected, was situated in Bucks county, Pennsylvania, about twenty miles north of Philadelphia. The Log College has long since disappeared; so that although the site on which it stood is well known to many in the vicinity, there is not a vestige of it remaining on the ground; and no appearance which would indicate that a house ever stood there. The fact is that some owner of the property, never dreaming that there was anything sacred in the logs of this humble edifice, had them carried away and applied to some ignoble purpose on the farm, where they have rotted away like common timber, from which, if any of them remain, they can no longer be distinguished. But that some small relic of this venerable building might be preserved, the late Presbyterian minister of the place, Rev. Robert B. Belville, some years ago, rescued from the common ruin so much of one of these logs as enabled him, by paring off the decayed parts, to reduce it to something of the form of a walking-staff; which, as a token of respect, and for safe keeping he presented to the late Rev. Samuel Miller, D.D., one of the oldest Professors of the Theological Seminary at Princeton, New Jersey.

The site of the Log College is about a mile from that part of Neshaminy creek where the Presbyterian church has long stood. The ground near and around it lies handsomely to the eye, and the more distant prospect is very beautiful; for while there is a considerable extent of fertile, well cultivated land, nearly level, the view is bounded to the north and west by a range of hills, which have a very pleasing appearance.

It may not be improper to observe that the late Rev. James P. Wilson, D.D., the learned and admired pastor of the first Presbyterian church in Philadelphia, was so pleased with the scenery and circumstances of this neighbourhood that he purchased a small farm, which is, I believe, as near to the site of the Log College as any other dwelling, except the one on the farm on which it was built. To this farm he retired when no longer able, through bodily weakness, to fulfil the arduous duties of the pastoral office. And here, in calm serenity, he spent the last years of his life.

If I were fond of projects, I would propose that a monument be erected to the founder of the Log College on the very site where the building stood, if the land could be purchased; but at any rate a stone with an inscription might be permanently fixed on or near the ground. The tradition respecting this humble institution of learning exists, not only in the neighbourhood, but has been extended far to the south and west.

The first Presbyterian ministers in this country were nearly all men of liberal education. Some had received their education in the universities of Scotland; some in Ireland; and others at one of the New England colleges. And though there existed such a destitution of ministers in this new country, they never thought of introducing any man into the ministry who had not received a college or university education, except in very extraordinary cases; of which, I believe, we have but one instance in the early history of the Presbyterian church. This was the case of a Welshman by the name of Evans, who, living in a place called the Welsh Tract, where the people had no public means of grace, began to speak to them of the things of God on the Sabbath and at other times; and his labours were so acceptable and useful that the presbytery, after a full trial of his abilities, licensed him to preach, and afterwards ordained him to the whole work of the ministry. They required him, however, to go through a course of study, under the direction of certain members of the Presbytery. There is, indeed, another case that may possibly fall into this class. 'The people of Cape May were without a pastor; Mr. Bradner, a candidate for the ministry, was willing to serve them, but had no authority to preach. In this emergency three of the nearest ministers, Messrs. Davis, Hampton and Henry, on their own responsibility, examined and licensed him.'[1] But as he was before a candidate, and a Scotchman, there is a strong probability that he was a liberally educated man.

There seems to be no written record of the existence of such an edifice as that which we are describing by any contemporary writer, except in the Journal of Rev. George Whitefield, the celebrated evangelist, who traversed this country several times, preaching everywhere with a popularity and success which have never been equalled by any other. It will be proper, therefore, to extract the paragraph which relates to this subject, as he gives the dimensions of the building, and expressly says that it had obtained the name of 'The College.' 'The place,' says he, 'wherein the young men study now, is in contempt called *The College*. It is a log house, about twenty feet long, and near as many broad; and to me it seemed to resemble the school of the old prophets, for their habitations were mean; and that they sought not great things for themselves is plain from those passages of Scripture, wherein we are told that each of them took them a beam to build them a house: and that at the feast of the sons of the prophets, one of them put on the pot, whilst the others went to fetch some herbs out of the field. All that we can say of most of our universities is, they are glorious without. From this despised place, seven or eight worthy ministers of Jesus have lately been sent forth; more are almost ready to be sent, and the foundation is now laying for the instruction of many others.' The Journal from which the preceding extract is taken was printed in Philadelphia by Benjamin

[1] See Records of the Synod of Philadelphia.

Franklin the same year in which Mr. Whitefield visited the Log College. From this testimony it appears that the name *College* was given to the building out of contempt by its enemies; but in this as in many other things, that which is lightly esteemed among men is precious in the sight of the Lord. Though as poor a house as perhaps was ever erected for the purpose of giving a liberal education, it was, in a noble sense, a College; a fountain from which, as we shall see hereafter, proceeded streams of blessings to the church. We shall again have occasion to advert to Mr. Whitefield's Journal, when we come to speak of the founder of this College; but we shall now proceed to finish what we have to say respecting the site and the building.

When the General Assembly of the Presbyterian Church in the United States determined, in the year 1811, to establish a Theological Seminary for the more thorough training of her candidates for the sacred office, there was much diversity of opinion respecting the most eligible site for the institution. Between Princeton, New Jersey, and Chambersburg, Pennsylvania, the chief competition existed; but there were a few persons who were strongly in favour of placing it on the very site of the Log College. The Rev. Nathaniel Irwin, then pastor of the church at Neshaminy, and a man of profound understanding, was earnestly desirous that it should be planted on the ground where a building had once stood to which the Presbyterian church owes so much. And to manifest his sincerity and zeal, Mr. Irwin left, in his will, one thousand dollars to the Seminary, on condition that it should be ultimately located on this site.

II

Memoir of the Rev. William Tennent, Sen.

A minister of the Irish Episcopal Church—Emigrates with his family to America—Applies for admission into the Synod and is received—Settles permanently at Neshaminy—Erects the Log College—Visits Whitefield, and is visited by him—His character and death.

We come now to give some account of the founder of the Log College. The Rev. William Tennent, sen., was a native of Ireland, where he was brought up and received a liberal education; but at what college or university is not known. It is probable, however, that he obtained his learning at Trinity College, Dublin, as he belonged originally to the Episcopal Church of Ireland, in which he took orders. By a small memorandum book kept by the Rev. William Tennent, sen., it appears that he was married to a daughter of the Rev. Mr. Kennedy, May, 1702, in the county of Down, in the north of Ireland; that he was ordained a deacon, in the Episcopal church of Ireland on the 1st day of July, 1704; and ordained priest on the 22nd of September, 1706. After entering the holy ministry, he acted as chaplain to an Irish nobleman. But there is no evidence that he was ever settled over a parish in that country; the reason assigned by the author of the Memoir of William Tennent, jr. was that he could not conscientiously conform to the terms imposed on the clergy of that kingdom. He remained in Ireland until he was past middle age. The truth is that very little is known of Mr. Tennent until he arrived in America. From Dr. Elias Boudinot, who was very intimate with the whole family, we learn that Mr. Tennent in Ireland became acquainted with the Rev. Mr. Kennedy, a distinguished Presbyterian preacher, who, having suffered persecution is his own country, exercised his ministry in Holland with great success. The only other notice of this zealous and evangelical preacher which has been found is in the 'Vindication' by the Rev. Samuel Blair, in which, speaking of the objections made to the revival, he says, 'Several have very sufficiently answered the objections against the work itself, as Mr. Edwards in New England, Mr. Dickinson in New Jersey, Mr. Finley in Pennsylvania, Mr. Robe and Mr. Webster in Scotland, and Mr. Kennedy in Holland.' He then remarks that Mr. Kennedy had published Mr. Edwards' 'Narrative', with attestations from Scotland, translated by him into the Dutch language. It would be very desirable to obtain some further information of this Mr. Kennedy, who is spoken of as a man of like spirit with Edwards, and Dickinson, and Robe, and Webster, and Finley. But probably there remains no earthly record of his labours, his sufferings, and successes.

Our attention has been directed to this man, not merely because Mr. Tennent became acquainted with him, but especially because he married his daughter, who was the mother of his four sons, and emigrated with him to America. And it is exceedingly probable that from this man Mr. Tennent imbibed his love of the Presbyterian system. Mr. Tennent's eldest son was no doubt called after his grandfather Kennedy, whose name was Gilbert.

In the Memoir of William Tennent, jr., it is said that his father arrived in America in the year 1718; but in the sketch of the life of Gilbert Tennent, in the Assembly's Magazine for May, 1805, 'that he came over in 1716,' which last is believed to be the more accurate statement. Upon his arrival, he settled first in the state of New York, where he resided for some time at East Chester, and then at Bedford. Not long after his emigration to America, Mr. Tennent applied to the Synod of Philadelphia to be received as a minister into their connexion. The Synod did not act hastily in this affair, but after full deliberation agreed to receive Mr. Tennent as a member of their body. Before doing this, however, they required him to lay before them in writing the reasons which had induced him to separate himself from the Episcopal church. And these reasons were ordered to be entered on record. The minute of the Synod, as found in the printed book of records of the Presbyterian church, is as follows: 'Mr. William Tennent's affair being transmitted by the committee [of overtures] to the Synod, was by them fully considered, being well satisfied with his credentials, and the testimony of some brethren here present;

as also, they were satisfied with the material reasons which he offered concerning his dissenting from the Established Church of Ireland; being put to a vote of the Synod, it was carried in the affirmative to admit him as a member of the Synod. Ordered, that his reasons be inserted on the Synod book *ad futuram rei memoriam.* The Synod also ordered that the moderator should give him a serious exhortation to continue steadfast in his now holy profession, which was done.'[1]

This transaction took place on the 17th day of September, 1718; it is probable, however, that Mr. Tennent's application was first made to the Synod the previous year; although nothing appears on the records relative to this matter. But in the short account of the Rev. William Tennent, sen., in the Assembly's Magazine, it is stated that after some delay he was received. And the minute recited above seems to speak of it as a thing before under consideration; for it would be very abrupt and unusual to speak of a first application in the language here used—'Mr. Tennent's affair,' &c., without any notice of any application made by him. It is probable that the application to Synod was made in the year 1717, which was the next year after his arrival.

Whether Mr. Tennent had the pastoral care of a church in the state of New York does not appear; but about the year 1721 he

[1] 'The reasons of Mr. William Tennent for his dissenting from the Established Church in Ireland, delivered by him to the Reverend Synod, held in Philadelphia, the 17th day of September, 1718.

'*Imprimis.* Their government by Bishops, Arch-Bishops, Deacons, Arch-Deacons, Canons, Chapters, Chancellors, Vicars, wholly anti-scriptural.

'2. Their discipline by Surrogates, and Chancellors in their Courts Ecclesiastic, without a foundation in the word of God.

'3. Their abuse of that supposed discipline by commutation.

'4. A Diocesan Bishop cannot be founded *jure divino* upon these Epistles to Timothy or Titus, nor any where else in the word of God, and so is a mere human invention.

'5. The usurped power of the Bishops at their yearly visitations, acting all of themselves, without the consent of the brethren.

'6. Pluralities of benefices.

'Lastly. The Churches conniving at the practice of Arminian doctrines inconsistent with the eternal purpose of God, and an encouragement of vice. Besides, I could not be satisfied with their ceremonial way of worship. These, &c., have so affected my conscience, that I could no longer abide in a church where the same are practised. Signed by
'WILLIAM TENNENT.'

received an invitation to settle at Bensalem, in Bucks county, Pennsylvania, to which place he removed his family, and continued to supply that small Presbyterian congregation until the year 1726, when he received a call to the Presbyterian church at Neshaminy, in the same county. In this place he continued the remainder of his life. And here, within a few steps of his own dwelling, he erected the building which has already been described; which though humble and even despicable in its external appearance, was an institution of unspeakable importance to the Presbyterian church in this country.

It may be proper to remark in this place that from all the accounts which we have, it appears that at this time the state of vital piety was very low in the Presbyterian church in America. And the same was true of the churches in New England. And this was remarkably the fact in regard to Great Britain. The ministers composing the Presbyterian church in this country were sound in the faith, and strongly attached to the Westminster Confession of Faith and Catechisms, as were also their people; and there were no diversities or contentions among them respecting the doctrines of the gospel; but as to the vital power of godliness, there is reason to believe that it was little known or spoken of. Revivals of religion were nowhere heard of, and an orthodox creed and a decent external conduct were the only points on which inquiry was made when persons were admitted to the communion of the church. Indeed, it was very much a matter of course for all who had been baptized in infancy to be received into communion at the proper age, without exhibiting or possessing any satisfactory evidence of a change of heart by the supernatural operations of the Holy Spirit. And the habit of the preachers was to address their people as though they were all pious, and only needed instruction and confirmation. It was not a common thing to proclaim the terrors of a violated law, and to insist on the absolute necessity of regeneration. Under such a state of things, it is easy to conceive that in a short time vital piety may have almost deserted the church, and that formality and 'dead orthodoxy' have been all that was left of religion. And nothing is more certain, than that when people have sunk into this deplorable state they will be disposed to manifest strong opposition to faithful, pointed preaching; and will be apt to view every appearance of revival with an unfavourable eye. Accordingly, when God raised up

B

preachers, animated with a burning zeal, who laboured faithfully to convince their hearers of their ruined condition, and of the necessity of a thorough conversion from sin, the opposition to them, both in Great Britain and this country, was violent. The gospel, among people in such a condition, is sure to produce strife and division between those who fall under its influence and those whose carnal minds urge them to oppose it. It was in such a state of the church that Mr. Tennent came to this country. What his own course of religious experience had been, we have no information; but he seems to have imbibed a warm, evangelical spirit, and to have been, in this country, distinguished for his zeal and efforts in promoting vital piety. When Mr. Whitefield first visited Philadelphia, Mr. Tennent lost no time in calling upon him. Though he lived nearly twenty miles from Philadelpia, yet no sooner did he hear of the arrival of this evangelical and successful preacher than taking with him some of his pious friends he repaired to the city, and from Mr. Whitefield's Journal, we learn that the visit was very acceptable to him; for he says, 'At my return home [from visiting a family] was much comforted by the coming of one Mr. Tennent, an old gray-headed disciple and soldier of Jesus Christ. He keeps an academy about twenty miles from Philadelphia, and has been blessed with four gracious sons, three of which have been, and still continue to be, eminently useful in the church of Christ. He brought three pious souls along with him, and rejoiced me by letting me know how they had been spoken evil of for their Master's sake. He is a great friend of Mr. Erskine, of Scotland; and as far as I can learn, both he and his sons are secretly despised by the generality of the Synod, as Mr. Erskine and his friends are hated by the judicatories of Edinburgh, and as the Methodist preachers (as they are called) are by their brethren in England.' This testimony of Mr. Whitefield goes to show that the course pursued by old Mr. Tennent and his sons was different from that of the other ministers of the Synod, to whom he stood in the same relation as Whitefield, Wesley, and their coadjutors to the great body of the clergy in England. Mr. Whitefield, on his return from New York, went to Neshaminy and spent some days with Mr. Tennent.

Here again we are glad to have the opportunity of using the very words of Mr. Whitefield.

'Nov. 22. [1739.] Set out for Neshaminy, (twenty miles distant from Trent Town), where old Mr. Tennent lives, and keeps an academy, and where I was to preach to-day, according to appointment. About 12 [o'clock] we came thither, and found about three thousand people gathered together, in the meeting-house yard. Mr. William Tennent, jr., an eminent servant of Jesus Christ, because we stayed beyond the time appointed, was preaching to them. When I came up, he soon stopped; sung a psalm, and then I began to speak, as the Lord gave me utterance. At first, the people seemed unaffected, but in the midst of my discourse, the power of the Lord Jesus came upon me, and I felt such a struggling within myself for the people, as I scarce ever felt before. The hearers began to be melted down immediately, and to cry much; and we had good reason to hope the Lord intended good for many. After I had finished, Mr. Gilbert Tennent gave a word of exhortation, to confirm what had been delivered. At the end of his discourse, we sung a psalm, and dismissed the people with a blessing: *O that the people may say Amen to it*! After our exercises were over we went to old Mr. Tennent's, who entertained us like one of the ancient patriarchs. His wife, to me seemed like Elizabeth, and he like Zachary; both, as far as I can learn, walk in all the commandments and ordinances of the Lord, blameless. Though God was pleased to humble my soul, so that I was obliged to retire for a while; yet we had sweet communion with each other, and spent the evening in concerting what measures had best be taken for promoting our dear Lord's kingdom. It happened very providentially that Mr. Tennent and his brethren are appointed to be a Presbytery by the Synod, so that they intend bringing up gracious youths, and sending them out from time to time into the Lord's vineyard. The place wherein the young men study, now is, in contempt, called the College, &c. Friday, Nov. 23: Parted with dear Mr. Tennent, and his other worthy fellow-labourers; but promised to remember each other publicly in our prayers.'

From the preceding extract we learn that Mr. Tennent was a man of congenial spirit with Mr. Whitefield, and that he was held in high esteem by this distinguished preacher and devoted servant of God. Of scarcely any other minister of any denomination does he make so honourable a mention, and to no other in this region did he pay so respectful an attention. It is certain, from the foregoing account, that Mr. Tennent was distinguished among his brethren as the open and zealous friend of vital piety and of revivals of religion. The character of his public preaching is nowhere given, and we are left to infer it from his character; or rather from the character of his pupils, of whom an account will be given hereafter. As a classical scholar, there can be no doubt of his eminence. The late Hon. Elias Boudinot, LL.D., who knew him well, says, 'that he was well skilled in the Latin language, that he could speak and converse in it with as much facility as in his vernacular tongue, and also, that he was proficient in the other ancient languages.' In confirmation of what he says about his skill in the Latin language, he relates that at the next meeting of the Synod of Philadelphia after his reception, he delivered before that body an elegant Latin oration. The writer of a sketch of the life of the Rev. Gilbert Tennent, inserted in the May number of the Assembly's Magazine, for the year 1805, says, respecting the Rev. William Tennent, sen.: 'He was eminent as a classical scholar. His attainments in science are not so well known; but there is reason to believe they were not so great as his skill in language. His general character appears to have been that of a man of great integrity, simplicity, industry, and piety.'

Mr. Tennent was, by his position at Neshaminy, a member of the Presbytery of Philadelphia; but when the division of the Synod took place, he attached himself to the New Brunswick Presbytery, to which his sons Gilbert and William belonged.

It appears from the published records of the Synod of Philadelphia that in the year 1737 a complaint was made to the Synod by a part of the congregation of Neshaminy against the Rev. William Tennent, their pastor: and also an answer to the same from another part of the said congregation. Both of these papers were read, article by article, and both parties heard at length what they had to say. Mr. Thomson was directed to prepare a minute which should express the mind of the Synod, in relation to this matter; which being done, was adopted, viz. 'That the reasons advanced by the disaffected party of that congregation, in justification of their non-compliance with the Synod's judgment in relation to them last year and their desire to be freed from Mr. Tennent as their pastor are utterly insufficient, being founded (as appears to us), partly upon ignorance and mistake, and partly (as we fear) upon prejudice. It is therefore ordered that the moderator recommend it to said people to lay aside such groundless dissatisfaction and return to their duty, which they have too long strayed from; otherwise, the Synod will be bound to treat them as disorderly.' This minute was unanimously approved.

The matter referred to as having been before the Synod the preceding year was that though Mr. Tennent had so long acted as the pastor of the church at Neshaminy, he had never been formally installed. In regard to which, the Synod had come to the following judgment: 'That it appears evident to the Synod, that Mr. Tennent having in all respects acted and been esteemed and looked upon, not only by the Synod, but by the congregation of Neshaminy, and particularly by the appellants themselves, as the minister and pastor of the people of Neshaminy, that he is still to be esteemed as the pastor of that people, notwithstanding the want of a formal instalment among them.'

For some time before his death his health was so feeble that he was unable to perform the duties of the pastoral office, and his pulpit was supplied by the Presbytery. In the year 1742, we find the following minute on the records of the Presbytery. 'Mr. William Tennent, sen., gave in to Presbytery a paper, setting forth his inability, by reason of advanced age, to discharge the work of the ministry unto the congregation of Neshaminy, over which for divers years past he has been overseer—desiring the Presbytery to grant to said congregation of Neshaminy such supplies as they can.' We find his name enrolled among the members of the New Brunswick Presbytery in the following year (1743), and in the same year he is mentioned as present when the Presbytery met to ordain Mr. Beatty as his successor. It is evident from this that he had resigned his charge, for Mr. Beatty is not said to have been ordained as his colleague. This seems to have been the last meeting of Presbytery which he ever attended. His connection with the congregation was, no doubt, dissolved at the time when he presented the paper stating his inability to fulfil the duties of a pastor: for in the same year a call was presented to Mr. William Robinson, which he declined; and after this, in 1743, Mr. Beatty having accepted the call of the people, was ordained their pastor in the month of October.

It is stated in the sketch of the life of Gilbert Tennent, in the Assembly's Magazine, that the Rev. William Tennent, sen. died in the year 1743; but this is not correct; for we find a record in the minutes of the New Brunswick Presbytery for the year 1746, of the following import: 'It is reported to the Presbytery that Mr. William Tennent, sen., deceased, since our last.' The exact date of his death was May 6, 1746, aged 73. This was communicated to the author by the Rev. Dr. Miller, who transcribed it from his tombstone.

He died at his own house, in Neshaminy, and came to the grave in a good old age, like a shock of corn fully ripe. He was buried in the Presbyterian burying-ground, where his tomb may be yet seen.

Mr. Tennent, as far as we know, never published anything. We have, therefore, no means of ascertaining his abilities as a writer; but the benefit he conferred on the church by his school can never be forgotten. The Presbyterian church is probably not more indebted for her prosperity, and for the evangelical spirit which has generally pervaded her body, to any individual than to the elder Tennent. Some men accomplish much more by those whom they educate than by their own personal labours. This should be an encouragement to such ministers as are obliged to resort to teaching for their support. If they are so favoured as to be the means of bringing forward a few pious youth, and preparing them for the ministry, they may do more good than if their whole lives had been spent in doing nothing else but preaching the Gospel. And it is good policy for Presbyterian ministers to establish schools, in their charges, wherever they are needed. And this they may do, without subjecting themselves to the drudgery of teaching all the time. Pious young men might be found, to whom such a situation would be a favour; and such institutions are often necessary to enable a minister to educate his own sons. When the means of acquiring a liberal education are brought to the doors of the people, many will avail themselves of the privilege who would never have thought of going abroad for the same purpose. The truth of this remark has been verified in almost every place where a good school has been established.

It is to be regretted that our materials for a memoir of the Founder of the Log College, are so scanty; but his usefulness must be estimated by the character of his pupils, of some of whom we shall have it in our power to give a more particular account; and to this part of our work we shall now address ourselves.

III

Memoir of the Rev. Gilbert Tennent

Gilbert Tennent—Birth—Education—Conversion—Licensure—Character by Dr. Finley—By Mr. Price—By Mr. Whitefield—Visit to Boston—Success of his ministry in New England, and in other places.

Having, in the preceding chapter, given some account of the Founder of this literary institution, let us now attend to the character of some of its principal pupils. The surest criterion by which to judge of the character of any school is to observe the attainments and habits of those educated in it. And, judging by this rule, a very high place must be assigned to the Log College, notwithstanding its diminutive and mean external appearance. And what was before said should be remembered, that this was the first seminary in which young men were trained for the gospel ministry within the limits of the Presbyterian Church. Before this school was opened, if a young man wished to become a minister in the Presbyterian Church, he must either repair to one of the New England colleges or go to Europe. It is morally certain, therefore, that few, if any, of those who were brought forward to the work could ever have reached the ministry had it not been for this school. Accordingly we find that, for a considerable time, nearly all the ministers composing the Synod were either from Great Britain, Ireland, or New England, except those who proceeded from this school. And of what character and abilities these were we shall soon see. The first on the list of students in this school was, no doubt, Mr. Tennent's eldest son, Gilbert. For though he had finished his education before the Log College was built, yet he received no other education than what he gained under the tuition of his father; and may, therefore, without impropriety be classed among the pupils of the institution.

Gilbert Tennent, the eldest son of the Rev. William Tennent, sen., was born in the county of Armagh, Ireland, April 5, in the year 1703, and was, therefore, thirteen or fourteen years of age when his father emigrated to this country. In setting up this school, no doubt, the father had a regard to the education of his four sons. Men who have themselves profited by education, and have become learned, cannot but feel a lively interest in the education of their children; and this motive has had its influence in the institution of numerous classical schools in this country besides the Log College. Judging by the result, however, all have reason to conclude that in the mind of this good man the education of his sons was viewed as subordinate to the prosperity of the Church; for every one of them became a minister of the gospel, and some of them ranked among the most distinguished who have ever laboured in the Presbyterian Church.

Gilbert Tennent, as has been remarked, received his education under the paternal roof before this school was opened, for at this time he was twenty-one or twenty-two years of age, and was soon able to be an assistant to his father in teaching the other students. And when we consider the eminence to which he rose as a preacher and as a writer, we need no other proof of the talents and skill of his reverend tutor.

Gilbert Tennent's first religious impressions of any permanency were experienced when he was about fourteen years of age. His serious concern about his salvation continued for several years before his mind was established in comfort and peace. During this period he was often in great agony of spirit, until at last it pleased God to give him 'the light of the knowledge of his glory in the face of Jesus Christ.' While he remained in the anxious state of mind which has been referred to, besides his other studies he pursued a course of theological reading; but living under the habitual impression that his spiritual condition was not good, he durst not think of entering the holy ministry. He therefore commenced the study of medicine, which he prosecuted for the space of a year. But about this time it pleased God to reveal himelf to him with so much clearness and comfort that all his doubts and sorrows and fears were dispelled, and the Sun of Righteousness arose upon him with healing under his wings. And no sooner was he satisfied of his saving interest in Christ than he felt himself called to seek the ministry, which he had before been deterred from thinking of. And here it may be proper to remark that often when God intends a man for eminent usefulness in the ministry, he leads him through deep waters, and causes him to drink freely of the cup of spiritual sorrow, that he may be prepared, by a long course of afflictive experiences, to sympathize with tempted and desponding believers; and may learn how to administer to them that consolation by which his own heart was at last comforted. Of this, religious biography furnishes many instructive examples. After due preparation and study, Mr. Gilbert Tennent presented himself as a candidate to the Presbytery of Philadelphia, of which his father was a member. Having passed the usual trials before the Presbytery to their great approbation, he received a licence to preach in May, 1726. This was the very year in which the Log College was opened; and as we learn from the documents to which we have had access that he was an usher or assistant to his father in the school, it seems altogether probable that he continued with his father in the school for one year at least; for by the Presbyterial Records it appears that he was not ordained and settled as a pastor until the autumn of the year 1727. This, then, is the only period in which he could have been a tutor in the Log College; for it was not in existence until 1726, and after he was ordained he was the regular pastor of an important church in another state; for he was called to take charge of the Presbyterian congregation in the city of New Brunswick, New Jersey. Before Gilbert Tennent settled at New Brunswick, he preached several Sabbaths in New Castle, on the Delaware, and received a call from the Presbyterian congregation in that place; which, however, he did not accept.

From his first entrance on the public work of the ministry, the preaching of Gilbert Tennent was very popular and attractive with all classes of hearers. He possessed uncommon advantages as a preacher. In person he was taller than the common stature, and well proportioned in every respect. His aspect was grave and venerable, and his address prepossessing. His voice was clear and commanding, and his manner in the pulpit was exceedingly earnest and impressive. His reasoning powers, also, were strong, and his language often nervous and indeed, sublime. No one could hear him without being convinced that he was deeply in earnest. His style was copious, and sometimes elegant. Indeed, in the vigour of his age, few preachers could equal him.

In the sermon preached at the funeral of Mr. Tennent, by Dr. Finley, he describes his character as follows: 'In his manners, at first view, he seemed distant and reserved; yet, upon nearer acquaintance, he was ever found affable, condescending and communicative. And what greatly endeared his conversation was an openness and undisguised honesty, at the greatest remove from artifice and dissimulation, which were the abhorrence of his soul while he lived. Besides, he was tender, loving, and compassionate; kind and agreeable in every relation; an assured friend to such as he esteemed worthy of his regards; and a common patron to all whom he apprehended were injured or distressed. He was of a truly public spirit, and seemed to feel the various cases of mankind in general; but sensibly partook of all the good or ill that befell his country. He needed no other motive to exert himself, than only to be persuaded that the matter in question was an important public good; and in such cases he was much regarded, not only because of his known integrity, but his generous and catholic disposition. For although he was a great lover of truth, and very zealous for its propagation, yet he was so far above a narrow, party spirit that he loved and honoured all who seemed to have "the root of the matter in them," and made it their business to promote the essentials of religion, though they were, in various points, opposed to his own sentiments. He was, moreover, an example of great fortitude and unshaken resolution. Whatever appeared to him subservient to the advancement of the Redeemer's kingdom, the salvation of souls, or the common good of mankind, he pursued with spirit; and what he did, he did with his might. If the end seemed to be attainable, great obstructions and difficulties in the way were so far from dispiriting that they animated him in his efforts; nor would he give up the point while one glimpse of hope remained. Hence, he accomplished many important matters which one less determined and enterprising would presently have relinquished as desperate. He would go through honour and dishonour, through "evil report and good report;" and though he had sensibility with respect to his character as well as other men, yet, if preserving it seemed at any time to require the omission of duty, or sinful compliances, he readily determined to expose himself to all risks; and if adhering to the will of God should be accounted "vile," he resolved that he would be "yet more vile."

'A great part of his life was a scene of unremitted labour. He studied hard, travelled much, and preached often, while his health and other circumstances permitted. He was "instant in season and out of season:" always about his Master's business. They who have journeyed or been often with him in company could not but observe his constant endeavours to do good by his conversation; to introduce some convincing or edifying topics; and his watching for proper opportunities for speaking for God. And very faithful was he in warning sinners of their danger, and persuading them to seek salvation in earnest. Thus, he showed how much religion was his element, and promoting it the delightful business of his life. How benevolent towards mankind he was and how precious immortal souls were in his esteem was evident from this, that every advantage accruing to them he reckoned clear gain to himself; nor were they "who divide the spoil" ever more joyful than I have known him to be on occasion of the hopeful conversion of sinners, whether by his own or the ministry of others. And often has his "soul wept in secret places for the pride" and obstinacy of those who refused to be reclaimed.

'His great reading, with his various and long experience of the workings of both grace and corruption in the heart, made him a wise and skilful casuist, who could resolve perplexing exercises of mind with clearness, [and enabled] him to comfort with those consolations, wherewith he in like cases had been comforted of God.

'He was a faithful attendant on the judicatories of the church, as was natural for one so anxiously concerned for the interest of religion as he was. And having observed the effects of a lax and negligent government in some churches, he became a more strenuous asserter of due and strict discipline. But above all other things, the purity of the ministry was his care; and, therefore, at the hazard of the displeasure of many and in the face of reproach, he zealously urged every scriptural method by which carnal and earthlyminded men might be kept from entering it, and men of piety and zeal as well as learning introduced.

'As Mr. Tennent's preaching was very alarming and awakening to careless sinners, so it was much blessed to this end, wherever he preached. And it was not only rendered effectual in producing conviction of sin, and exciting desires to flee from the wrath to come, but also to comfort mourners in Zion, and to encourage the timid and self-diffident. The atoning blood of the Redeemer, that only sovereign balsam, was applied to their recent or festering wounds. For while, at one time, when he thundered the terrors of the law, the heavens seemed to gather blackness, and a tempest of wrath appeared ready to be hurled on the heads of the guilty; at other times, when he exhibited the riches of the grace and provisions of the gospel, the heavens seemed to smile, the clouds were dispelled, and the sky became serene. The almighty God was shown to be their refuge, and underneath were the everlasting arms. Then his exhilarating words dropped upon them as the dew.'

The preceding full-length portrait is, with some slight alterations in the language, from the pen of one well qualified to judge in such matters, and who, by a long and intimate acquaintance, had the best opportunities of knowing the true character of the man whom he undertakes to describe. The Rev. Dr. Finley, President of New Jersey College, the author of the foregoing sketch, was himself one of the alumni of the Log College. It is possible, however, that the cordial friendship which he had long cherished for Gilbert Tennent and the early admiration which he felt for his talents and virtues might insensibly lead him to give rather too high a colouring to the portraiture which he has delineated. One thing is apparent to all who attentively consider what Dr. Finley has written, that, however just the prominent traits may be, the shading which more or less belongs to every human character is wanting. Undoubtedly, Gilbert Tennent had his imperfections, and they were sometimes sufficiently visible. But, on the whole, it must be confessed that he was a very eminent minister of Jesus Christ, and was made the instrument of performing a great work in his day. His memory ought to be precious in the Presbyterian church. Dr. Finley says, 'that the seals of his ministry in New Brunswick and parts adjacent, where he first exercised his ministry, were numerous. Many have I known in those and other parts where he only preached occasionally, whose piety was unquestioned who owned him for their spiritual father; and many have I heard of in different places.'

Though Dr. Finley's description of the character of Gilbert Tennent is full, it will be satisfactory to have the testimony of some other distinguished persons respecting him. The Rev. Mr. Prince, a pious and learned minister of Boston, speaks of Mr. Tennent in the following terms: 'In private conversation I found him to be a man of considerable parts and learning, free, gentle, and condescending. From his own various experience, his reading the most eminent writers on experimental divinity, as well as the Scriptures, and from his conversing with many who had been awakened by his ministry in New Jersey, he seemed to have as deep an acquaintance with the experimental part of religion as any I have conversed with. And his preaching was as searching and rousing as ever I heard.' 'He seemed to have such a lively view of the divine Majesty—of the spirituality, purity, extensiveness, and strictness of the law, with his glorious holiness, and displeasure at sin; his justice, truth, and power in punishing the damned, that the very terrors of God seemed to rise in his mind afresh, when he displayed and brandished them in the eyes of unreconciled sinners.' And the same writer speaks of his remarkable discrimination and skill in detecting hypocrites, 'and laying open their many vain and secret refuges, counterfeit resemblances, their delusive hopes, their utter impotence, and impending danger of destruction.'

It will be gratifying to learn what Mr. Whitefield's opinion was of the subject of this memoir. And this, we have given very freely and fully in his Journal to which reference has already been made. 'Nov. 13, [1739]. Left Trenton about six in the morning, had a sweet and pleasant journey, and reached Brunswick, about thirty miles distant, about one o'clock. Here we were much refreshed with the company of Mr. Gilbert Tennent, an eminent dissenting minister, about forty years of age, son to that good old man who came to see me on Saturday, at Philadelphia. God, I find, has been pleased greatly to bless his labours. He and his associates are now the burning and shining lights of this part of America. He recounted to me many remarkable effusions of the blessed Spirit, which have been sent down among them. And one may judge of their being true and faithful soldiers of Jesus Christ because they are every where spoken evil of by natural men. The devil and carnal ministers rage horribly against them. Several pious souls came to see me at his house, with whom I took sweet counsel.' 'Wednesday, Nov. 14. Set out early from Brunswick, with my dear fellow-travellers, and my worthy brother and fellow-labourer, Mr. Tennent. As we passed along, we spent our time most agreeably in telling what God had done for our souls.'

Upon their arrival at New York, Mr. Whitefield goes on to say, 'I went to the meeting house to hear Mr. Gilbert Tennent preach,

and never before heard I such a searching sermon. He went to the
bottom, indeed, and did not daub with untempered mortar. He
convinced me more and more that we can preach the gospel of
Christ no further than we have experienced the power of it in our
own hearts. Being deeply convicted of sin, and being from time
to time driven from his false bottom and dependencies by God's
Holy Spirit at his first conversion, he has learned experimentally
to dissect the heart of the natural man. Hypocrites must either
soon be converted or enraged at his preaching. He is a "son of
thunder", and does not regard the face of man. He is deeply sensible
of the deadness and formality of the Christian church in these
parts, and has given noble testimonies against it.'

A higher testimony and from higher authority could not be
given upon earth. It is doubtful whether Mr. Whitefield has ever
expressed so high an opinion of any other preacher of any denomination. Indeed, it is probable that he never met with a man
of a more perfectly congenial spirit with his own. As Mr. Whitefield
was doubtless honoured to be the instrument of the conversion
of more souls than any other preacher of his age, or perhaps of
any age since that of the apostle Paul, so Mr. Tennent, among
orthodox preachers, undoubtedly deserves to be placed next to
him, both in the abundance of his labours and the wonderful
success which attended his ministry.

When in the year 1740, Mr. Whitefield returned from Boston,
he persuaded and urged Mr. Gilbert Tennent to make a preaching
tour through New England as far as Boston, to water the good seed
which he had there sown by his preaching on his late visit. At
that time, there was but little intercourse between the middle and
eastern colonies; and no ecclesiastical connection between the
Presbyterian and Congregational churches. Mr. Whitefield's
preaching, attended by the mighty power of God, not only was the
means of the conviction and conversion of many of his hearers;
but he also excited a host of enemies, who pursued him with
unrelenting hostility; and among his opposers were reckoned,
both in this country and in Great Britain, the majority of the
clergy and of professors of religion; thus verifying the words of
our Lord, 'If they have persecuted me, they will also persecute
you; if they have kept my sayings they will keep yours also.'
Mr. Tennent must have been inflamed with a very ardent zeal,
situated as he was, the pastor of a church and the father of a

family, to set off in the depth of winter to preach to a strange people, among whom he probably had not a single acquaintance, either among the clergy or the laity. But invincible resolution was a prominent trait in his character. Mr. Whitefield made no journeys without several attendants; men who cheerfully ministered unto him, as did Timothy, and Luke, and Silas, and Mark, and others, to Paul. But Mr. Tennent appears to have gone on this self-denying and evangelical tour alone. He was influenced by no curiosity to see a country not before visited; nor could he have had any secular motive to induce him to perform so laborious a service as that in which he now engaged.

As Mr. Whitefield's preaching had enkindled a considerable flame in Boston, Mr. Tennent directed his course immediately to that city, where he arrived on the 13th of December, 1740; and here he continued for nearly three months, preaching almost every day, with extraordinary power and success. There were, however, many there who were ready to welcome him; and several of the excellent ministers of the town cordially received this zealous preacher, and opened their pulpits—and, indeed, some of them gave them up to him while he continued in the place. Among those who received him joyfully was the Rev. Thomas Prince, the author of 'The Christian History,' from whose pen we are favoured with an account of Mr. Tennent's manner of preaching, during his ministry in Boston. 'It was,' says he, 'both terrible and searching. It was for matter, justly terrible, as he, according to the inspired oracles, exhibited the dreadful holiness, justice, law-threatenings, truth, power, and majesty of God, and his anger with rebellious, impenitent, and Christless sinners: the awful danger they were in every moment of being struck down to hell, and damned forever, with the amazing miseries of that place of torment. By his arousing and scriptural preaching, deep and pungent convictions were wrought in the minds of many hundreds of persons in that town; and the same effect was produced in several scores, in the neighbouring congregations. And now was such a time as we never knew. The Rev. Mr. Cooper was wont to say, that more came to him in one week, in deep concern, than in the whole twenty-four years of his preceding ministry. I can say also the same, as to the numbers who repaired to me.' 'By a letter of Mr. Cooper, one of the evangelical ministers of Boston, to a friend in Scotland, it appears he had had about six hundred different persons to visit

him on the concerns of their souls, in three months' time. And
Mr. Webb, another of the pious Boston ministers, informs me
he has had, in the same space, above a thousand.'

But it will be satisfactory to hear Mr. Tennent's own account
of this visit, which is found in a letter addressed to Mr. Whitefield,
by whose urgent entreaty he was persuaded to undertake the
journey. This letter has been preserved in that excellent book,
'Gillies' Historical Collections.' of which we are glad to learn a
new edition has been recently published in Scotland.

'VERY DEAR BROTHER,—In my return home, I have been
preaching daily; ordinarily, three times a day, and sometimes
oftener: and through pure grace, I have met with success much
exceeding my expectations. In the town of Boston there were
many hundreds, if not thousands, as some have judged, under
soul-concern. When I left the place, many children were deeply
affected about their souls, and several had received consolation.
Some aged persons in church communion, and some open opposers
were convinced. Divers of young and middle aged were converted,
and several negroes. The concern was rather more general at
Charlestown. Multitudes were awakened, and several had received
great consolation; especially among the young people, children,
and negroes. In Cambridge, also, in the town and in the college,
the shaking among the dry bones was general, and several of the
students have received consolation." He then proceeds to name
more than twenty towns to which the revival had extended; and
in most of which he had preached on his return home. 'In New
Haven,' says he, 'the concern was general, both in the college
and in the town. About thirty students came on foot, ten miles,
to hear the word of God. And at Milford, the concern was
general. I believe, by a moderate calculation, divers thousands
have been awakened. Glory to God on high! I thank you, sir,
that you did excite me to this journey. I have had good information
that on Long Island God has blessed my poor labours on my passage
to New England. The work of God spreads more and more. My
brother William has had remarkable success this winter at
Burlington. Mr. John Cross has had remarkable success at Staten
Island; and many, I hear, have been awakened by the labours of
Mr. Robinson, in New York government. Mr. Mills has had
remarkable success in Connecticut, particularly at New Haven.

And I hear that Mr. Blair has had remarkable success in Pennsylvania.'

On the subject of this great revival, which extended from Massachusetts to Georgia, the ministers of the Synod were greatly divided. For while some approved the work, and were principal instruments in promoting it, a majority considered it an ebullition of enthusiasm which tended neither to the glory of God, nor to the real benefit of immortal souls; and concerning Mr. Whitefield and his preaching, there was an entire dissension. This difference relating to the great and vital interests of religion, produced exasperation. The friends of the revival considered all who opposed it as setting themselves in opposition to a glorious work of God's grace, and they could not but view all who openly spoke against the revival or opposed it in any way to be the enemies of God. Hence, they too hastily took up the opinion that all those ministers who disapproved the work were unconverted men; that they were mere formalists, and knew nothing of the vital power of religion, but trusted to a mere profession of orthodoxy, and that if in words they did not deny the truths of God, they did in fact: and though they might acknowledge the truth in theory, it was with them a 'dead orthodoxy,' which they held in unrighteousness. On the other hand, the opposers of the revival blamed the kind of preaching which the revivalists adopted; especially the dwelling so much on the terrors of the law, and the torments of the damned. They charged the leaders in the revival with encouraging enthusiastic raptures, and making religion to consist too much in strong emotion and violent excitement, attended often with bodily affections. They were also greatly offended with the harsh, uncharitable spirit with which they were denounced and misrepresented by the preachers on the other side; and their opposition to no one, unless Mr. Whitefield be an exception, was greater than to Mr. Gilbert Tennent. Indeed, all must acknowledge that among the friends and promoters of the revival he stood preeminent; and in the harshness of his censures, and the severity of his denunciation, he went far before all his brethren. It cannot be doubted that before the commencement of this extraordinary revival of religion the Presbyterian church in America was in a most deplorable state of deadness and formality; and that the necessity of a change of heart was very little inculcated from the

C

pulpit, or understood by the people. Here it may be remarked, that the founder of the Log College and all the pupils of that school were warm friends of the revival, and exerted themselves with all their might to promote the good work.

In all great revivals, where the people are under strong excitement, there will be some things which the judicious must regret; and, no doubt, there were many such things in this great and extensive awakening; but it was a dangerous mistake to repudiate the whole work on account of some irregularities.

IV

Memoir of the Rev. Gilbert Tennent

(CONTINUED)

Rev. Gilbert Tennent's contest with the Synod—Severity of his censures —New Brunswick Presbytery protest against the Synod's act— Violate it—Are excluded irregularly from the Synod—Form a separate body—Judgment of their conduct.

We come now to a period of Gilbert Tennent's life, in which he was called to act a very conspicuous part in the affairs of the Presbyterian church. A great schism took place in the Synod, in bringing about which, it must be admitted, he had his full share. It took place, indeed, by the expulsion of himself and the other members of the New Brunswick Presbytery from the Synod; but he had provoked his opponents by one of the most severely abusive sermons which was ever penned, called 'The Nottingham Sermon,' because it was preached at that place. In the protests which he and Mr. Samuel Blair presented to the Synod, in 1740, the majority of the members of the Synod were exhibited in a very unenviable light. Mr. Gilbert Tennent felt himself called in providence to attempt to arouse the Presbyterian church from its profound sleep of carnal security, and to bring about a reformation in the body; but the majority of the clergy were opposed to his measures, and disparaged what had already been done. He seems, therefore, to have considered them as the enemies of the spiritual kingdom of Christ; and that it was his duty, in imitation of Christ and the ancient prophets, in the plainest and most solemn manner, to denounce and expose their hypocrisy, as did our Lord that of the Pharisees. But here he made a grand mistake. He could not read the hearts of his opponents, and, therefore, had no authority to pronounce a sentence of condemnation on them. He should have remembered that precept of our Lord, 'Judge not that ye be not judged.' A difference of opinion from him respecting the true nature of the revival and concerning Mr. Whitefield's character, furnished no sufficient ground for him to censure and denounce them as he did; and, especially, as a part of them, at least, were excellent men, and sound and judicious theologians. They were not the enemies of vital godliness, but were opposed to what they apprehended to be spurious religion. We may now see that they erred in their judgment, and pursued a course which was very injurious to the people under their care; and that they committed a great fault in opposing a glorious work of God on account of some irregularities which accompanied it. One of the greatest causes of complaint against Mr. Gilbert Tennent and his 'New-light' brethren was that in violation of order and propriety they passed beyond the bounds of their own Presbytery, and intruded into congregations under the care of other ministers. This these brethren attempted to justify by the sound maxim employed by the apostles when forbidden to preach by the Jewish rulers, 'that we should obey God rather than men.' But it may well be doubted whether, in the circumstances in which they were placed, the maxim was applicable. The ministers into whose congregations they intruded belonged to the same Synod with themselves, and had as good a right to judge what was right and expedient as the 'New Side' ministers.

We think, therefore, that Mr. Tennent was much to be blamed for the course which he pursued in this controversy with the Synod; especially, in the harshness, censoriousness, and bitterness which he manifested towards them; particularly, in the sermon before mentioned; and that his course can by no means be justified. He does, indeed, appear in a very unamiable light, and as exceedingly deficient in the meekness and charity of the gospel, in this whole controversy. He, doubtless, believed that he was doing God service, and that duty required him to pursue the course and manifest the spirit which he did. After the separation had taken place, and the heat of the controversy had cooled, he seems to have been sensible that he had not done justice to the majority of the Synod; for he wrote and published a large pamphlet called 'The Pacificator,' in which he strongly pleads for peace, and a re-union of the separated parts of the Presbyterian Church. This desirable event was, after a division which lasted seventeen years, and after long negotiation, accomplished; and Mr. Gilbert Tennent entered cordially into the measure. Whatever mistakes he fell into arose from error of judgment, in regard to duty. He was, doubtless, actuated by a sincere and glowing zeal for the honour of the Redeemer, and the salvation of souls. Like the sun, he was a burning and a shining light; but like that luminary, had some dark spots, which, in some measure, marred the beauty and symmetry of his otherwise estimable character. His natural disposition appears to have been severe and uncompromising; and he gave strong evidence of being very tenacious of all his opinions; and not very tolerant of those who dissented from his views, as appears by the controversy which he had with the Rev. Mr. Cowell, of Trenton, and which he brought before the Synod. But with all his faults he was an extraordinary man, raised up by Providence to accomplish a great work. We of the Presbyterian Church are more indebted to the men of the Log College for our evangelical views and for our revivals of religion than we are aware of. By their exertions, and the blessing of God on their preaching, a new spirit was infused into the Presbyterian body; and their views and sentiments respecting experimental religion have prevailed more and more; until at last opposition to genuine revivals of religion is almost unknown in our church. It is not my purpose to enter into the ecclesiastical transactions in which Mr. Tennent acted an important part any further than is necessary to form a judgment of his Christian and ministerial character. They who desire to see a lucid view of the ecclesiastical transactions of that period are referred to Dr. Hodge's 'Constitutional History of the Presbyterian Church;' or they may go to the fountain head, by consulting the 'Records of the Transactions of the Synod,' recently given to the public by the Presbyterian Board of Publication.

We have seen that a great schism was produced in the Presbyterian body by a difference of opinion among the ministers of the Synod respecting the great revival which pervaded many of the churches. But though this was the proximate cause of the division, by those who attentively consider the history of that time, and especially the 'Records' of the Synod itself, it will be seen that this event was actually produced by the Log College. At first view, this will seem very improbable, but when all the documents are read, and all the circumstances of the church weighed and compared, it will appear exceedingly probable that the erection of this school of the prophets was, innocently, the cause of the breach which took place in 1741. Here it will be necessary to enter

somewhat minutely into a consideration of the condition of the
church prior to the commencement of the revival. A liberal education was, from the beginning, considered an indispensable qualification for the gospel ministry in the Presbyterian Church. The
usual evidence of having received such an education was a diploma
from some college or university in Europe or America. The
Presbyterian ministers, before the erection of the Log College,
had nearly all received such an education. We know of but one
exception, and that was Mr. Evans, whose case has already been
mentioned. There existed no college in any of the middle states
where young men seeking the ministry could obtain the requisite
learning. Until this school was instituted, no young man could
enter the Presbyterian ministry without going to Scotland or New
England for his education; and this amounted pretty nearly to
closing the door against all candidates who were brought up in
the Presbyterian Church; for very few in those days could bear
the expense of acquiring a liberal education, by going to any
college or university on this or the other side of the Atlantic. The
church, therefore, had to depend for a supply of ministers on
emigration from Scotland, Ireland, or New England. Most of
those who came to settle in the Presbyterian Church came from
Ireland; except that those Presbyteries which bordered on New
England received a supply of ministers from that region. It must
be evident at once that this condition of the church was very
unfavourable to her prosperity; for often those who came across
the ocean were not men of the best character. They were often
mere adventurers, and sometimes had crossed the Atlantic to
escape from the censure incurred by their misconduct; and it was
exceedingly difficult in those days to ascertain the true character
of a foreigner coming here as a minister of the gospel; for though
such men commonly exhibited ample testimonials from abroad,
too often these were forged. Several instances of this very thing
occurred. As the ministers who came in from New England were
all brought up Congregationalists and had habits and customs not
congenial with those of the Scottish Presbyterians, their accession
to the body had a tendency to produce confusion and strife. The
sons of the pilgrims and the descendants of Scottish Presbyterians,
though holding substantially the same creed, have never readily
amalgamated into one uniform mass, but the habits and prejudices
of each have been preserved, and kept the people distinct for

several generations, though living contiguously to each other. There seemed, therefore, to be an urgent necessity for some seminary to be erected within the limits of the Presbyterian Church, where young men might be educated for the ministry. It is indeed wonderful that the Synod had not paid earlier attention to this subject, as being essential to the prosperity of the church. But as far as appears, no classical school had been erected in any part of the Synod, until the Rev. William Tennent connected himself with the Presbyterian Church, and set up a school at his own door in Neshaminy. It is probable that Mr. Gilbert Tennent was the first candidate licensed in the Presbyterian Church who was educated within its limits. As he was thirteen or fourteen years of age when his father arrived, it is probable that his classical education was commenced before he left Ireland; though the principal part of his education must have been acquired here; and no doubt, under the paternal roof. Although we have connected Mr. Gilbert Tennent with the Log College, it must be in the character of a teacher rather than a student; for in the very year in which his father removed to Neshaminy, he was licensed to preach. This was the year 1726.

Though Gilbert Tennent had received no diploma from any college, yet he passed his trials before the mother Presbytery of Philadelphia with great credit to himself and much to the satisfaction of the Presbytery. It was now seen that young men could be well prepared for the ministry at home, without going to distant colleges. As Mr. William Tennent, the father, had been, as far as is known, the sole instructor of his son, who as soon as licensed attracted public attention, and was seen to be an able preacher, the conclusion was easily drawn that he would be an excellent person to train up young men for the ministry. But though the thing appeared thus to many plain and pious people, others were apprehensive that by educating young men in this way the literary qualifications of candidates would necessarily be greatly diminished. The school, however, went on prosperously, and a number of young men who had the ministry in view resorted to the Log College to pursue their education; and here they were not only taught the classics, but studied divinity also; so that this institution was a theological seminary, as well as a college. How many years they were occupied with these studies does not appear; but a number of persons educated in this school were licensed by the

Presbyteries, after undergoing such trials as were usually pre-scribed to candidates in Scotland and Ireland. Some of them, as we shall see, became eminent in the church, and were much distinguished as powerful and evangelical preachers. Still the impression existed, and grew stronger, that this course of instruc-tion was not sufficient. To men educated in the universities of Europe, furnished with so many professors, and other advantages, it seemed preposterous to suppose that a man could acquire adequate learning for the ministry in this little paltry log cabin; and instructed, principally, by one teacher. They began, therefore, in the Synod, to talk of establishing a Synodical school, and to express dissatisfaction with the course of study in the Log College, as it was contemptuously called. None doubted of old Mr. Tennent's classical scholarship; but it was believed that his proficiency in the arts and sciences was by no means equal to his classical learning. As young men were still entering the church from this school, the Synod adopted a rule that no Presbytery should license any young man until he had passed an examination on his literary course before a committee of Synod. Two large committees, one for the northern part of the Synod, and the other for the south, were appointed, before whom young men were to appear and submit to an examination. This rule gave great dissatisfaction to the Tennents and their friends; for they per-ceived, at once, that this rule was intended to bear on the students of the Log College, and they believed it to be a high-handed measure, entirely inconsistent with the rights of Presbyteries, who, as they had the power of ordaining ministers, ought to possess the power of judging of their qualifications. What rendered the measure more odious to them, they had just succeeded in getting a Presbytery set off, in New Jersey, which included most of the friends of the Log College. Their object in getting this Presbytery erected, as they confessed to Mr. Whitefield, was that they might license such young men as they deemed properly qualified for the office; and, in their opinion, fervent piety was the first and principal qualification. Though they believed a classical education necessary, yet it seems that they lightly esteemed some parts of learning, which the other members of the Synod thought requisite. While they were blamed for being too lax in their demands of a knowledge of literature and science, they seriously charged the majority of the Synod with neglecting to make a thorough

examination into the piety of their candidates. On several occasions, Mr. Gilbert Tennent brought this matter before the Synod,
and obtained from them some formal resolutions in favour of
inquiring carefully into the personal piety of the candidates.

When the order was passed rendering it necessary for candidates
to appear before a committee of the Synod, Mr. Gilbert Tennent
and his friends entered their protest against the regulation. But to
be more exact in regard to this first measure, which divided the
Synod into two parties, it will be proper to observe that the
regulation adopted in the year 1738 was occasioned by an overture
from the Presbytery of Lewes, in which they say, 'That this part
of the world, where God has ordered our lot, labours under
grievous disadvantage for want of the opportunities of universities
and professors skilled in the several branches of useful learning;
and that many students from Europe are especially cramped in
prosecuting their studies, their parents removing to these colonies
before they have an opportunity of attending the college, after
having spent some years at the grammar school; and that many
persons born in this country groan under the same pressure, whose
circumstances are not able to support them to spend a course of
years in the European or New England colleges, which discourages
much, and must be a detriment to our church, for we know that
natural parts, however great and promising, for want of being
well improved, must be marred in their usefulness, and cannot
be so extensively serviceable to the public; and that want paves
the way for ignorance, and this for a formidable train of sad
consequences. To prevent this evil, it is humbly proposed, as a
remedy, that every student, with approbation not pursuing the
usual courses, in some of the New England or European colleges
approved by public authority, shall, before he be encouraged by
any Presbytery for the sacred work of the ministry, apply himself
to this Synod, and that they appoint a committee of their members,
yearly, whom they know to be well skilled in the several branches
of philosophy, divinity, and the languages, to examine such
students in this place, and finding them well accomplished in these
several parts of learning, shall allow them a public testimony from
the Synod, which, till better provision be made, will, in some
measure, answer the design of taking a degree in college. And,
for the encouragement of students, let this be done without
putting them to further expenses than attending. And let it be an

objection against none where they have studied, or what books; but let all encouragement be only according to merit, &c.' The Synod, by a great majority, approved the overture, and proceeded to appoint two committees, the one for the region north of Philadelphia, and the other for the country south of that city.

It does not appear that any dissent or protest was entered on the minutes at the time, but the next year the Presbytery of New Brunswick sent up a remonstrance. The paper containing the objections to the act of the Synod of the preceding year is not on the records; but the Synod, upon hearing it, agreed to reconsider the subject, and after due deliberation resolved to substitute the following instead of the act complained of. 'It being the first article in our excellent Directory for the examination of the candidates for the sacred ministry, that they be inquired of what degrees they have taken in the university, &c. And it being often-times impracticable for us, in these remote parts of the earth, to obtain an answer to these questions of those who propose them-selves to examination, many of our candidates not having enjoyed the advantage of a university education, and it being our desire to come to the nearest conformity to the incomparable prescrip-tions of the Directory that our circumstances will admit of, and after long deliberation of the most proper expedients to comply with the intentions of the Directory, where we cannot exactly fulfil the letter of it: the Synod agree and determine that every person who proposes himself to trial, as a candidate for the ministry, and who has not a diploma or the usual certificate from a European or New England university, shall be examined by the whole Synod or its commission as to these preparatory studies, which we generally pass through at the college; and if they find him qualified, they shall give him a certificate, which shall be received by our respective Presbyteries as equivalent to a diploma or certificate from the college, &c.' But this form of the act was no more acceptable to the New Brunswick Presbytery than the former; the next day, therefore, they entered a protest against the said act. This protest was signed by the four Tennents, Samuel Blair, and Eleazar Wales, ministers, and by four elders. The Synod, it appears, were determined to bring the pupils of the Log College under their own examination before they would suffer any more of them to be received as members of the Synod, or to preach as candidates in the churches. The friends of this institution were exceedingly averse to having their young men examined by the Synod; either because they were conscious that they would be found defective in some of the branches usually pursued in the college course; or, because they were of opinion that the major part of the Synod were prejudiced against this humble institution, and against all who were connected with it. Probably both these considerations had their weight in leading them to oppose so strenuously a measure which to us seems reasonable and necessary, to guard the ministry against the intrusion of unqualified candidates. For it appears that this examination by the Synod was not intended to interfere with the right of Presbyteries to examine their candidates, but to be a substitute for a diploma, which the Directory seemed to require. For when a young man presented his certificate to a Presbytery, if, upon examination, they were not satisfied, they could reject him notwithstanding his certificate.

But the fact was, that the New Brunswick Presbytery had already committed themselves. At their very first meeting, in August, 1738, they took on trial a certain Mr. Rowland, one of the scholars of the Log College, in direct violation of the act of the Synod. After the Synod had reconsidered the matter, and re-enacted the same thing, in different words, this Presbytery proceeded with the trials of Mr. Rowland, licensed him to preach the gospel, and, not long afterwards, ordained him. The Synod refused to recognize Mr. Rowland as a member of their body; for, though they did not deny that by the act of the Presbytery he was a real minister; yet they alleged that they had a right to determine who should and who should not become members of their own body. Henceforth the parties became much exasperated against each other. The friends of the Log College saw that the act of the Synod was directed against that institution, for there was no other school at that time in the bounds of the Synod where young men were trained for the ministry. This was not all. The act implied a reflection on all those who had before entered the ministry from this school. The majority of Synod were grievously offended that one of their Presbyteries, and one too just created, should so disregard the authority of the supreme judicatory of the church as to act in open defiance of an act formed after much discussion and deliberation in the Synod.

One thing necessary to be known in order to form an impartial judgment respecting the dispute which arose in the Synod, but which cannot at this distance of time be accurately ascertained, is what sort of education was actually received at this famous institution. Was it as solid and thorough as could be obtained within the limits of the Presbyterian church? If so, even if compared with that which was given in the universities of Europe it was in some parts defective, this was no good reason why the institution should be frowned upon by the Synod. Instead of this, they ought to have recognized and cherished it, and should have endeavoured to raise it higher, and to enlarge its advantages. As far as we have observed, this school, although already it had produced a number of distinguished preachers, is never once mentioned in the minutes of the Synod; except in their letter to President Clapp, of which further notice will be taken. It is true that most of the members of Synod had enjoyed the advantages of a university education in Europe or New England; and it cannot be supposed that equal advantages could be had in the little log cabin at Neshaminy. But it is a well-known fact, that men's eminence in learning does not always correspond with the privileges enjoyed. If we compare Gilbert Tennent, Samuel Blair, Samuel Finley, William Tennent, jr., and John Blair, with an equal number of their opposers, they certainly will not suffer in public opinion by the comparison. One advantage which they possessed who were educated in the Log College was that the spirit of piety seems to have been nourished in that institution with assiduous care. All, as far as we can learn, who proceeded from this school were men of sound orthodoxy, evangelical spirit, glowing zeal, and in labours very abundant. They had, we have reason to believe, the teaching of the Holy Spirit; and without the advantages which others enjoyed, they became 'burning and shining lights.' They were the friends and promoters of revivals of religion, which their censurers bitterly opposed. Still, we do not justify their irregular and insubordinate acts. Gilbert Tennent and Samuel Blair were men of invincible firmness—a firmness bordering on obstinacy. They were the leaders in this warfare. They saw a great harvest before them, and the Lord seemed to attend their labours everywhere with a blessing; and they were led to think that mere forms of order and regulations of ecclesiastical bodies were of trivial importance, compared with the advancement of the Redeemer's kingdom, and the salvation of souls. They felt, as did the apostles and first reformers, that they were called to go everywhere preaching the gospel, without regard to prescribed limits of Presbyteries or congregations; especially, as they observed that many pastors neglected to inculcate on their hearers the necessity of a change of heart, and that the people were as really perishing for lack of knowledge as they were under Jewish or Popish instructors. They felt themselves bound, therefore, to preach far and wide, wherever the people would hear them; and although there was irregularity in this, judging by human and ecclesiastical rules, yet I doubt not that in the main their zealous and exhausting labours have met with a large reward. Weak enthusiasts or fierce fanatics may abuse the principle on which they acted; but the same thing occurred at the time of the blessed Reformation from popery. We must not neglect to do all the good we can, because some may pervert our example to sanction their own lawless proceedings.

I cannot express how much the Presbyterian Church in these United States is indebted to the labours of this very corps, who studied successfully the sacred oracles in the Log College; or more probably, under the beautiful groves which shaded the banks of the Neshaminy. There they studied, and there they prayed, and there they were taught of God.

But I do not mean to justify all that was done by these zealous men. As was admitted before, they did not act towards their brethren in the ministry with brotherly affection and Christian meekness. Gilbert Tennent indulged himself in very unwarrantable language in speaking of men clothed with the same office as himself, and members of the same Synod. Nothing could have justified his treatment of them, unless he had been inspired to know that they were a set of hypocrites; or, unless their lives had been wicked, or their faith heretical, none of which things were alleged against them.

But while it is admitted that Mr. Gilbert Tennent was a principal instrument in provoking a majority of the Synod to exscind the New Brunswick Presbytery, it does not appear that either he or his friends wished to bring about a separation in the church. Their object was to produce a reformation, if possible, among the ministers, and in the churches under the care of the Synod; though it must be acknowledged that their zeal led them to make use of unjustifiable means to accomplish the desired end. It need not, therefore, be a matter of surprise that Gilbert Tennent was among the first to seek a reconciliation and re-union of the parties.

To promote this object he wrote and published a pamphlet, as was before said, entitled, 'The Pacificator,' in which he reasons strongly in favour of peace and union. Between the contending parties there existed, really, no difference on doctrinal points; except that the New Side were blamed for dwelling too much on the terrors of the law, and insisting too strongly on the necessity of legal conviction for sin. On church government there was scarcely a shade of difference. The members of the New Brunswick Presbytery were disposed to consider Presbyteries as the origin of ecclesiastical power; while the majority of the Synod probably thought that all the power of the church was concentrated in the Synod, then the supreme judicatory. The same difference of opinion still exists in the Presbyterian Church, for while some are of opinion that Synods and General Assemblies possess limited powers, defined by the constitution of the church, and that all ecclesiastical power emanates from the Presbyteries, which they consider the *essential* body in our Church government, there are others who consider the Synod in no other light than a larger Presbytery, and the General Assembly, as it were, a universal Presbytery, possessing all the powers of the inferior judicatories. Whichever of these be the more correct theory of our Presbyterian Church government, the Presbytery of New Brunswick has always been firm in maintaining the rights of Presbyteries against the encroachments of the higher judicatories. Certainly, our higher judicatories were constituted by the junction of Presbyteries. In Scotland, the General Assembly existed before there were either Presbyteries or Synods, and all church power descended from that body; but not so with us, where Presbyteries first existed, of which the higher judicatories were formed. This schism in the Presbyterian Church in America lasted about seventeen years, although negotiations for a reconciliation were going on a great part of this time, chiefly by the members of the Presbytery of New York, who were absent from the meeting of Synod at which the disruption occurred.

V

Memoir of the Rev. Gilbert Tennent
(CONTINUED)

Mr. Gilbert Tennent removes to Philadelphia to be the pastor of the Second Presbyterian Church—Mission to Great Britain for the College of New Jersey—Exertions to get a commodious church erected—His Sickness and Death—Eulogy on his character—His Publications.

The preaching of Mr. Whitefield, in Philadelphia, was the means of the conversion of many souls. A number of these, with others who agreed with them in sentiment, and were admirers of Mr. Whitefield's preaching, and friends of the revival, had formed a new Presbyterian congregation in that city. Being desirous to obtain a pastor of like views and sentiments with themselves, and one possessed of talents and eloquence suited to such a station, they turned their eyes upon the Rev. Gilbert Tennent. Their call to him was presented in May, 1743, just two years after the rupture of the Synod, which took place in the same city. Mr. Tennent did not hesitate to accept this call, as he saw that the sphere of his influence would be greatly enlarged. He was, therefore, regularly released from his pastoral charge in New Brunswick, where he had preached for sixteen years. In the important station on which he now entered, he continued to exercise his ministry with great fidelity and diligence for twenty years. During this whole period, comprehending more than one half of his ministerial life, he seems to have lived in peace with all men. The fiery edge of his zeal had worn off, and he had found by experience that neither people nor ministers were ever rendered better by vituperative attacks from the pulpit or the press. During the whole of the latter part of his life, Mr. Gilbert Tennent, as far as has come to our knowledge, never had any controversy with any of his brethren, but seems to have conducted himself in a friendly and peaceable

manner toward all men. From this it would seem that he was not
of a quarrelsome or litigious spirit. It may hence be fairly inferred
that the warm controversies in which he engaged with his brethren
of the Synod of Philadelphia were entered into conscientiously and
on principle. We have no doubt that in this whole concern he was
at the time fully persuaded that he was doing God service, and
performing a painful duty toward his opposing brethren, which
he could not with a good conscience omit. But as was before said,
we are of opinion that he was mistaken, and proceeded on an
erroneous principle; and there is good reason to think that he was
of the same opinion himself in this latter part of his life.

The only interruption of his pastoral labours in Philadelphia
was occasioned by a mission to Great Britain, in conjunction with
the Rev. Samuel Davies, of Virginia, for the College of New
Jersey. At the request of the Trustees of New Jersey College, the
Synod of New York appointed these two gentlemen to cross the
Atlantic, to solicit funds for the College. The mission was in a
good degree successful; but of this our only account is found in
the diary of the Rev. Mr. Davies. It does not appear that Mr.
Tennent ever kept any journal or diary, at home or abroad. From
Mr. Davies's journal we learn that he and Mr. Tennent went on
board a vessel bound for London, November 17, 1753, and on the
next day set sail. They arrived in London on the 25th of December,
and were well received. We are unable to give any account of
Mr. Tennent's preaching, and its effects on the people whom he
addressed, for he and Mr. Davies seem to have been separated
from each other for the most part. But in regard to the direct
object of their mission, he says, under date of April 7, 1754, 'We
have had most surprising success in our mission; which, notwithstanding the languor of my nature, I cannot review without
passionate emotions. From the best information of our friends,
and our own observation on our arrival here, we could not raise
our hopes above £300, but we have already got about £1200. Our
friends in America cannot hear the news with the same surprise,
as they do not know the difficulties we have had to encounter;
but to me it appears the most signal interposition of Providence I
ever saw.'

It appears from the journal of the Rev. Samuel Davies that by
means of Mr. Tennent's 'Nottingham Sermon,' which some
person unfriendly to him and his mission had sent over to England,

strong prejudices had been excited against him before his arrival; so that he was rarely invited to preach in the dissenting pulpits of London. And it is probable that during his whole visit to Great Britain he was under a cloud, which must have rendered his visit unpleasant, and yet was a just chastisement for preaching and publishing that very uncharitable discourse.

While Mr. Gilbert Tennent was in Great Britain, a friend to the conversion of the Indians put into his hands two hundred pounds sterling, to be made use of by the Synod of New York in sending missionaries to these heathen tribes. This seems to have excited, for a time, a considerable missionary spirit among the ministers in connection with this Synod. Several pastors, who had charges, went on temporary missions; and Mr. John Brainerd devoted himself wholly to the work among the tribes who resided in New Jersey.

John Brainerd was the brother of David, whose devoted missionary life is so well known, and has had so powerful an effect in exciting the missionary spirit in Great Britain as well as America. His brother succeeded him, supported by the same society in Scotland which had supported himself. But after some time he relinquished the missionary work, and accepted a pastoral charge in the town of Newark, New Jersey. The contribution from Scotland was now withdrawn, as there was no missionary among the Indians. But when Mr. Tennent returned with the afore-mentioned sum, appropriated to this object, the Synod of New York renewed their missionary enterprise; and as the very name of Brainerd was precious to the Indians of New Jersey, Mr. John Brainerd, by the advice of the Synod, resigned his charge, and returned to the Indians.

'The Rev. Messrs. Tennent and Davies, when in Great Britain, received from various persons in London the sum of £296 17s., "for the education of such youth for the ministry of the gospel, in the College of New Jersey, as are unable to defray the expenses of their education, who appear upon proper examination to be of promising genius, Calvinistic principles, and in the judgment of charity experimentally acquainted with the work of saving grace, and to have distinguished zeal for the glory of God, and the salvation of men." The annual interest of the aforesaid sum only was to be appropriated. To this sum was added, by another donor,

D

£10 7s. 6d., making the whole of this charitable fund to be £307 4s. 6d.

'The money aforesaid was by Messrs. Tennent and Davies put into the hands of the Trustees of New Jersey College, to be applied to the education of such youth, of the character above mentioned, as shall be examined and approved by the Synod of New York, (or by what name soever that body of men may be hereafter called) and by them recommended to the trustees of said college, and to be divided among such youths, in proportion as said Synod shall think fit. To the above sums fifty pounds sterling were added by an individual, making the whole sum £357 4s. 6d.'[1]

A report has attained some currency that Mr. Tennent and Mr. Davies did not perfectly harmonize when on this mission; but though it is possible that some coolness may have arisen between these eminent ministers, there is not any written document in which we have found the least hint of any difference. From the suavity of Mr. Davies's disposition and the perfect politeness of his manners, we cannot think that there is any foundation for the report. The men, it is true, in natural disposition were not altogether congenial; for while the manners of one were polished and calculated to please, it is probable those of the other were rough, blunt, and not at all courtly. We shall, therefore, dismiss this report as one of the thousands which have no probable foundation. No doubt Mr. Davies carried off the palm as to popularity in London and other places; and if Mr. Tennent was at all susceptible of the feelings of envy, which are very natural to the human heart, and the remains of which are often found lurking in the hearts of ministers as well as others, he might have felt badly in finding himself eclipsed by a much younger man. But, as was said, we have no right to charge him with any such feeling, and we are confident that Mr. Davies's treatment of him must have been uniformly respectful and affectionate; for it was so to everybody.

After Mr. Tennent's settlement in Philadelphia, he exerted himself with great energy and perseverance to get a good house of worship erected for the congregation which he served. Indeed, at that time the building of such an edifice as that which, by his

[1] This fund was nearly all lost during the revolutionary war.

indefatigable exertions, was erected at the north-east corner of the intersection of Mulberry (or Arch) and Third streets, for the second Presbyterian church in Philadelphia, was a great work. Very few of the Presbyterian denomination then possessed much wealth. Mr. Tennent not only obtained nearly all the subscriptions for the building, but actually superintended the work in person, and assiduously watched over it, from its commencement to its completion. After some time the congregation added a handsome steeple to the building.

Such men as Mr. Gilbert Tennent always appear greatest in times of excitement and stirring activity. It may well be doubted whether his preaching was as awakening and impressive after his removal to Philadelphia as it was before. Some change in his views and feelings as to the best method of promoting religion had taken place, it would be very natural to suppose. The warmth of his religious feelings had in some measure cooled, and the violence of his zeal had, by time and experience, been mitigated. From this time he seems to have gone along as quietly as other ministers around him. We thus judge, because we have never heard of any remarkable effects of his preaching after his settlement in Philadelphia. There is another thing which ought not to be overlooked. In a great city the hearers are more fastidious than in the country, and will not tolerate so much liberty of digression, and so frequent departures from good taste and correct composition. Before Mr. Gilbert Tennent went to Philadelphia, though, doubtless, he studied his sermons carefully, and digested his matter under a sufficient variety of heads, yet he preached without having written his discourses, and like all ardent preachers, gave himself great indulgence in pursuing any new train of ideas which was presented during the time of preaching. But when settled in a great city, he thought it necessary, for the sake of correctness, to write his sermons, and read them from the pulpit. This circumstance alone, probably, produced a great alteration in his mode of preaching. Many men who preach admirably when free to follow the thoughts which they have arranged, or to pursue such as spring up at the time, when confined to a discourse written in the study appear to be very much cramped, and lose much of their vivacity and natural eloquence. The writer once conversed with a plain and pious man who in early life being apprenticed to a trade in Philadelphia attended Mr. Tennent's ministry. We asked him respecting his manner of preaching. He answered simply, 'that Mr. Tennent was never worth anything after he came to Philadelphia;' 'for,' said he, 'he took to reading his sermons, and lost all his animation.' This testimony came from a class not sufficiently considered, when the best mode of preaching is under consideration. Our reference is too much to the taste of men of cultivated minds, who form but a small part of any congregation; and even these, when pious, are better pleased with blundering simplicity joined with animation, than with cold accuracy when the most solemn truths are delivered without emotion.

Though Mr. Tennent, however, probably lost a considerable portion of his early vehemence and impressiveness, which can be well enough accounted for by the mere increase of years, without supposing any real diminution of zeal, yet his discourses, as appears by those published, were various and instructive. This will appear more clearly when we come to speak of his writings.

The interest of Mr. Gilbert Tennent in revivals and his joy at the conversion of sinners continued unabated. For in March, 1757, an extraordinary revival of religion occurred in the New Jersey college, concerning which he thus speaks in the preface to one of his volumes of sermons: 'In March last, I received a letter from the College of New Jersey, informing me of an extraordinary appearance of the Divine power and presence there, and requesting I would come and see. With this kind motion I gladly complied; and having been there some time, had all the evidence of the aforesaid report, which could be in reason desired.' He then inserts a letter from his brother William, giving a particular account of the nature and progress of the work; which was addressed to the Rev. Dr. Finley, and the autograph of which the writer has seen.[1]

For about three years before his death, Mr. Tennent became very infirm, so that he was unable to go through the duties which devolved upon him as the pastor of a large city congregation. In December, 1762, the congregation got leave to present a call to the Rev. George Duffield, D.D., then of Carlisle, to be a co-pastor with Mr. Tennent. This call Dr. Duffield declined to accept, and the congregation remained without another pastor until Mr. Tennent's death; which event occurred in the year 1764, in the sixty-second year of his age.

[1] See Appendix, I.

Of the circumstances of his death, Dr. Finley, in his funeral sermon, says but little. In the general, he informs us that, 'as he lived to the Lord, so death was his unspeakable gain; and his being conscious of it made him ardently wish for the pleasing hour when he should enter into the joy of his Lord.' . . . 'He had an habitual unshaken assurance of his interest in redeeming love, for the space of more than forty years; but eight days before his death he got a more clear and affecting sense of it still. And though he lamented that he had done so little for God, and that his life had been comparatively unprofitable; yet he triumphed in the grace of Jesus Christ, who had pardoned all his sins; and said his assurance of salvation was built on the Scriptures, and was more sure than the sun and moon.'

His congregation placed a monumental stone over his remains, in the middle aisle of the church in which he had so long preached. The inscription on this stone was written by his friend Dr. Finley, in classical Latin. When this church was remodelled, his remains and those of Dr. Finley also, were removed to the cemetery of the Second Presbyterian Church, in Arch street, between Fifth and Sixth streets.

After Mr. Tennent's death, there was a eulogy on his character published in Philadelphia by a young gentleman of that city, from which some extracts will be made, as serving to show in what estimation he was held in the place where he spent more than twenty years of his life. We expect, in discourses of this kind, some exaggeration; but as this eulogy was addressed to the public, who were well acquainted with the person eulogized, it must have a general foundation of truth; and the reader, by making an allowance for the strong expressions of the partial writer, may form a pretty correct opinion of the true character of the person celebrated.

After an introduction this writer goes on to say:

'He whose memory these pages are intended to celebrate, was distinguished in a very remarkable manner by his eminent endowments of mind; a love of learning that nothing could abate; an intense application that no recreations could divert. His great proficiency in the several branches of literature, while the powers of his soul were but just opening, raised the expectations of all that knew him. What recommended these amiable accomplishments was that they were early adorned with the charms of Divine grace. It was his study to remember his Creator in the days of his youth. As he often inculcated the necessity and manifold advantages of early piety, so he might with propriety have added his own experience of them, as an inducement to the votaries of gaiety and pleasure to embrace the pleasures that flow from true religion. He had no sooner experienced what it was to pass from death unto life, and from a state of nature to a state of grace, than he formed a resolution of spending his time, his talents, and his all, in the service of God, in his sanctuary; previously to the accomplishment of which design, he devoted himself wholly to the study of the sacred scriptures, and his own heart, and not merely to a dry system of speculative notions. He was too sensible of the importance of that arduous office, to rush into it without suitable preparation. He knew too well the worth of precious immortal souls to recommend any other foundation for the hopes of their future happiness, than what he was well assured would stand the test of beating rains and descending showers. . . . The manner in which he usually preached, and the indifference with which he treated all secular advantages, abundantly evinced that neither a love of popular applause nor a desire of promoting his own affluence and ease could have been any inducement to him to assume the holy function. But, on the contrary, an ardent love to God, and a desire to advance his glory in the world, by proclaiming pardon and reconciliation through the atoning blood of his crucified Son, were his only motives for the choice of that noble, disinterested profession. As he entered into the ministry in the prime of life, when his bodily constitution was in its full vigour, he devoted his juvenile strength and ardour of mind to the service of the church, at a time when their exertion was of the greatest importance. Few that knew Mr. Tennent in that season of life can speak of him without some pleasing emotions. The good old Puritan spirit that had for a series of years been asleep, seemed to revive and blaze forth in him with a genuine lustre. He was, indeed, like the harbinger of his Master, "a burning and a shining light," in the church. His undissembled piety, his fervent zeal, his pungency of address, and his indefatigable assiduity in the performance of every ministerial duty were remarkably eminent. He might truly be styled a Boanerges. As he knew the composition and make of the human heart, so he knew how to speak to it;

and all his discourses were aimed at the fountain of impurity and sin. He knew that a reformation that did not take its rise in the heart could not be of long continuance, or pleasing in the sight of God; and, therefore, he always strove to convince his hearers that a thorough renovation of it was necessary to salvation.

'As his presence was venerable, and his voice commanding, so his very appearance in the pulpit filled the minds of his hearers with a kind of religious awe. . . . The thunderings and mighty vociferations of Mount Sinai seemed to roar from the sacred desk, when he denounced the wrath of God against him that transgressed but once God's law, which he knew to be spiritual, and that nothing but a perfect obedience—which man in his fallen state is unable to perform—would satisfy its demands. Hence, he made it his constant practice to sound the alarm of God's curse abiding on the whole human race; and taught that to doom man to ever-lasting misery would be highly consistent with the mercy and justice of Jehovah. But while he enforced the truth of inspiration, "that in Adam all die," he was no less warm in proclaiming "that in Christ all shall be made alive." And as he knew how to wound, so he knew how to pour the oil of consolation on the bleeding conscience. The blood of Jesus, that sacred healing balm, was his grand *catholicon* for sin-sick souls. This alone was what he recommended as sufficient to procure ease to the trembling sinner; with the love of God to man—in sending his beloved Son into the world to redeem a race of rebel sinners, by bearing on the accursed tree the heavy punishment due to man's enormous crimes, in order to translate him to the regions of eternal joy.

'The beginning of his ministry was employed in long and tedious itinerations. And wherever he had a prospect of doing good, however remote the place might be from his friends, and however repugnant to his own ease, he needed no other induce-ment, but cheerfully undertook the pleasing task.

'Fatigues and toils from which even worldly men in the prosecu-tion of an earthly good shrink back, he joyfully engaged in; and with a degree of perseverance peculiar to himself bravely overcame those difficulties which to some minds appeared insurmountable. . . . It pleased God, in a very gracious manner, to crown his labours with success. The energy of the divine Spirit accompanied his ministrations. Wherever he went the kingdom of Satan trembled; the desolate and solitary places bloomed like the rose before him; and he became the happy instrument of turning many from the error of their ways to the living God.

'His knowledge in divinity, in which he made great proficiency, was entirely derived from the Bible; and whatever truth it enforced as duty, he inculcated; his arguments for the one and motives for the other were all taken from those inspired pages, which he prized above all human writings, and valued as the charter by which he possessed the hope, and ere long expected the full enjoyment of a blessed eternity.

'Sensible how much man is dependent upon God for every blessing he enjoys, and that the best way to keep the flame of devotion alive in his own soul was to maintain a constant inter-course with heaven, he made prayer his chief and most delightful employment. This was the very breath of his soul. . . . His manner of praying was such as evidence it to be not the mere language of the passions, but a rational, solemn, and animated address to the great Father of spirits.

'After having laboured for many years, with much success, in New Brunswick, where he was settled, by the advice of his brethren he accepted an urgent call from the Second Presbyterian church in Philadelphia, while the society was in its infant state; and continued to exercise his pastoral functions there for upwards of twenty years, with a degree of watchfulness and fidelity scarcely to be paralleled. He considered himself as the shepherd of his flock, and made it his practice to lead them to the green pastures and living fountains of salvation, with the care of one that knew he must render an account at the last day. Nay, he considered himself the father of his people, and as his beloved children he counselled, warned, and reproved them with all the tenderness and solicitude of a father's heart. He was, indeed, a faithful watchman, that never failed to give warning of impending danger. The rich and the poor, the black and white had equally free access to his person, and ever found him ready to hear their complaints and solve their doubts.

'What he preached in the pulpit, his life preached out of it. His disposition—naturally calm—was still more sweetened with that holy temper which the gospel of Christ inspires. A genuine serenity and cheerfulness dwelt upon his countenance, which he never failed to diffuse on all around him. He was charitable to the poor; kind to all men; a lover of all that loved the Lord Jesus, whatever mode of worship they professed; and much beloved in all the tender endearments of domestic life, as a husband, a father, a master, and a friend.

'There is nothing in this world, methinks, more grand or illustrious than the old age of a man who has devoted his whole time, and spent his whole life in promoting the spiritual interests of his fellow-creatures. . . . The review of his life fills the soul with a pleasure which none but such as experience it can conceive. Whilst he sees no ill-spent time to sting his conscience with remorse, nor feels any attachment to the transitory things of this world, he beholds a calm haven prepared for his repose, where the storms and billows of affliction can reach him no more. . . . In this light should we contemplate Mr. Tennent. His soul, like the setting sun, broke through the clouds of infirmity. There was a dignity and grandeur in his old age. Wisdom bloomed upon his silver locks; and while the cold hand of time snowed upon his locks, his heart glowed with redoubled love for the church. . . . Nor more dreadful to the man of ease in his possessions is the approach of the king of terrors, than he was welcome to this eminent servant of God. Every symptom of his approaching dissolution, instead of filling his soul with alarms, rather filled him with comfort, and made him impatiently long for the kind stroke that should dismiss his soul. After having borne a long and tedious illness with the most invincible fortitude and resignation, the friendly messenger at last came with the joyful summons. . . . And with full confidence in the merits and atonement of his dear Redeemer, he gently fell asleep.'

The following is the most accurate list of Mr. Gilbert Tennent's works which the author has been able to collect:

1 . In the year 1735, Mr. Tennent published his 'Solemn Warning to the secure World, from the God of Terrible Majesty; or, the Presumptuous Sinner Detected, his Pleas Considered, and his Doom Displayed.' This volume was printed in Boston.

2. 'Sermons on Sacramental Occasions,' by Divers Authors. A small duodecimo volume. The sermons are all by Mr. Gilbert Tennent, except two; one by his brother William, and the other by the Rev. Samuel Blair. It would seem that at the time when this volume was published, no books were printed either in New York

or Philadelphia; for the manuscript was sent to Boston, and printed there in the year 1739.

3. Two Sermons of the Rev. John Tennent, with a Preface, containing a memoir of him, to which is added, 'An Expostulatory Address to Saints and Sinners,' by Gilbert Tennent. Printed in Boston, in the year 1735.

4. 'The Espousals, or a Passionate Persuasion to a Marriage with the Lamb of God.' Newport, 1741.

5. His next publication was, probably, his famous 'Nottingham Sermon,' in which he lashed his brethren of the Synod so severely, that it had much influence in leading to the separation which soon followed.

6. 'The Examiner Examined' was written in the year 1740, and is an answer to a pamphlet written against him by an anonymous author, after his visit to New England.

7. 'The Pacificator,' a large pamphlet, the object of which was to bring about a reunion of the dissentient parties in the Presbyterian church.

8. A small quarto volume of sermons, twenty-three in number. These Discourses appear to have been the commencement of a body of Divinity. The subjects treated are, 'The Chief End of Man—The Divine Authority of the Sacred Scriptures—The Being and Attributes of God, and the Trinity.' Preached in Philadelphia, in 1743.

9. Two sermons, preached at Burlington, N. J., on a day of Public Fasting, 1749. They are dedicated to Governor Belcher. The texts are, Matt. 6. 16–18, and Jonah 3. 8.

10. 'Sermons on Important Subjects, adapted to the perilous state of the British Nation.' 1758.

We do not know where Mr. Tennent obtained his degree of Master of Arts. It would be natural to suppose that it was conferred by the Trustees of the College of New Jersey; but his name is not on the catalogue; while we find there the names of some of his contemporaries, who received honorary degrees. As he was a Trustee of New Jersey College, it is probable that this honour was conferred on him by Yale or Harvard, or possibly by one of the Scotch universities.

11. A Funeral Sermon, occasioned by the death of Captain William Grant. Preached in Philadelphia, 1756.

12. The last publication of Mr Gilbert Tennent was, 'A Sermon on the Nature of Religious Zeal. Its Excellency and Importance opened and urged.' Preached in Philadelphia, January 27, 1760.

The style of these several publications is very diverse, as they were composed at different periods of Mr. Tennent's life, on different subjects, and in different circumstances. In all his writings perspicuity and force are manifest characteristics of his style; but there is a great want of simplicity and ease. Throughout the whole, the doctrines inculcated are rigidly orthodox, according to the Westminster Confession. In his didactic discourses he shows himself not only to be a profound thinker, but a well-read theologian; and often quotes the standard Latin writers of systematic theology, as one who had been accustomed to read them. While he manifests an ardent zeal in defence of the 'doctrines of grace,' he never loses sight of the importance of experimental religion and practical godliness. In conformity with the custom of the age, he too much abounds in divisions and subdivisions, and is too fond of technical words and phrases. His practical discourses, however, are often both pungent and searching.

It is somewhat remarkable, that while so many old authors have been republished in our day, none of the writings of Gilbert Tennent have ever passed to a second edition. A selection from his works should be published, that we might not only have a sketch of the lives of the divines of the Log College, but a specimen of their theology.

VI

Memoir of the Rev. Gilbert Tennent
(CONTINUED)

Mr. Gilbert Tennent's letter to the Rev. Thomas Prince, containing many interesting particulars of the state of religion in New Brunswick, and vicinity; and also in Philadelphia, and various other places.

The preceding memoir of Gilbert Tennent was drawn up before the writer met with the following letter from his own pen, addressed to the Rev. Thomas Prince, of Boston, and published in his 'Christian History,' dated August 24, 1744, soon after Mr. Tennent had removed to Philadelphia. This letter sheds a satisfactory light on several parts of Mr. Tennent's life, which all other accounts leave in obscurity, as for example, the success of his ministry in New Brunswick, while the pastor of that church; and also in Staten Island, where he had a congregation in which his labours appear to have been blessed. It is a sad evidence of the retrograde march of Presbyterianism in some parts of our country that after the lapse of a complete century there is not a vestige of a Presbyterian congregation in that island; nor has there been within the memory of any person living. Even the part of the island in which this congregation was located cannot now be ascertained.

Such parts of Mr. Tennent's letter as have no bearing on his own life have been omitted, but we have retained much the larger part, and in his own language.

EXTRACTS from the letter of the Rev. Gilbert Tennent, to the Rev. Thomas Prince of Boston, published in the 'Christian History' of the latter.

'I am glad it pleased the sovereign God to make my poor labours of any service among you. I desire ever to bless his name for that undeserved mercy. I am thankful for the "Christian History," and well pleased with the design and management of the work. I hope it will be a means in God's hand of conveying with honour to posterity a *memorial* of the late blessed revival of religion, which has been so virulently opposed by many.'

Here he introduces a long extract from a public attestation to the reality of the work of grace in the late revival, which was prefixed to Mr. Dickinson's 'Display of Special Grace.' This public testimony was subscribed by Gilbert Tennent, William Tennent, Samuel Blair, Richard Treat, Samuel Finley, and John Blair. Some parts of this paper will not be out of place here, as, no doubt, it was drawn up by Gilbert Tennent.

'If any should inquire what we mean by the work of God, we think the judicious author of the following dialogue (Mr. Dickinson) has given a plain and pertinent answer, to which we give our approbation. "A work of conviction and conversion spread not long since in many places of these provinces with such power and progress as even silenced for a time the most malignant opposers. They were either afraid or ashamed openly to contradict such astonishing displays of the divine Almightiness in alarming multitudes of secure sinners out of their fatal stupor, and exciting in them the utmost solicitude about the everlasting concerns of their souls; many of whom gave us a rational and scriptural account of their distress, and afterwards of their deliverance from it, agreeable to the method of the gospel of Christ. Their comforts as well as their sorrows appeared, by all the evidence we can have of such things, to be agreeable to scripture and reason.

'It is shocking to think that any should dare to oppose a work attended with such commanding evidence as has been among us. We would beseech all such solemnly to answer the following paragraph of the Rev. Mr. Robe, minister of the gospel in Kilsyth, Scotland, in his preface to his "Narrative," which is as follows: "I seriously beg of any who are prejudiced against this dispensation of God's extraordinary grace, and look upon it as a delusion, that they will show themselves so charitable, as to direct me and other ministers, what we shall answer distressed persons of all ages, who come to us crying bitterly that they are undone, because of unbelief and other sins—'What shall we do to be saved!' And as a young girl about twelve, who had been in distress for some time called upon me in the house where I was, and asked me with great sedateness, 'What shall I do to get Christ?', shall we tell them that they are not Christless, and are not unconverted, when we evidently see many of them to be such? Shall we tell them that their fears of the wrath of God are all but delusion, and that it is no such a dreadful thing that they need to be much afraid of it? Shall we tell persons lamenting their cursing, and swearing, Sabbath-breaking, and other immoralities, that it is the devil that now makes them see these evils to be offensive to God, and destructive to their souls? Shall we tell them, who, under the greatest uneasiness, inquire of us what they shall do to get an interest and faith in Jesus Christ, that Satan is deluding them, when they have, or show any concern this way? In fine, shall we pray and recommend it to them to pray to God, to deliver them from such delusions? It would be worse than devilish to treat the Lord's sighing and groaning prisoners at this rate; and yet such treatment is a natural consequence of reckoning this the work of the devil, and a delusion."

'I may add that both our Presbyteries of New Brunswick and New Castle have, in their declaration of May 26, 1743, printed at Philadelphia, manifested their cordial concurrence with the protestation of the Presbytery of New York, in which are these words, viz.: "We protest against all those passages which have been published in these parts which seem to reflect on the work of divine power and grace, which has been carrying on in so wonderful a manner in many of our congregations; and declare to all the world that we look upon it to be the indispensable duty of all our ministers to encourage that glorious work, with their most faithful and diligent endeavours." '

This public protestation was signed by Jonathan Dickinson, Ebenezer Pemberton, Daniel Elmore, Silas Leonard, John Pierson, Simon Horton, and Azariah Horton, ministers; and by Nathaniel Hazard, Timothy Whitehead, and David Whitehead, elders. Now the concurrence of the Presbyteries of New Brunswick and New Castle with the aforesaid Protest is expressed in the following words, in the 5th page of their Declaration: 'With this Protestation of our reverend and other brethren we heartily agree.' And in the 13th page they declare, 'that they could not come into a

state of settled constant communion with such as had protested
against them, until they received competent satisfaction; especially
concerning their opposition to and reflections upon the work of
God's grace, and success of the gospel in the land.'

'I trust I may say to the glory of God's grace, that it pleased
the most high God to let me see considerable success in the places
where I laboured statedly many years before I came hither.

'The labours of the Rev. Mr. Frelinghuysen, a Dutch Calvinist
minister, were much blessed to the people of New Brunswick, and
places adjacent; especially about the time of his coming among
them, which was about twenty-four years ago.

'When I came there, which was about seven years after, I had
the pleasure of seeing much of the fruits of his ministry; divers of
his hearers, with whom I had the opportunity of conversing,
appeared to be converted persons, by their soundness in principle,
Christian experience, and pious practice; and these persons
declared that the ministrations of the aforesaid gentleman were the
means thereof. This, together with a kind letter which he sent me,
respecting the dividing the word aright, and giving to every man
his portion in due season, through the divine blessing, excited me
to greater earnestness in ministerial labours. I began to be very
much distressed about my want of success; for I know not for
half a year or more after I came to New Brunswick that any one
was converted by my labours, although several persons were at
times affected transiently. It pleased God, about that time, to
afflict me with sickness, by which I had affecting views of eternity.
I was then exceedingly grieved I had done so little for God, and
was very desirous to live one half year more, if it was his will,
that I might stand upon the stage of the world, as it were, and
plead more faithfully for his cause, and take more earnest pains
for the salvation of souls. The secure state of the world appeared
to me in a very affecting light; and one thing, among others,
pressed me sore, that I had spent so much time in conversing
about trifles, which might have been spent in examining people's
states, and persuading them to turn unto God. I therefore prayed
to God that he would be pleased to give me one half year more,
and I was determined to promote his kingdom with all my might,
and at all adventures. This petition God was pleased to grant
manifold, and to enable me to keep my resolution in some measure.

'After I was raised up to health, I examined many about the grounds of their hope of salvation, which I found in most to be nothing but as the sand. With such I was enabled to deal faithfully and earnestly, in warning them of their danger, and urging them to seek converting grace. By this method many were awakened out of their security, and of these, divers were to all appearance effectually converted; but some that I spoke plainly to were prejudiced. And here I would have it observed that as soon as an effectual door was opened, I found many adversaries, and my character was covered with unjust reproaches, which through divine goodness did not discourage me in my work. I did then preach much on original sin, repentance, the nature and necessity of conversion, in a close, examinatory, and distinguishing way: labouring in the mean time to sound the trumpet of God's judgments, and alarm the secure by the terrors of the Lord, as well as to affect them with other topics of persuasion: which method was sealed by the Holy Spirit, in the conviction and conversion of a considerable number of persons, at various times, and in different places, in that part of the country, as appeared by their acquaintance with experimental religion and good conversation.

'I may further observe that frequently at sacramental seasons in New Brunswick there have been signal displays of the divine power and presence. Divers have been convinced of sin by the sermons there preached, some converted, and many much affected with the love of God in Jesus Christ. O the sweet meltings that I have seen on such occasions among many! New Brunswick did then look like a field the Lord had blessed. It was like a little Jerusalem, to which the scattered tribes with eager haste repaired at sacramental solemnities; and there they fed on the fatness of God's house, and drank of the rivers of his pleasures. But alas! the scene is now altered!

'While I lived in the place aforesaid, I do not remember that there was any great ingathering of souls at any one time; but, through mercy, there were frequently gleanings of a few here and there, which in the whole were a considerable number. But having never taken a written account of them, I cannot offer any precise conjecture at their number, and shall therefore leave it to be determined at the judgment-day. But at Staten Island, one of the places where I statedly laboured, there was, about fifteen or sixteen years agone, a more general concern about the affairs of salvation, which hopefully issued in the conversion of a pretty many. Once in the time of a sermon from Amos 6. 7, before which the people were generally secure, the Spirit of God was suddenly poured out on the assembly; the people were generally affected about the state of their souls; and some to that degree that they fell upon their knees in the time of the sermon, in order to pray to God for pardoning mercy. Many went weeping home from the sermon; and then the general inquiry was, "What must I do to be saved?" I may further observe that some few of those that I hope were converted in the places aforesaid were compelled to cry out in the public assembly, both under the impressions of terror and love. During the late revival of religion, New Brunswick felt some drops of the spreading rain, but no general shower.

'As to Philadelphia, where, by the providence of God, I now labour stately, many have been hopefully converted here during the display of God's grace in this land. The Rev. Mr. Whitefield was the instrument God was pleased to *improve*, principally in the awakening and conversion of sinners here; yet the labours of others have been attended with some success. This town, by all that I can learn, was in deep security generally before Mr. Whitefield came among them, but his preaching was so blessed that a great number were brought under a religious concern about the salvation of their souls; multitudes were "inquiring the way to Zion with their faces thitherward, weeping as they went." Some years since there were so many under soul-sickness in this place that my feet were pained in walking from place to place to see them. And there was then such an eagerness to hear religious discourse that when they saw me going to a house they would flock to it; and under what was spoken, they were sometimes generally, and to all appearance deeply affected. And thus it was in more public assemblies; there were sometimes general meltings. And though several persons have lost their religious impressions, and "returned with the dog to his vomit," and some others have fallen into erroneous sentiments, yet God has preserved many from those evils, who give a rational and scriptural account of their conversion, and crown the same by their practice. Neither is it strange that some should be carried away here by the fair speeches and cunning craftiness of those that lie in wait to deceive; seeing that the greater part in this place have never had the advantage of a strict religious education, and therefore were never well fixed in the thorough

E

knowledge of a consistent system of principles. None that I know of in this town that were well acquainted with the doctrines of religion in their connection and established in them have been turned aside by the tempests and tricks of errorists.

'The last Sabbath in May last I gave the sacrament of the Lord's Supper; the first time that it was dispensed to the society to which I belong—considered as a society. The number of communicants was above one hundred and forty. Those persons I examined about their gracious state, as well as doctrinal knowledge; and, upon trial, almost all of them gave scriptural and satisfactory account of the ground of their hope. Now the chief of these, according to their own account, have been brought to Christ during the late revival of religion. And there are divers other persons, who, in a judgment of charity, have got saving benefit during the late marvellous manifestation of God's grace, who do not join in communion with us.

'Though there is in many a considerable decay as to their liveliness and affectionateness in religion, yet through divine goodness they grow more humble and merciful; and it is evident by their conversation that the general bent of their heart is for God. Since I have come here, my labours seem to be chiefly serviceable to instruct and establish the great truths of religion and to comfort pious people. There have been but a few instances of conviction and conversion in this town that I know of.

'In some places of this province, some years ago, particularly in Nottingham, Fagg's Manor, Whiteclay Creek, Neshaminy, and elsewhere, there have been such general lamentations in the time of preaching that the speaker's voice has been almost drowned with the cries of the distressed, even after they have been entreated again and again to restrain themselves; yea, and sometimes when the speaker discoursed in a gospel strain, divers persons in this province have fallen down to the ground in the time of sermon, as though they were stabbed with a sword. And what though some have lost their impressions and relapsed into their sordid impieties, this is no more than what the Scriptures inform us did happen in the apostolic times; yet it is well known that many of them, so far as we are capable of judging by men's speech and practice, have been brought to a sound conversion.

'I think it needless here to offer a reply to the cavils of opposers, which are as numerous as insidious and impertinent. But this I must say, that mine eyes and ears have seen and heard so much of the appearance and fruits of the late revival of religion that I must reject religion altogether and turn infidel, if I should dispute and oppose the same. May it please the gracious God to pardon those unhappy men who have set themselves in opposition to the work of the most high God, and painted it in black and odious colours, and let them see their sin and danger before it be too late.

'Dear sir, I did not think, when I began to write, to offer any more than our prefatory attestation; but being urged to mention something of what I have seen and heard, and finding a pleasure in the subject, I have added, with the strictest regard to truth and soberness, these few hasty hints, concerning some matters of fact which I know to be true; and shall leave to your discretion to do with them as you shall see meet.

'I am, sir, yours, &c.,

'GILBERT TENNENT.

'August 24, 1744.'

VII

The College of New Jersey

The Log College, the germ from which proceeded the College of New Jersey.

At the time of the disruption of the church, when the New Brunswick Presbytery was excluded by an arbitrary determination of the majority of the Synod, the whole Presbytery of New York were absent. This Presbytery contained several members of high standing in the church, such as Dickinson and Burr; and although this Presbytery had not been actually engaged in the controversy with the ministers of Pennsylvania respecting the revival, and respecting Mr. Whitefield, yet they sympathized on these subjects with the new Brunswick Presbytery. They were, therefore, much dissatisfied with the proceedings of the Synod in the excision of this body; which, if they had been present, they could probably have prevented. When, therefore, the Synod met the year following the disruption, these brethren exerted themselves to get the Synod to receive again the excluded brethren. When repeated efforts to procure a restoration of the excluded brethren were without success, they withdrew from the Synod, and connected themselves with the Presbytery of New Brunswick; and these, with the Presbytery of New Castle, formed a Synod, and took the name of the Synod of New York, which in a short time considerably outnumbered the old Synod.

The Log College, which had done so much and so good service, was now evidently on the decline. Its venerable founder, through the infirmities of old age, was no longer able to act with the energy of his former years; and, indeed, his strength had so much failed that soon after this time he was under the necessity of applying to the Presbytery for aid in the discharge of his pastoral duties. There was, therefore, every prospect of the speedy extinction of this humble school of the prophets. But the need of a literary institution of a high character, where candidates for the ministry might be fully trained, became more evident every day. The time for the establishment of a college in the bounds of the Synod of New York seemed to be auspicious. While the Synod of Philadelphia were labouring to establish a school for training young men at New London, the Synod of New York were exerting themselves to erect a college which should stand upon a level with any other institution in the country.

Messrs. Dickinson and Burr, the former, pastor of the Presbyterian Church in Elizabethtown, and the latter, in Newark, took the lead in this enterprise. Both these distinguished divines were graduates of Yale College; but just at this time their minds probably experienced some alienation from their *alma mater*, on account of the harsh treatment which Mr. David Brainerd had received from the officers of that college; for he had been expelled merely for a harsh word, spoken in a private company, and overheard by a student who happened to be passing the door, who knew not to whom it referred. But the persons present, contrary to every rule of propriety, were forced by the faculty to testify to whom reference was had. Mr. Brainerd, at the time of his expulsion, was a member of the Junior Class. Having applied to the Presbytery of New York, he was taken under their care, and having manifested a strong desire to go and preach the gospel to the heathen in our land, the Commissioners appointed by the Society in Scotland, to employ a missionary to the Indians, selected Mr. Brainerd. It appears that President Clapp, in his letter to the Synod of Philadelphia, complained of the New York Presbytery for receiving under their care persons who had left the college under censure, where the reference was undoubtedly to David Brainerd. A strong desire was now felt both by Mr. Brainerd and his friends to get the stigma removed from his character. To effect this the Commissioners who had employed Mr. Brainerd deputed the Rev. Mr. Burr, one of their number, to go to New Haven at the commencement, when his class were about to be graduated, to endeavour to have him restored. Jonathan Edwards also, who then became acquainted with Mr. Brainerd, and formed a strong attachment to him, used all his influence to accomplish the object; but their efforts were ineffectual. The faculty of the college remained inflexible, or as it may more properly be termed, obstinate. They did offer that if he would return and remain another year in college, without giving offence, they would then give him his degree. But this could not be done without disconcerting the whole plan of the mission for which he was engaged, and in which he became so eminently successful. The attachment of all the members of the New York Synod to Mr. Brainerd was warm, and deservedly so. This affair, it is very probable, quickened the zeal of these excellent men to get up a college of their own. Some years ago, the writer heard the relict of the late Dr. Scott, of New Brunswick, say, that when she was a little girl she heard the Rev. Mr. Burr declare in her father's house, in Newark, 'If it had not been for the treatment received by Mr. Brainerd at Yale, New Jersey college would never have been erected.' How many influences are made to combine and operate, when Providence has the design of giving existence to an institution which has affected and will still affect the happiness of thousands!

It was a circumstance favourable to the views of the friends of a new college that Mr. Belcher, a man of humble piety and great public spirit, was then the acting governor of New Jersey. It was, therefore, not found difficult to enlist the zeal and exertions of this excellent man in the contemplated enterprise.

The first charter for a college which was obtained was not satisfactory to governor Belcher, and he succeeded in obtaining from the royal authority the very ample charter under which the college is now governed and instructed. Mr. Edwards refers to this matter, in a letter addressed to the Rev. Doctor Erskine of Edinburgh, who took a lively interest in the enterprise, and requested some information respecting the prospects of the college.

'You desire to be informed respecting the present state of New Jersey College, and of things of a religious nature respecting the Indians. As to the former, viz., the state of New Jersey college, by the last accounts I had, it is in somewhat of an unsettled state. Governor Belcher had a mind to give them a new charter that he thought would be more for the benefit of the society. Accordingly the draft of a new charter was drawn, wherein it was proposed to make considerable alteration in the corporation of trustees—to leave out some of the former trustees, and that the governor and four of the council of that province should be put in their place. These two things made considerable uneasiness, viz., leaving out part of the trustees, and making it a part of the constitution, that the governor and so many of the council should be members of the corporation. . . . As to governor Belcher himself, he appears thoroughly engaged to promote virtue and vital religion in those parts. The disposition of governor Belcher may in some measure be seen in the following extract of a letter from him, in answer to one I wrote to him on a special occasion.

Burlington, New Jersey, Feb. 5th, 1748.

' "You will, sir, be sure of me as a friend and father to the missionaries this way; and of all my might and encouragement for spreading the everlasting gospel of God our Saviour, in all parts and places where God shall honour me with any power and influence. As to myself, sir, it is impossible to express the warm sentiments of my heart for the mercies without number with which I have been loaded by the God who has fed me all along to this day; and my reflection on his goodness covers me with shame and blushing, for I know my utter unworthiness, and that I am less than the least of all his mercies. I would, therefore, abhor myself, and repent in dust and ashes. You are sensible, my good friend, that governors stand in a glaring light, and their conduct is watched by friends and enemies; the one often unreasonably applaud, while the other, perhaps, too justly censure. Yet in this I am not anxious, but to approve myself to the Searcher of hearts, from whose mouth I must hear pronounced, at the great and general audit, those joyful words, 'Enter thou,' &c.; or that terrible sentence, 'Depart from me,' &c. Join me then in thankfulness to God for all the blessings and talents he has entrusted me with, and in prayer that I may employ them to his honour and glory, to the good of the people over whom he hath placed me, and so to the comfort of my own soul; that I may always remember, that he who ruleth over men must be just, ruling in the fear of God." '

Mr. Edwards goes on to say of his correspondent, 'In another letter which I received, dated Burlington, New Jersey, May 31, 1748, he says as follows:

' "I will prostrate myself before my God and Saviour, and on the bended knees of my soul (abhorring myself in every view) I will beg for a measure of divine grace and wisdom; that so I may be honoured in being an instrument in advancing the kingdom of

the blessed Jesus in this world, and in that way be bringing forth
fruit in old age. I bless God, my Heavenly Father, that I am not
ashamed of the cross of Christ; and I humbly ask the assistance
of sovereign grace that in times of temptation I may never be a
shame to it; I mean that my conversation may always be such as
becometh the gospel of Christ. And I tell you again that all such
as minister at the altar, and in the course of their ministry approve
themselves faithful to the great Head of the Church will not only
find my countenance and protection, but my love and esteem.

' "As to our embryo college, it is a noble design, and, if God
pleases, may prove an extensive blessing. I have adopted it for a
daughter, and hope it may become an *alma mater* to this and the
neighbouring provinces. I am getting the best advice and assistance
I can in the draft of a charter, which I intend to give to our infant
college; and I thank you, sir, for all the kind hints which you have
given me for the service of this excellent undertaking; and as
St. Luke says of Mary, *'she kept all these things and pondered them
in her heart,'* so you may depend what you have said about the
college will not be lost on me; but as far as God shall enable me,
I will lay out and exert myself in every way to bring it to maturity,
and thus to advance its future welfare and prosperity; for this,
I believe, will be acceptable in the sight of God our Saviour, a
relish for true religion and piety being a great stranger to this part
of America. The accounts I receive from time to time give me
reason to believe that Arminianism, Arianism, and even Socinian-
ism, in destruction of the doctrines of free grace, are daily propagated in the New England colleges. How horribly and how
wickedly are these poisonous notions rooting out those noble
principles on which our excellent ancestors founded those
seminaries! And how base a return is it in the present generation
to that God who is constantly surrounding them with goodness
and mercy! And how offensive is it in the eyes of that God who
is jealous of his glory, and will take vengeance on his adversaries,
and reserveth wrath for his enemies! And from these things I am
glad to thank you for your book, wrote in consequence of the
memorial from Scotland for promoting a concert of prayer. I am
much pleased with this proposal, and with your arguments to
encourage and corroborate the design. The two missionaries you
mention, Spencer and Strong, I am told are at Boston. I have
once and again desired Mr. Brainerd to assure them of my kindness

and respect. But their affairs have not yet led them this way. I rejoice in their being appointed to carry the gospel in its purity to the Six Nations; and when Mr. Brainerd and they proceed to Susquehanna, they shall have all my assistance and encouragement, by letters to the king's governors where they may pass, and my letters to the sachem or chief of those Indians." '

It has been judged expedient to insert both these letters in our account of the origin of New Jersey College, as they will serve to give the reader a better idea of the father and founder of this institution than any thing to which we can refer him. For although the character of governor Belcher has come down to us marked with piety and benevolence, these are the only memorials of the man from his own pen with which we are acquainted. But from these fragments of correspondence we see how deep was his humility, how fervent his zeal for the promotion of truth and piety, and his willingness to bear the reproach of the cross. And as to his public spirit in promoting the cause of virtue and literature, the College of New Jersey is a standing memorial. The good already accomplished by this College cannot be calculated, and we trust that it is destined to be a blessing to the community for ages to come.

We seem, however, to have lost sight of the design of this chapter, which was to show that the Log College was the germ of the College of New Jersey. But a little consideration will serve to convince the impartial reader of the reality of this connection. The Log College had done its work, and a great and good work it was. But the progress of the country, the proceedings of the old Synod, and the general sense of the community, made it evident that a literary institution of a higher order than the log cabin on the plains of Neshaminy was urgently needed; and the members of the new Synod were, no doubt, stimulated to exertion in this enterprise by the example of the other body, who were now engaged in establishing a school at New London.

The ministers who now exerted themselves in the establishment of the New Jersey College were all the friends of the Log College; and most of them had received their training, both in classical and theological learning, within the walls of this humble institution. Besides Dickinson and Burr, who were graduates of Yale College, the active friends and founders of Nassau Hall were the Tennents,

Blairs, Finley, Smith, Rogers, Davies, and others who had received their education in the Log College, or in schools instituted by those who had been instructed there. As this enterprise was entered on during the separation of the Presbyterian Church, those ministers connected with the old side took no part in it; and this, especially, because they had planned an institution for themselves, of which we propose to give some account in the ensuing chapter.

It is not my purpose to write the history of the New Jersey College; this will be done by another hand. This institution was commenced in Elizabethtown under its first President, the Rev. Jonathan Dickinson, a man of superior abilities both as a preacher and a writer, and truly evangelical; a friend of revivals, and a zealous promoter of missions among the aborigines of this country. He deserves to stand in the foremost rank among the fathers of the Presbyterian Church in these United States. Upon his decease the school was removed to Newark, and placed under the tuition and care of the Rev. Aaron Burr, another distinguished man, whose piercing intellect and commanding eloquence qualified him to be a leader in such an enterprise. No permanent site for the college had yet been selected. Elizabethtown and Newark were too near the borders of the State; New Brunswick was thought of, and the trustees came near fixing it there; but Providence overruled it, and Princeton, then a very small and inconsiderable village, was selected to be the seat of a college which has always been dear to a large portion of the Presbyterian Church. Here a large number of her sons received their education; for after the union of the two dissentient parties in 1758, nearly all candidates for the ministry in the Presbyterian Church finished their education in Nassau Hall. And to this day no literary institution enjoys more favour and is held in higher estimation than this venerable college. May her trustees and instructors never forget the principles on which the institution was founded!

A venerable friend,[1] in conversing with the writer on the subject of the Log College, observed that this humble institution was not only the germ of New Jersey College, but several other colleges which have been useful to the church and state, and have risen to high estimation in the country; and mentioned Jefferson, Hampden Sidney, and Washington College in Virginia; all which were founded and taught originally by students from Princeton.

[1] Rev. Matthew Brown, D.D.

And we need not stop here, for these in their turn have given rise to many other schools and colleges, where the same system of education, and the same principles of religion are adopted. Thus we see how much good may arise from a small beginning. As the stately oak originated in a small acorn, so an obscure school in the midst of the forest becomes a nursery, from which proceed not only eminent men but other and higher schools of learning, by which our country is enlightened and adorned. Let this fact encourage all who have it in their power to institute good schools of useful and solid learning, and to be liberal in encouraging and endowing academies and colleges and aiding poor scholars who possess talents to acquire a liberal education.

If our free institutions are long preserved, it will be by the means, under Providence, of religion and learning. Without the benign influence of knowledge and virtue, a free republican government cannot long exist; and without the influence of religion and good education, men are not fit for such freedom as is now enjoyed under our free and happy government. The immigration of so many thousand foreigners into our country renders it doubly necessary to exert every nerve to diffuse knowledge and sound principles of religion among the people. Let us have public schools, supported by the state, normal schools for the education of teachers, and parochial schools, in which every denomination may inculcate that religion which they believe to be founded in truth. Evangelical Christians need not contend about what shall be taught in schools, for if those truths in which they are all agreed shall be faithfully inculcated on our youth, there will not be any very glaring defect in the system of religious instruction. Those points in which they differ may be reserved for their consideration at a riper age. But *let the Bible be the text-book in every school, whether high or low.*

VIII

The New London School

As we have given a brief history of the Log College, the first
school erected within the bounds of the Presbyterian Church in
this country, and also of the New Jersey College, of which it was
the germ, it will not be considered an unsuitable digression to say
something of another school, which was established by the Synod
of Philadelphia after the rupture which has been described took
place. The want of an institution of classical and scientific education
was deeply felt; but what course to pursue was a problem not easy
to be solved. The Log College had been in successful operation
about fifteen years before the exclusion of the New Brunswick
Presbytery; but it appears from the statement of a former chapter
that it had never given general satisfaction to the Synod. And now
this school and all its friends and supporters were separated from
the Synod; so that the need of a school where candidates might
obtain at least the ground-work of a liberal education was felt to
be urgent. This matter, therefore, became the subject of frequent
deliberation and mutual consultation among the ministers. A
public meeting was at length agreed upon, and the business was
entered upon in good earnest. The Presbyteries of Philadelphia,
New Castle, and Donegal appointed certain of their members to
meet in the Great Valley, Nov. 16, 1743, to take into consideration
the subject of a plan for educating young men for the holy ministry.
After conference and deliberation, they resolved that this business
could not be properly managed unless the Synod would undertake
it; they therefore referred the further consideration of the subject
to that reverend body, but agreed that in the mean time a school

should be opened for the education of youth. When this matter, the ensuing year, was brought before the Synod, they adopted the plan as their own, and took the school under their care, and agreed upon the following plan for carrying it on.

'1. That there be a school kept open where all persons who please may send their children, and be there instructed gratis in the languages, philosophy, and divinity.

'2. In order to carry on this design, it is agreed that every congregation under our care be applied to for yearly contributions, more or less, as they can afford, and as God may incline them to contribute until Providence open the door for our supporting the school in some other way.

'3. That if any thing can be spared besides what is required to support a master and tutor, that it be employed by the trustees in buying books and other necessaries for said school, and for the benefit of it, as the trustees shall see proper.

'And Mr. Alison is chosen master of said school, and has the privilege of choosing an usher under him, to assist him; and the said Mr. Alison is exempted from all public business, save only attending church judicatories, and what concerns his particular pastoral charge. And the Synod agree to allow Mr. Alison twenty pounds per annum, and the usher fifteen pounds.' They then proceeded to appoint from their own body trustees for the management of the affairs of the school. To these trustees it belonged to visit the school, and direct the whole course of instruction, and to report to the Synod the condition of the school. (See Records of the Presbyterian Church, p. 174).

From what is here stated, it appears that Mr. Alison was the pastor of a church, and consequently the school was situated in his own vicinity. Where he received his education is not known to the writer, but it seems probable that he came over a probationer; for we have an account of his ordination in the Records referred to above, but no account of his licensure. Doubtless he stood very high as a scholar in the opinion of the Synod; and from the tradition which has come down respecting him, he was a very accomplished man. The estimation in which he was held as a scholar may be also inferred from the fact that he was invited to take charge of an academy, instituted in Philadelphia, over which he presided for many years.

The Synod of Philadelphia had now a school under their own

care, and an able teacher; but as they had manifested so great a reluctance to receive the pupils of Mr. Tennent's school, without a better education than could be afforded by a grammar-school, they could not for consistency's sake be satisfied with the course of instruction in their own school, where there were no more professors than in the Log College. They, therefore, thought of a plan of sending their young men for a short period to Yale College, to receive a diploma, if they could make an arrangement with the faculty and trustees of the college that would suit them. Messrs Andrews and Cross were appointed to write a letter to the president and corporation of the aforesaid college. This letter is not on record; neither is President Clapp's answer. But on receiving his letter they appointed a large committee to prepare a letter in answer, which is preserved in the Records of the Church, (pp. 185, 186, 187.) This letter has been several times referred to, and is an important document to cast light on the affairs of the church at that time and before the schism. Several things stated as facts in this narrative depend for their authority on this letter. It will be proper, therefore, to lay a considerable part of it before the reader. It serves to show what views the Synod entertained of the Log College, and what steps they had taken to establish a school under the superintendence of the Synod.

As we have neither the letter written by the Synod to President Clapp, nor his answer, the precise nature of the application made cannot now be ascertained, but from the reply to President Clapp's letter, which is on record, we may learn generally what the request or proposal was which they made. In this letter, dated May 30, 1746, they express their thanks to the president and fellows of Yale College, for considering their request, and expressing a readiness to promote the interests of learning and religion in the Presbyterian Church. It appears, however, that President Clapp wished for more particular information respecting the synodical school, and also the present state of the Synod. In answer to his inquiries they say: 'Some years ago our Synod found the interest of Christ's kingdom likely to suffer in these parts for want of a college for the education of young men. And our supplies from Europe, or New England, were few in proportion to the numerous vacancies in our growing settlements. Mr. William Tennent set up a school among us, where some were educated, and afterwards admitted to the ministry *without sufficient qualifications, as was judged by many of the Synod*. And what made the matter look worse, those that were educated in this private way denied the usefulness of some parts of learning that we thought very necessary. It was therefore agreed to try to institute a college, and apply to our friends in Britain, Ireland, and New England, to assist us. We wrote to the Association of Boston on this head, and had a very favourable answer. But when we were thus projecting our plan, and appointing commissioners to Britain, &c., to promote the thing, the war with Spain was proclaimed, which put a stop to our proceedings then. The Synod then came to a public agreement to take all private schools where young men were educated for the ministry so far under their care as to appoint a committee of our Synod to examine all such as had not obtained degrees in the European or New England colleges, and give them certificates if they were found qualified, which was to serve our Presbyteries instead of a college diploma till better provision could be made. Mr. Gilbert Tennent cried out that this was to prevent his father's school from training gracious men for the ministry; and he and some of his adherents protested against it, and counteracted this our public agreement, admitting men to the ministry which were judged unfit for that office; which course they persisted in, though admonished and reproved by us for such unwarrantable proceedings. While these debates subsisted, Mr. Whitefield came into the country, whom they drew into their party to encourage divisions; and they and he have been the sad instruments of dividing our churches. And by his interest, Mr. Gilbert Tennent grew hardy enough to tell our Synod he would oppose their design of getting assistance to erect a college wherever we should make application, and would maintain young men at his father's school in opposition to us. This, with his and his adherents' divisive practices, obliged the Synod to exclude him and others of his stamp from their communion. In this situation our affairs grew worse; for our vacancies were numerous, and we found it hard in such troubles to engage gentlemen from New England or Europe to come among us, such as our best friends in those places could recommend as steadfast in the faith, and men of parts and education. Upon this the Synod erected a school in 1744. It was agreed that the said school should be opened under the inspection of the Synod, where the languages, philosophy and divinity should be taught gratis to all that should comply with the regulations of the school, being persons of good character and behaviour. They appointed a master and a tutor for this business, who were to be paid by such contributions as the Synod could obtain for this purpose; and agreed from year to year to appoint trustees to meet twice a year to inspect the master's diligence and method of teaching, and direct what authors are chiefly to be read in the several branches of learning; to examine the scholars as to their proficiency and good conduct; apply the money procured to such uses as they judge proper; and who order all affairs relating to the school. The trustees are yearly to be accountable to the Synod, and to make report of their proceedings and state of the school. And it is agreed that after the said scholars pass the course of study prescribed them, they shall be publicly examined by the said trustees and such ministers as the Synod shall think fit to appoint.'

We are not informed that this negotiation with the president of Yale College resulted in anything practical. It does not appear that the Synod ever sent any of their young men to Yale College to finish their education. Indeed, the necessity for such a measure soon passed away, as the College of New Jersey in a short time after this was instituted and rapidly rose into credit. Dr. Alison, the principal of their school at New London, was invited to Philadelphia, to take charge of an academy which a number of gentlemen had erected in that city. It was not long before this academy was constituted a college, in which Dr. Alison was appointed the vice-provost and professor of Moral Philosophy. To this institution the young men belonging to the Synod of Philadelphia directed their attention, and here they commonly finished their education. But after the union of the two Synods, in 1758, candidates from all the Presbyteries were accustomed to resort to New Jersey College; especially after Dr. Witherspoon became the president.

Dr. Alison's departure from the Synod's school at New London seems to have been its death-blow. From the Records of the Synod of Philadelphia, it appears that Dr. Alison relinquished his station without receiving the approbation, either of the Presbytery of New Castle, of which he was a member, or of the Synod. His course was viewed as irregular by the Synod, but they were well satisfied with the thing itself; and when they met, a reference from the Presbytery of New Castle was laid before them, relative to this matter, when the following minute was adopted and placed on record, viz: 'The Synod having deliberately considered the affair of Mr. Alison's removal to Philadelphia, referred to them by the Presbytery of New Castle, judge that the method he used is contrary to the Presbyterian plan. Yet, considering the circumstances which urged him to take the method he used were very pressing, and that it was indeed almost impracticable to him to apply for the consent of Presbytery or Synod in the orderly way; and further being persuaded that Mr. Alison's being employed in such a station in the academy has a favourable aspect in several respects, and a very probable tendency not only to promote the good of the public but also of the church, as he may be serviceable to the interests thereof in teaching philosophy and divinity, as far as his obligations to the academy will permit, we judge that his proceedings in said affair are in a great measure excusable. Withal, the Synod advises that for the future its members be very cautious, and guard against such proceedings as are contrary to our known and approved methods in such cases.'

As we are not aware that any memoir of Dr. Francis Alison has been published; and as he was one of the most accomplished scholars who has adorned the Presbyterian Church in these United States, it seems desirable to preserve his memory from utter oblivion by giving a large extract from the funeral sermon preached on the occasion of his death by his friend and successor, the Rev. John Ewing, D.D. Dr. Alison died Nov. 20, 1777, in Philadelphia, where he had long resided.

'This discourse administers comfort and consolation under the loss of our pious friends and relations, who have died the death of the righteous, and had a just foundation to entertain the hope of a glorious immortality. Whatever reasons we have to mourn under the loss we sustain, by being deprived of their counsel, their prayers, or their conversation, yet we have no reason to be grieved on account of the exchange they have made, of a world of sin and sorrow for joys inconceivable and full of glory. They have fought the good fight of faith; they have finished their course; they are discharged from the Christian warfare, and are exalted to an unfading crown of righteousness and glory. These considerations afford consolation to the church of God, and to all its members, when those who were stationed by its glorious Head as watchmen upon her walls are removed by death; and particularly under the

F

heavy stroke which the interests of religion and learning this day
feel in America by the much lamented death of the Rev. Dr.
Francis Alison.

'However the partialities of friendship for the deceased have
carried funeral eulogies to a very exceptionable and unjustifiable
length on many occasions, yet I am persuaded that you will readily
acknowledge that there is but little danger of an extreme of this
kind in paying this tribute to the memory of a man whose private
virtues commanded the esteem of all that knew him, and whose
extensive public usefulness has erected a lasting monument to
his praise. To be silent on this occasion would argue an un-
pardonable insensibility to the interests of religion and learning,
and would be an instance of injustice to the man who for more than
forty years has supported the ministerial character with dignity
and reputation, and to whom America is greatly indebted for that
diffusion of light and knowledge, and that spirit of liberty and
inquiry which this day places many of her sons upon a level with
those of the oldest nations of Europe. All who knew him
acknowledge that he was frank, open, and ingenuous in his natural
temper; warm and zealous in his friendships; catholic and enlarged
in his sentiments; a friend to civil and religious liberty; abhorring
the intolerant spirit of persecution, bigotry, and superstition,
together with all the arts of dishonesty and deceit. His humanity
and compassion led him to spare no pains nor trouble in relieving
and assisting the poor and distressed by his advice and influence,
or by his own private liberality; and he has left behind him a
lasting testimony of the extensive benevolence of his heart in
planning, erecting, and nursing, with constant attention and
tenderness, the charitable scheme of the Widows' Fund, by which
many helpless orphans and destitute widows have been seasonably
relieved and supported; and will, we trust, continue to be relieved
and supported so long as the Synods of New York and Philadelphia
shall exist.

'Blessed with a clear understanding and an extensive liberal
education, thirsting for knowledge, and indefatigable in study
through the whole of his useful life, he acquired an unusual fund
of learning and knowledge, which rendered his conversation
remarkably instructive, and abundantly qualified him for the
sacred work of the ministry and the painful instruction of youth
in the college. He was truly a scribe well instructed unto the

kingdom of heaven, a workman that needed not be ashamed, for he rightly divided the word of truth, and was peculiarly skilful in giving to every one his portion in due season. In his public exhibitions he was warm, animated, plain, practical, argumentative, and pathetic; and he has left a testimony in the consciences of thousands who attended upon his ministry, that he was willing to spend and be spent to promote their salvation, and that he failed not to declare to them the whole counsel of God, while he endeavoured to save himself and those that heard him. And we have reason to hope that the bountiful Redeemer, whom he served in his spirit, has greatly honoured him by making him instrumental in the salvation of many, who shall be the crown of his rejoicing in the day of the Lord. His solicitude for the interests of the Redeemer's kingdom, and his desires to engage young men in the sacred work of the ministry, and to promote the public happiness by the diffusion of religious liberty and learning through the once untutored wilds of America induced him to open a public school in New London about thirty-six years ago, at which time there was scarcely a shadow of learning in the Middle States; and he generously instructed all that came to him without fee or reward, accounting himself amply paid by the propagation of that spirit of inquiry, that thirst for learning, and those generous and public-spirited attempts to found and establish colleges in the states which we now see.

'Animated by a laudable spirit and a generous concern for the public good, some gentlemen in this city erected an academy here about thirty years ago, and invited him to take the instruction and oversight of it. They pursued the same benevolent design until a college was afterwards added, in which he was constituted vice-provost, and professor of moral philosophy. In this laborious employment he has ever since acquitted himself with distinguished honour, fidelity and success, to the extensive dissemination of that public spirit which was so early raised and so successfully cultivated by this faithful and industrious servant of the public. And to the spreading influence of those numerous gentlemen who have received the first rudiments of their education from him, we cannot but attribute in a great measure those pleasing prospects which we now entertain, of seeing the sacred lamp of science burning with a brighter flame, and scattering its invigorating rays over the unexplored deserts of this extensive continent, until the whole world be involved in the united blaze of knowledge, liberty and religion. In short, he was "a burning and a shining light." and one of the brightest luminaries that ever shone on this western world.

'He is now discharged from the labours of mortality, and is gone, we trust, to receive the approbation of that compassionate Redeemer whom he so faithfully served. For he often expressed his hopes in the mercy of God unto eternal life, and told me but a few days ago, "that he had no doubt but that, according to the tenor of the gospel covenant, he would obtain the pardon of his sins through the great Redeemer of mankind, and enjoy an eternity of rest and glory in the presence of God." It was this comfortable prospect that animated him to uncommon fidelity and industry in all the duties of life, and enabled him to bear the lingering dissolution of his body with patience and resignation, until he fell asleep in Jesus.

'Let us, then, who survive our friends, endeavour to be followers of them who by faith and patience have inherited the promises. Let the solemnities of this mournful day, in which an afflicted family, the college in this city, the congregation in which he so long laboured in word and in doctrine, the church of Christ, and the community at large, have felt a painful wound, teach us to live the life of the righteous, that we may also have hopes of the divine approbation at our death. Let those virtues and graces which shone with a distinguished lustre in the private life and the public conduct of our departed friend engage us all who have in one way or other enjoyed the benefit of his pious and useful labours to remember him who has spoken to us the word of God, and considering the issue of his conversation imitate his faith. That gracious God who has told us that the righteous shall be had in everlasting remembrance expects that they should concur in accomplishing that comfortable promise, and not counteract it by burying their eminent virtues in an ungrateful oblivion. Let us so remember them as that we may feel their constraining efficacy to excite in us a laudable emulation.

'And now, my friends, let me close the present address with a word to you who have long enjoyed his ministerial labours. You are now deprived of an opportunity of hearing the word of God from his mouth; of listening to his warm and pathetic entreaties to be reconciled to God through a Redeemer; of joining with him in ardent supplications to the throne of grace; and of receiving any further instructions from his labours among you. We cannot but trust that some of you will have reason to bless God eternally that he has, in his wise providence, placed you under his ministry, while our solicitude for your salvation makes us fear that others of you may yet remain barren and unfruitful under all the cultivation of divine grace by the hand of this faithful watchman in Israel. You are, therefore, this day addressed by this mournful dispensation of divine providence, and called to make a solemn pause, and to consider what improvement you have made of his labours; to recollect the compassionate warnings he has given you of your danger, the warm expostulations he has made with you, and the strong cries he has often raised to the God of mercy for your salvation. And if you have any grateful remembrance of his pious and useful labours, let me exhort and entreat you to discover it by a constant and careful attendance upon the means of grace with which you are yet favoured. These are appointed to bring you to God and to glory, to the spirits of just men made perfect, and all the first-born sons of glory above. It is not long before you shall be deprived of all these golden opportunities to secure your eternal salvation; and let this awakening consideration excite us to speak, and you to hear the word of God, that our mutual account at the bar of our Judge may be joyful.'

IX

Memoir of the Rev. John Tennent

Birth—Religious Exercises and Conversion—Entrance into the ministry—Settlement at Freehold, Monmouth County—Great Success—Early Death.

Although John Tennent was younger than his brother William, being the third son of the Rev. William Tennent, sen., yet, on several accounts, it seems expedient to place the short memoir of him before that of his elder brother. It would seem from all that we can learn respecting these men that John was licensed to preach the gospel before William. This was probably owing to the fact that William Tennent, jr. suffered much loss of time by severe sickness, as will hereafter appear. Or it may have been the case that William was engaged longer than his brother in assisting his father in teaching in the Log College. But whatever may have been the case, it is certain that the Rev. John Tennent was settled in the ministry some years before his brother; and that the Rev. William Tennent was not settled as a pastor, until after the death of his brother John, when he became his successor in the church at Freehold, as will appear when we give a memoir of him; and it is principally on this account that we place John foremost.

The third son of the Rev. William Tennent, sen. was born in the county of Armagh, in Ireland, in the year 1707, Nov. 12, and was therefore only nine years of age when his father came to America. The whole of his education he obtained under the paternal roof, and in the Log College which his father had founded at Neshaminy.

Of his conversion to God we have an interesting narrative from the pen of his brother, Gilbert, written after his death, and prefixed to some of his sermons, which were published in a pamphlet after his decease, from which the following is an extract:

'His conviction of his sin, danger, and misery, was the most violent in degree of any I ever saw. For several days and nights together he was made to cry out in the most dolorous and affecting manner, almost every moment. The words which he used in his soul-agony were these: "O my bloody, lost soul! What shall I do? Have mercy on me, O God, for Christ's sake." Sometimes he was brought to the very brink of despair, and would conclude, surely God would never have mercy on such a great sinner as he was. And yet his life was unstained with those scandalous extravagances by which too many in their youth are ensnared. His natural predominant sin was rash anger; and the worst I ever knew him guilty of was some indecent haste in this way, on account of which he was afterwards exceedingly humbled, and against which he became very watchful. His passionateness cost him many a deep sob, heavy groan, and salt tear. After it pleased God to confer his grace upon him, he was remarkably altered in this particular, and gained in a great measure an ascendency over his besetting sin. Whilst under conviction his distress was such as to induce him to make an open confession of his sins to almost all that came near him, and also to beg their prayers in his behalf at a throne of grace. And this he did in the most earnest and beseeching manner. His dolorous groans and vehement importunity were such as greatly to affect even strangers who came to see him. And he earnestly and frequently begged of God that he would humble him to the dust, and beneath the dust.

One morning, about break of day, after great wrestling through the night and day preceding, he took occasion to speak as surprisingly as ever I heard any mortal about the morning star, longing and praying that the blessed Jesus, the true, the bright, the beautiful Morning Star, who brought the light and day into a dark world, would appear in mercy to his poor soul; and then, at the rising of the sun, he entreated that the Sun of righteousness might shine upon his disconsolate, dejected, wretched soul, with beams of mercy and salvation. His heart appeared to be sick, soresick, with panting after Christ, so as to be ready to burst in pieces. I have through the riches of free grace been favoured with the sight of many a convinced sinner, but never did I behold any other in such a rack of acute and continued anguish, under the dismal apprehensions of impending ruin and endless misery from the vengeance of a just and holy God.

'Perceiving such evident signs of deep conviction, humiliation, and earnest desire, I offered to him for his comfort all the most encouraging invitations and promises adapted to his case; and sometimes endeavoured to persuade him that he had an interest in these promises, since God had wrought in him those conditions on which the blessings were suspended. But although this would sometimes yield him a temporary relief, yet in a little while he would break forth again with the most doleful lamentations, complaining that no promise in the book of God belonged to him, and denying that any of these conditions to which the promises were made had been wrought in him. The truth is, his wound was so deep that none but God's arm could heal it. But it pleased God, after an agony almost uninterrupted for four days and four nights, during which he cried out incessantly as described above, that he would make his consolations as eminent and conspicuous as his convictions had been severe. It is worthy of remark that for some time before it pleased the Almighty to shed abroad the beams of his love and mercy on his soul, he was much exercised with sorrowful and piercing reflections on account of his hypocrisy. He judged himself to be a pharisee and a hypocrite for crying out as he had done; and yet the sharpness of his inward pain was such that he could not prevent it, therefore he would have all people out of the room, that he might pray and mourn alone.

'One morning when I went to see him, I perceived a great alteration in his countenance; for he who an hour before had looked like a condemned man going to be put to some cruel death now appeared with a cheerful, gladsome countenance, and spoke to me in these words: "O brother, the Lord Jesus has come in mercy to my soul. I was begging for a crumb of mercy with the dogs, and Christ has told me that he will give me a crumb." Then he desired me to thank God in prayer, which I did more than once. He also requested me to praise God by singing part of a psalm, which I complied with, and sang the 34th. It was, indeed, surprising to hear this person singing the praises of God with more clearness, energy, and joy, than any of the spectators who had crowded in on this extraordinary and solemn occasion. And that, especially, when it is considered that now it was ten o'clock in the forenoon, whereas at three o'clock in the same morning he was speechless for some minutes, and thought by all present to be expiring in death. The consolations of God had such an influence upon him that about an hour or two afterwards he walked about thirty rods to see his brother William, who was then extremely sick, nigh unto death, and thought by most to be past all human hope of recovery. He said he must see his brother, to tell him what God had done for his soul, that he might praise God on his account before he died. And when he entered the room where his brother was lying, his joy appeared to overflow, and he addressed him in the following words: "O brother, the Lord has looked with pity on my soul. Let the heavens, earth, and sea, and all that in them is, praise God!" But being exposed too soon to the cool air, he fell into a fever, and then called in question that eminent discovery of God's love which he had experienced. But it was not long before he was again comforted; and from this time a great change in his conversation was manifest. And while he experienced many seasons of the sealing of God's covenant love, yet in the intervals he was often dejected and distressed with doubts and fears respecting his own state.

'He gave the best evidence of a change of heart in the conscientious and diligent performance of all Christian duties, even of those most opposite to our corrupt nature, such as secret prayer and fasting. He was a tender-hearted, courteous relative, and of a very sympathetic spirit. His respectful and affectionate treatment of his reverend and aged father and his kind mother merits an honourable mention. His great soul disdained any thing that was mean, and inclined him to the most noble and generous actions that were within his power.

'He was endowed by his Creator with a natural quickness of apprehension, copiousness of fancy, and fluency of expression, which served to qualify him eminently for the office of a preacher. He had made no contemptible progress in the learned languages, and also in philosophical and theological studies; but he particularly excelled in the polemical and casuistical branches of divinity. He was well known to be an expert disputant and casuist; but that which crowned his other attainments, and made them appear with beauty and lustre, was his unfeigned and eminent piety.

'His attainments in the Christian graces were eminently conspicuous in the following particulars. First, his humility. He was wont to speak of himself in the most abasing terms, saying that he thought himself one of the worst creatures the creation bore; and on his dying bed he desired his relations to forbear any funeral encomiums upon him when he was gone, for he declared with vehemence that he was not worthy of them. When admitted to preach he would often, in his private studies, take the Bible in his hand, and would walk up and down the room weeping and mourning that although there was a treasury of precious truth contained in that blessed book, he understood so little of them. A sense of the greatness of the ministerial work, and of his ignorance and unfitness for it was often a very oppressive burden to him. It was a striking evidence of the low opinion which he entertained of himself, that he never could be persuaded that a holy God would bless the labours of a person every way so mean and so unworthy as he felt himself to be. And when informed that certain persons had been convinced under his ministry, he could not for some time believe that the work was genuine, until further conviction was afforded by bright and incontestable evidences.

'His love to Christ was manifest to all who had the opportunity of hearing his earnest and importunate prayers. Indeed, Christ and him crucified was the end at which he aimed, the sacred centre in which all the lines of his life terminated. Christ was the object of his supreme love and highest admiration.

'He possessed also a flaming zeal for the establishment and promotion of the Messiah's kingdom. It was his oft-repeated petition that God would make him serviceable to his church, and that he would not suffer him to live merely to devour the alms of the church, but that he would rather remove him to himself before he became useless.'

When Mr. John Tennent had finished his preparatory studies in the Log College, he presented himself to the Presbytery of Philadelphia; and after passing with credit the usual trials he was licensed to preach the gospel.

Soon after Mr. Tennent's licensure he visited the congregation of Freehold, in the county of Monmouth, New Jersey, which was now without a pastor. This congregation owed its origin to some Scotch people who were cast on the Jersey shore, the vessel Caledonia, in which they sailed, having been stranded on our coast. These people, being thus by the providence of God cast upon this land, determined to take up their abode in the country, near to the place where they reached the shore; and being Presbyterians, they were not content to live without the ordinances of public worship, according to the creed and usages of the church of Scotland. They accordingly set about building a house of worship, which was situated a few miles east of the present church of Freehold, where the remains of the old building and a grave-yard are yet to be seen. Mr. Boyd, the first licentiate of the Presbytery of Philadelphia was their first minister, but died within less than two years. For some time afterwards this congregation was supplied by the Rev. Joseph Morgan, but he having left them early in the year 1730, they invited young Mr. Tennent to preach to them as a candidate. Being a young man of uncommon modesty and humility, he was very reluctant to go, and even after he had consented to visit them, as his brother William, in his letter to Mr. Prince, of Boston, informs us, he regretted the engagement very much, for it seemed to him that they were a people whom God had given up for the abuse of the gospel. But though he went under this cloud of discouragement, his first labours among this people were remarkably blessed. On his first visit he preached four or five Sabbaths, and found among the people a serious disposition to attend to the concerns of their souls, and to search the Scriptures to see whether the things which they heard from the pulpit were so. And he was assisted to preach with so much freedom, that he told his brother William that he was fully per-suaded that Christ Jesus had a large harvest to bring home there; and though they were a poor broken people, yet if they called him he would go to them, though he should be under the necessity of begging his bread. On the 15th of April, 1730, they assembled, and gave him a unanimous call, which he accepted, and was ordained November 19th of the same year.

'His labours in this congregation.' according to his brother Gilbert, 'were attended with three notable qualities—prudence, diligence, and success,' Though the time was short which he was permitted to remain among them, yet his labours were abundant. His race was swift and vehement; and his heart was so fixed on the work of God that he could not be persuaded to desist from his public labours, even when his body was emaciated and debilitated by a consumptive disease, and when, in the judgment of physicians, it was prejudicial to his broken constitution.

'In his public discourses, not to mention the justness of his method, the beauty of his style, and the fluency of his expression, by which he chained his not unwilling hearers to his lips, he was very awakening and terrible to unbelievers in denouncing and describing with the most vehement pathos and awful solemnity the terrors of an offended Deity, the threats of a broken law, and the miseries of a sinful state. And this subject, he insisted much upon, because he, with many others, found it the most effectual and successful means to alarm secure sinners. He used a close, distinguishing, and detecting method in the application of his sermons; which, with his pungent mode of expression, was very piercing and solemn. But, as Dr. Watts observes of Mr. Gouge, he knew the pity of Immanuel's heart as well as the terrors of Jehovah's hand. He was as tender and compassionate in his addresses to gracious souls as faithful to brandish and apply the law's lancet to the secure: and he was as willing to do the one as the other. But, indeed, he was very cautious of misapplying the different portions of the word to his hearers; or of setting before them only a common mess, and leaving it to them to divide among themselves, as their fancy and humour directed them; for he well knew that was the bane of preaching.

'Once more, he was a successful preacher. When he was under trials for the ministry, he was much exercised with doubts, difficulties, and distresses about his call to this great and awful trust; but it pleased God to dissipate these clouds, and to afford to his perplexed and anxious mind abundant satisfaction respecting this matter, by the numerous seals which crowned his public labours; for as the famous Rutherford says, "it is not probable that God would seal a blank." It may be truly said of him that he gained more poor sinners to Christ in that little compass of time which he had to improve in the ministerial work, which was about three and a half years, than many in the space of twenty, thirty, forty, or fifty years. Many souls have and will have reason through eternity to bless God that ever they saw him. But though he was thus honoured with smiles of heaven upon his labours; and though favoured with the kind regards of a loving and generous people, who had it been possible would have plucked out their own eyes and have given them to him; so that no minister before was ever the object of a more respectful regard and sympathy; yet was he far from being exalted in his own mind, but through grace retained a just, grateful, and humble sense of God's distinguishing goodness and his own unworthiness.

'As he drew near to his end, his love for his people and concern for their welfare increased. He would often express himself to one of his brothers in such language as the following, "I am grieved for my people, for I fear they will be left to wander as sheep without a shepherd; or get one that will pull down what I have poorly endeavoured to build up." His brother, who watched with him in his sickness, has frequently overheard him in the deep silence of the night, wrestling with God by prayer, sobs and tears, for his people. Yea, when so reduced by consumption that he could scarce walk alone, he bore the pains of this lingering disease with unbroken patience, and silent submission to his Father's pleasure, until it pleased God to open a door of escape to his captive soul, through the ruins of his decayed frame.

'On Saturday evening—the last evening of his life—he was seized with a violent pang of death which was thought by his attendants to be his last; from which unexpectedly recovering and observing a confusion among them, he addressed one whom he saw uncommonly affected, with a cheerful countenance, in the following words, "I would not have you think the worse of the ways of holiness, because you see me in such agonies of distress, for I know there is a crown of glory in heaven for me, which I shall shortly wear." Afterwards, in the night, he often prayed, "Come Lord Jesus! O Jesus, why dost thou linger?" Some time before day, he repeated with humble confidence the last words of David, "Although my house be not so with God, yet hath he made with me an everlasting covenant, ordered in all things and sure; for this is all my salvation and all my desire." 2 Sam. 23. 5.

'About the break of day, he called his brother William to prayer, and earnestly desired him to implore Heaven for his speedy removal, for, he said, he longed to be gone. About eight or nine o'clock of the next day, which was the Sabbath, his desire was granted, when it pleased his Master to translate him to that great assembly of the just, "the church of the firstborn," there to celebrate an eternal Sabbath, in praises and songs of triumph.

'A few minutes before he expired, holding his bother William by the hand, he broke out into the following rapturous expressions; "Farewell, my brethren, farewell father and mother; farewell world, with all thy vain delights. Welcome, God and Father—welcome, sweet Lord Jesus! Welcome death—welcome eternity. Amen!" Then with a low voice, he said, "Lord, Jesus, come Lord

Jesus!" And so he fell asleep in Christ, and obtained an abundant entrance into the everlasting kingdom of his God and Saviour.'

He was buried in the grave-yard near to the church where he preached, and where his tombstone may yet be seen. The Rev. Jonathan Dickinson, of Elizabethtown, composed for his tombstone the following epitaph:

> 'Who quick grew old in learning, virtue, grace,
> Quick finished, well-yielded to death's embrace:
> Whose mouldered dust, this cabinet contains,
> Whose soul triumphant, with bright seraphs reigns;
> Waiting the time 'till heaven's bright concave flame,
> And the last trump repairs his ruined frame.'

Much praise cannot be awarded to the poetry of the foregoing epitaph, but it serves to show in what estimation Mr. Tennent was held by one of the most eminent theologians of his day.

His death occurred on the 23rd day of April, 1732, in the twenty-fifth year of his age.

Mr. Gilbert Tennent, with the memoir of his brother John, published also one of his sermons. The subject is 'Regeneration'; and is treated in a clear discriminating manner.

As far as can be judged from the accounts which have come down to us respecting this young pastor, and from the aforesaid discourse, there is reason to conclude that both in piety and talents he was not inferior to any one of his brothers; and that if he had lived to the usual period of human life, he would have been 'a burning and a shining light' in the church.

The people of his charge were greatly attached to him, and exceedingly lamented his death. There is still extant the fragment of an old manuscript book, kept by the session of his church, in which is contained the following entry:

'A mournful providence and cause of great humiliation to this poor congregation, to be bereaved in the flower of youth, of the most laborious, successful, well-qualified, and pious pastor this age afforded; though but a youth of twenty-four years five months and eleven days.'

In this record he is called 'the reverend and dear Mr. John Tennent.'[1]

It may be gratifying to some to know the names of some of the principal families which constituted the congregation of Freehold, which have been taken from the record before mentioned. Among them we find Ker, Craig, Forman, Anderson, Newall, Gordon, Lloyd, Crawford, Henderson, Robinson, Rhea, Watson, Wilson, Campbell, Covenhoven, Little, Cumming, English, &c.

[1] See Appendix, II.

X

Memoir of the
Rev. William Tennent, Jr.

Preliminary Remarks—Mr. Tennent's birth and education—Sickness, apparent death, and recovery—State of his mind during his trance—Settlement and ordination as successor to his brother at Freehold—Marriage—Character as a pastor and success in the ministry—Trial for Perjury—Extraordinary means of deliverance—The close of life.

The following memoir of the Rev. William Tennent, jr. was originally published in 'The Assembly's Missionary Magazine,' in the year 1806; and although it was not accompanied with the author's name, it was well understood to be from the pen of the Hon. Elias Boudinot, LL.D., who was well acquainted with all the members of this remarkable family. But although Dr. Boudinot prepared this memoir for the press, the greater part of the narrative was written, at his request, by the late Dr. Henderson of Freehold, one of the elders of the Freehold church, and a man distinguished for his piety, integrity, veracity, and patriotism. This original manuscript is now in the possession of the Historical Society of New Jersey. From it we learn that the history of Mr. Tennent's trial, which occurred soon after his settlement in the ministry, and when Dr. Henderson was too young to be a competent witness, was received from his father, who was then an elder in the church of Freehold, of which Mr. William Tennent was the pastor. There can be no doubt about the authenticity of the facts here stated, however they may be accounted for. The writer has heard the same facts from elderly persons who never had seen this published account; and they were so public that they were generally known, not only to the people of this part of the country, but they were currently reported and fully believed in other states. The writer has heard them familiarly talked of in Virginia, from his childhood. It is a matter of some regret that the record of this trial cannot be found, yet papers have been discovered among the archives of the state, in which reference is made to this transaction. The following is the narrative:

'Among the duties which every generation owes to those who are to succeed it, we may reckon the careful delineation of the characters of those whose example deserves and may invite imitation. Example speaks louder than precept, and living practical religion has a much greater effect on mankind than argument or eloquence. Hence, the lives of pious men become the most important sources of instruction and warning to posterity; while their exemplary conduct affords the best commentary on the religion they professed. But when such men have been remarkably favoured of God with unusual degrees of light and knowledge, and have been honoured by the special and extraordinary influences of his Holy Spirit, and by the most manifest and wonderful interpositions of divine Providence in their behalf, it becomes a duty of more than common obligation to hand down to posterity the principal events of their lives, together with such useful inferences as they naturally suggest. A neglect of this duty, even by persons who may be conscious of the want of abilities necessary for the complete biographer, is greatly culpable, for, if the strictest attention be paid to the truth of the facts related, and all exaggeration or partial representation be carefully avoided, the want of other furniture can be no excuse for burying in oblivion that conduct, which, if known, might edify and benefit the world.

'The writer of these memoirs has difficulties of a peculiar kind to encounter, in attempting to sketch the life of that modest, humble, and worthy man, whose actions, exercises, and sentiments he wishes to record. Worldly men, who are emulous to transmit their names to following ages, take care to leave such materials for the future historian as may secure the celebrity which they seek. But the humble follower of the meek and lowly Jesus, whose sole aim is the glory of God in the welfare of immortal souls, goes on from day to day as seeing Him who is invisible, careful to approve himself only to the Searcher of hearts, regardless of worldly fame or distinction, and leaving it to his heavenly Father to reward him openly in the day of final account. The writer of such a man's life must principally rely on a personal acquaintance with him, and the communications of his intimate friends, for the information

G

which shall be imparted to the public. In these circumstances it is peculiarly embarrassing if some of the facts to be recorded are of such a nature that it is most desirable to have their authenticity so fully established that incredulity shall be confounded, and the sneer of the sceptical and profane lose its effect. But the writer of the following narrative, though placed in these circumstances, and having such facts to detail, has nevertheless determined to proceed. He has refreshed and corrected his own recollection by the most careful inquiries that he could possibly make of others, until he is well assured that what he shall state is incontestable truth. From the very nature of several things of which an account will be given, they do not indeed admit of any other direct testimony than that of the remarkable man to whom they relate. But if there ever was a person who deserved to be believed unreservedly on his word, it was he. He possessed an integrity of soul and a soundness of judgement which did actually secure him an unlimited confidence from all who knew him. Every species of deception, falsehood, and exaggeration he abhorred and scorned. He was an Israelite indeed in whom there was no guile. With such materials, then, as have been mentioned, and for a work of such character as has been hinted, the writer has undertaken his task. He has undertaken what he would most gladly have resigned to an abler hand; but from which, as no other offered, he *dared* not withhold his own. He could wish that speculative and even unbelieving minds might be instructed and convinced by these memoirs. But his principal object, and that in which he trusts he shall not be entirely disappointed, is to direct, assist, and comfort pious souls, groaning under the pressure of the calamities which they often have to endure in their pilgrimage through the wilderness of this world.

'The Rev. Wm. Tennent, of Freehold, New Jersey, was the second son of the Rev. Wm. Tennent, sen., and was born on the 3rd day of June, 1705, in the county of Armagh, in Ireland, and was just turned of thirteen years when he arrived in America. He applied himself with much zeal and industry to his studies, and made great proficiency in the languages, particularly in the Latin. Being early impressed with a deep sense of divine things, he soon determined to follow the example of his father and elder brother, by devoting himself to the service of God in the ministry of the gospel. His brother Gilbert being called to the pastoral charge of the church at New Brunswick, in New Jersey, and making a very considerable figure as a useful and popular preacher, William determined as he had completed his course in the languages, to study divinity under his brother. Accordingly he left his father's house with his consent, and by his advice, and went to New Brunswick. At this departure from home, which was considered as his setting out in life, his father addressed him with great affection, commending him to the favour and protection of that God from whom he himself had received so much mercy, and who had directed him in all his migrations. He gave him a small sum of money, as the amount of all he could do for him, telling him that if he behaved well and did his duty, this was an ample provision for him; and if he should act otherwise, and prove ungrateful to a kind and gracious God, it was too much and more than he deserved. Thus, with a pittance, and the blessing of a pious and affectionate parent, of more consequence than thousands of pounds, the young student set out in the world.

'After a regular course of study in theology, Mr. Tennent was preparing for his examination by the Presbytery as a candidate for the gospel ministry. His intense application affected his health, and brought on a pain in his breast, and a slight hectic. He soon became emaciated, and at length was like a living skeleton. His life was now threatened. He was attended by a physician, a young gentleman who was attached to him by the strictest and warmest friendship. He grew worse and worse, till little hope of life was left. In this situation, his spirits failed him, and he began to entertain doubts of his final happiness. He was conversing one morning with his brother in Latin on the state of his soul when he fainted and died away. After the usual time he was laid out on a board, according to the common practice of the country, and the neighbourhood were invited to attend his funeral on the next day. In the evening, his physician and friend returned from a ride in the country, and was afflicted beyond measure at the news of his death. He could not be persuaded that it was certain; and on being told that one of the persons who had assisted in laying out the body thought he had observed a little tremor of the flesh under the arm, although the body was cold and stiff, he endeavoured to ascertain the fact. He first put his own hand into warm water, to make it as sensible as possible, and then felt under the arm, and at the heart, and affirmed that he felt an unusual warmth, though no one else could. He had the body restored to a warm bed, and insisted that the

people who had been invited to the funeral should be requested
not to attend. To this the brother objected as absurd, the eyes
being sunk, the lips discoloured and the whole body cold and stiff.
However, the doctor finally prevailed, and all probable means
were used to discover symptoms of returning life. But the third
day arrived, and no hopes were entertained of success but by the
doctor, who never left him night or day. The people were again
invited, and assembled to attend the funeral. The doctor still
objected, and at last confined his request for delay to one hour,
then to half an hour, and finally to a quarter of an hour. He had
discovered that the tongue was much swollen and threatened to
crack. He was endeavouring to soften it, by some emollient ointment
put upon it with a feather, when the brother came in, about the
expiration of the last period, and mistaking what the doctor was
doing for an attempt to feed him manifested some resentment,
and in a spirited tone said, "It is shameful to be feeding a lifeless
corpse;" and insisted with earnestness that the funeral should
immediately proceed. At this critical and important moment,
the body to the great alarm and astonishment of all present opened
its eyes, gave a dreadful groan and sunk again into apparent death.
This put an end to all thoughts of burying him, and every effort was
again employed in hopes of bringing about a speedy resuscitation.
In about an hour the eyes again opened, a heavy groan proceeded
from the body, and again all appearance of animation vanished.
In another hour life seemed to return with more power, and a complete revival took place to the great joy of the family and friends,
and to the no small astonishment and conviction of very many
who had been ridiculing the idea of restoring to life a dead body.

'Mr. Tennent continued in so weak and low a state for six weeks,
that great doubts were entertained of his final recovery. However,
after that period he recovered much faster, but it was about twelve
months before he was completely restored. After he was able to
walk the room, and to take notice of what passed around him, on a
Sunday afternoon, his sister, who had stayed from church to attend
him, was reading in the Bible, when he took notice of it and asked
her what she had in her hand. She answered that she was reading
the Bible. He replied, "What is the Bible? I know not what you
mean." This affected the sister so much that she burst into tears,
and informed him that he was once well acquainted with it. On
her reporting this to the brother, when he returned, Mr. Tennent

was found, upon examination, to be totally ignorant of every trans-action of life previous to his sickness. He could not read a single word, neither did he seem to have any idea of what it meant. As soon as he became capable of attention, he was taught to read and write, as children are usually taught, and afterwards began to learn the Latin language under the tuition of his brother. One day, as he was reciting a lesson in Cornelius Nepos, he suddenly started, clapped his hand to his head, as if something had hurt him, and made a pause. His brother asking him what was the matter, he said that he felt a sudden shock in his head, and now it seemed to him as if he had read that book before. By degrees his recollection was restored, and he could speak the Latin as fluently as before his sickness. His memory so completely revived that he gained a perfect knowledge of the past transactions of his life, as if no difficulty had previously occurred. This event, at the time, made a considerable noise, and afforded, not only matter of serious contemplation to the devout Christian, especially when connected with what follows in this narration, but furnished a subject of deep investigation and learned inquiry to the real philosopher and curious anatomist.

'The writer of these memoirs was greatly interested by these uncommon events; and, on a favourable occasion, earnestly pressed Mr. Tennent for a minute account of what his views and apprehensions were while he lay in this extraordinary state of suspended animation. He discovered great reluctance to enter into any explanation of his perceptions and feelings, at this time; but, being importunately urged to do it, he at length consented, and proceeded with a solemnity not to be described.

' "While I was conversing with my brother," said he, "on the state of my soul, and the fears I had entertained for my future welfare, I found myself, in an instant, in another state of existence, under the direction of a superior being, who ordered me to follow him. I was accordingly wafted along, I know not how, till I beheld at a distance an ineffable glory, the impression of which on my mind it is impossible to communicate to mortal man. I immediately reflected on my happy change, and thought,—Well, blessed be God! I am safe at last, notwithstanding all my fears. I saw an innumerable host of happy beings surrounding the in-expressible glory, in acts of adoration and joyous worship; but I did not see any bodily shape or representation in the glorious appearance. I heard things unutterable. I heard their songs and hallelujahs of thanksgiving and praise with unspeakable rapture. I felt joy unutterable and full of glory. I then applied to my conductor, and requested leave to join the happy throng; on which he tapped me on the shoulder, and said, 'You must return to the earth.' This seemed like a sword through my heart. In an instant, I recollect to have seen my brother standing before me, disputing with the doctor. The three days during which I had appeared lifeless seemed to me not more than ten or twenty minutes. The idea of returning to this world of sorrow and trouble gave me such a shock, that I fainted repeatedly." He added, "Such was the effect on my mind of what I had seen and heard that if it be possible for a human being to live entirely above the world and the things of it, for some time afterwards I was that person. The ravishing sound of the songs and hallelujahs that I heard, and the very words uttered, were not out of my ears when awake, for at least three years. All the kingdoms of the earth were in my sight as nothing and vanity; and so great were my ideas of heavenly glory that nothing which did not in some measure relate to it could command my serious attention."

'The author has been particularly solicitous to obtain every confirmation of this extraordinary event in the life of Mr. Tennent. He accordingly wrote to every person he could think of likely to have conversed with Mr. T. on the subject. He received several answers; but the following letter from the worthy successor of Mr. Tennent, in the pastoral charge of his church, will answer for the author's purpose:

' "MONMOUTH, NEW JERSEY, December 10th, 1805.

' "*Dear Sir:*—Agreeably to your request, I now send you in writing the remarkable accounts which I sometime since gave you verbally respecting your good friend, my worthy predecessor, the late Rev. William Tennent, of this place. In a very free and feeling conversation on religion, and on the future rest and blessedness of the people of God (while travelling together from Monmouth to Princeton), I mentioned to Mr. Tennent that I should be highly gratified in hearing, from his own mouth, an account of the *trance* which he was said to have been in, unless the relation would be disagreeable to himself. After a short silence, he proceeded, saying that he had been sick with a fever, that the fever increased, and he by degrees sunk under it. After some time (as his friends informed him) he died, or appeared to die, in the same manner as persons usually do; that in laying him out, one happened to draw his hand under the left arm, and perceived a small tremor in the flesh; that he was laid out, and was cold and stiff. The time for his funeral was appointed, and the people collected; but a young doctor, his particular friend, pleaded with great earnestness that he might not then be buried, as the tremor under the arm continued; that his brother Gilbert became impatient with the young gentleman, and said to him, *'What! a man not dead, who is cold and stiff as a stake?'* The importunate young friend, however, prevailed; another day was appointed for the burial, and the people separated. During this interval many means were made use of to discover, if possible, some symptoms of life, but none appeared excepting the tremor. The doctor never left him for three nights and three days. The people again met to bury him, but could not even then obtain the consent of his friend, who pleaded for one hour more; and when that was gone, he pleaded for half an hour, and then for a quarter of an hour; when, just at the close of this period, on which hung his last hope, Mr. Tennent opened his eyes. They then prised open his mouth, which was stiff, so as to get a quill into it, through which some liquid was conveyed into the stomach, and he by degrees recovered.

' "This account, as intimated before, Mr. Tennent said he received from his friends. I said to him, 'Sir, you seem to be one indeed raised from the dead, and may tell us what it is to die, and what you were sensible of while in that state.' He replied in the following words: 'As *to dying*—I found my fever increase, and I became weaker and weaker, until *all at once* I found myself in heaven, as I thought. I saw no shape as to the Deity, *but glory all unutterable!*' Here he paused, as though unable to find words to express his views, let his bridle fall, and lifting up his hands, proceeded, 'I can say, as St. Paul did, I heard and I saw things all unutterable; I saw a great multitude before this glory, apparently in the height of bliss, singing most melodiously. I was transported with my own situation, viewing all my troubles ended and my rest and glory begun, and was about to join the great and happy multitude, when one came to me, looked me full in the face, laid his hand upon my shoulder and said, "You must go back." These words went through me; nothing could have shocked me more;

I cried out, Lord, must I go back? With this shock I opened my eyes in this world. When I saw I was in the world I fainted, then came to, and fainted for several times, as one probably would naturally have done in so weak a situation.'

' "Mr. Tennent further informed me that he had so entirely lost the recollection of his past life and the benefit of his former studies that he could neither understand what was spoken to him, nor write, nor read his own name. That he had to begin all anew, and did not recollect that he had ever read before, until he had again learned his letters, and was able to pronounce the mono-syllables, such as *thee* and *thou*. But that as his strength returned, which was very slowly, his memory also returned. Yet notwith-standing the extreme feebleness of his situation, his recollection of what he saw and heard while in heaven, as he supposed, and the sense of divine things which he there obtained continued all the time in their full strength, so that he was continually in something like an ecstacy of mind. 'And,' said he, 'for three years the sense of divine things continued so great, and everything else appeared so completely vain, when compared to heaven, that could I have had the world for stooping down for it, I believe I should not have thought of doing it.' "

'It is not surprising, that after so affecting an account, strong solicitude should have been felt for further information as to the words, or at least the subjects of praise and adoration, which Mr. Tennent had heard. But when he was requested to com-municate these, he gave a decided negative, adding, "You will know them, with many other particulars, hereafter, as you will find the whole among my papers;" alluding to his intention of leaving the writer hereof this executor, which precluded any further solicitation.[1]

[1] 'It was so ordered, in the course of divine Providence, that the writer was sorely disappointed in his expectation of obtaining the papers here alluded to. Such, however, was the will of heaven! Mr. Tennent's death happened during the revolutionary war, when the enemy separated the writer from him, so as to render it impracticable to attend him on a dying bed; and before it was possible to get to his house, after his death (the writer being with the American army at the Valley-Forge), his son came from Charleston, and took his mother, and his father's papers and property, and returned to Carolina. About fifty miles from Charleston, the son was suddenly taken sick and died among entire strangers; and never since, though the writer was left executor to the son also, could any trace of the father's papers be discovered by him.'

'The pious and candid reader is left to his own reflections on this very extraordinary occurrence. The facts have been stated, and they are unquestionable. The writer will only ask whether it be contrary to revealed truth or to reason, to believe that in every age of the world, instances like that which is here recorded have occurred, to furnish *living testimony* of the reality of the invisible world, and of the infinite importance of eternal concerns?

'As soon as circumstances would permit, Mr. Tennent was licensed, and began to preach the everlasting gospel with great zeal and success. The death of his brother John, who had been some time settled as minister of the Presbyterian church at Free-hold, in the county of Monmouth, New Jersey, left that congregation in a destitute state. They had experienced so much spiritual benefit from the indefatigable labours and pious zeal of this able minister of Jesus Christ that they soon turned their attention to his brother, who was received on trial, and after one year was found to be no unworthy successor to so excellent a predecessor. In October 1733, Mr. Tennent was regularly ordained their pastor, and continued so through the whole of a pretty long life; one of the best proofs of ministerial fidelity.

'Although his salary was small (it is thought under £100), yet the glebe belonging to the church was an excellent plantation, on which he lived, and which, with care and good farming, was capable of maintaining a family with comfort. But his inattention to the things of this world was so great that he left the management of his temporal concerns wholly to a faithful servant, in whom he placed great confidence. After a short time he found his worldly affairs were becoming embarrassed. His steward reported to him that he was in debt to the merchant between 20*l.* and 30*l.*, and he knew of no means of payment, as the crops had fallen short. Mr. Tennent mentioned this to an intimate friend, a merchant of New York, who was on a visit at his house. His friend told him that this mode of life would not do, that he must get a wife to attend to his temporal affairs, and to comfort his leisure hours by conjugal endearments. He smiled at the idea, and assured him it never could be the case unless some friend would provide one for him, for he knew not how to go about it. His friend told him he was ready to undertake the business; that he had a sister-in-law, an excellent woman, of great piety, a widow of his own age, and one peculiarly suited in all respects to his character and circumstances. In short, that she was every thing he ought to look for; and if he would go with him to New York the next day, he would settle the negotiation for him. To this he soon assented. The next evening found him in that city, and before noon the day after, he was introduced to Mrs. Noble. He was much pleased with her appearance; and when left alone with her, abruptly told her that he supposed her brother had informed her of his errand; that neither his time nor inclination would suffer him to use much ceremony, but that if she approved the measure, he would attend his charge on the next Sabbath and return on Monday, be married and immediately take her home. The lady with some hesitation and difficulty at last consented, being convinced that his situation and circumstances rendered it proper. Thus in one week she found herself mistress of his house. She proved a most invaluable treasure to him, more than answering every thing said of her by an affectionate brother. She took the care of his temporal concerns upon her, extricated him from debt, and by a happy union of prudence and economy, so managed all his worldly business that in a few years his circumstances became easy and comfortable. In a word, in her was literally fulfilled the declaration of Solomon, that "a virtuous woman is a crown to her husband, and that her price is far above rubies." Besides several children who died in infancy, he had by her three sons who attained the age of manhood; John, who studied physic, and died in the West Indies when about thirty-three years of age; William, a man of superior character, and minister of the Independent church in Charleston, South Carolina, who died the latter end of September or beginning of October, A.D. 1777, about thirty-seven years old; and Gilbert, who also practised physic, and died at Freehold before his father, aged twenty-eight years. Few parents could boast three sons of a more manly or handsome appearance; and the father gave them the most liberal education that the country could afford.

"Mr. Tennent's inattention to earthly things continued till his eldest son was about three years old, when he led him out into the fields on a Lord's day after public worship. The design of the walk was for religious meditation. As he went along, accidentally casting his eye on the child, a thought suddenly struck him, and he asked himself this question: "Should God in his providence take me hence, what would become of this child and his mother, for whom I have never taken any personal care to make provision?

How can I answer this negligence to God and to them?" The impropriety of his inattention to the relative duties of life, which God had called him to, and the consideration of the sacred declaration, "that he who does not provide for his own household has denied the faith, and is worse than an infidel," had such an impressive effect on his mind that it almost deprived him of his senses. He saw his conduct, which before he thought arose entirely from a deep sense of divine things, in a point of light in which he never before had viewed it. He immediately attempted to return home, but so great was his distress that it was with difficulty he could get along; till all at once he was relieved by as suddenly recurring to that text of scripture, which came into his mind with extraordinary force: "But unto the tribe of Levi Moses gave not any inheritance; the Lord God of Israel was their inheritance." Such, however, was the effect of this unexpected scene on Mr. Tennent's mind and judgment that ever afterwards he prudently attended to the temporal business of life, still, however, in perfect subordination to the great things of eternity; and became fully convinced that God was to be faithfully served, as well by discharging relative duties in his love and fear, as by the more immediate acts of devotion. He clearly perceived that every duty had its proper time and place, as well as motive; that we had a right and were called of God to eat and drink and to be properly clothed; and of course that care should be taken to procure those things, provided that all be done to the glory of God. In the duties of a gospel minister, however, especially as they related to his pastoral charge, he still engaged with the utmost zeal and faithfulness; and was esteemed by all ranks and degrees, as far as his labours extended, as a fervent, useful, and successful preacher of the gospel.

'His judgement of mankind was such as to give him a marked superiority, in this respect, over his contemporaries, and greatly aided him in his ministerial functions. He was scarcely ever mistaken in the character of a man with whom he conversed, though it was but for a few hours. He had an independent mind, which was seldom satisfied on important subjects without the best evidence that was to be had. His manner was remarkably impressive; and his sermons, although seldom polished, were generally delivered with such indescribable power that he was truly an able and a successful minister of the New Testament. He could say things from the pulpit which, if said by almost any other man, would have been thought a violation of propriety. But by him they were delivered in a manner so peculiar to himself, and so extremely impressive, that they seldom failed to please and to instruct. As an instance of this, the following anecdote is given, of the truth of which the writer was a witness.

'Mr. Tennent was passing through a town in the state of New Jersey, in which he was a stranger and had never preached, and stopping at a friend's house to dine, was informed that it was a day of fasting and prayer in the congregation, on account of a very remarkable and severe drought, which threatened the most dangerous consequences to the fruits of the earth. His friend had just returned from church, and the intermission was but half an hour. Mr. Tennent was requested to preach, and with great difficulty consented, as he wished to proceed on his journey. At church the people were surprised to see a preacher wholly unknown to them and entirely unexpected ascend the pulpit. His whole appearance, being in a travelling dress, covered with dust, wearing an old-fashioned large wig, discoloured like his clothes, and a long meagre visage, engaged their attention, and excited their curiosity. On his rising up, instead of beginning to pray, as was the usual practice, he looked around the congregation with a piercing eye and earnest attention, and after a minute's profound silence he addressed them with great solemnity in the following words: "My beloved brethren! I am told you have come here to-day to fast and pray; a very good work indeed, provided you have come with a sincere desire to glorify God thereby. But if your design is merely to comply with a customary practice or with the wish of your church officers, you are guilty of the greatest folly imaginable, as you had much better have stayed at home and earned your three shillings and sixpence (at that time the stated price for a day's labour); but if your minds are indeed impressed with the solemnity of the occasion, and you are really desirous of humbling yourselves before Almighty God, your Heavenly Father, come, join with me, and let us pray." This had an effect so uncommon and extraordinary on the congregation that the utmost seriousness was universally manifested. The prayer and the sermon added greatly to the impressions already made, and tended to rouse the attention, influence the mind, command the affections, and increase the temper which had been so happily produced. Many had reason to bless God for his unexpected visit, and to reckon this day one of the happiest of their lives.

'The writer having requested of the present Rev. Dr. William M. Tennent a written account of an anecdote relative to his uncle, which he had once heard him repeat verbally, received in reply the following letter:

' "ABINGTON, January 11th, 1806.

' "*Sir*—The anecdote of my venerable relative, the Rev. William Tennent, of Freehold, which you wished me to send to you, is as follows:

' "During the great revival of religion which took place under the ministry of Mr. Whitefield and others distinguished for their piety and zeal at that period, Mr. Tennent was laboriously active, and much engaged to help forward the work; in the performance of which he met with strong and powerful temptations. The following is related as received in substance from his own lips, and may be considered as extraordinary and singularly striking.

' "On the evening preceding public worship, which was to be attended next day, he selected a subject for the discourse which was to be delivered, and made some progress in his preparations. In the morning he resumed the same subject, with an intention to extend his thoughts further on it, but was presently assaulted with a temptation that the Bible which he then held in his hand was not of Divine authority, but the invention of man. He instantly endeavoured to repel the temptation by prayer, but his endeavours proved unavailing. The temptation continued, and fastened upon him with greater strength as the time advanced for public service. He lost all the thoughts which he had on his subject the preceding evening. He tried other subjects, but could get nothing for the people. The whole book of God, under that distressing state of mind, was a sealed book to him; and to add to his affliction, he was, to use his own words, '*shut up in prayer.*' A cloud, dark as that of Egypt, oppressed his mind.

' "Thus agonized in spirit, he proceeded to the church, where he found a large congregation assembled, and waiting to hear the word; and then it was, he observed, that he was more deeply distressed than ever, and especially for the dishonour which he feared would fall upon religion through him that day. He resolved, however, to attempt the service. He introduced it by singing a psalm, during which time his agitations were increased to the highest degree. When the moment for prayer commenced, he arose, as one in the most perilous and painful situation, and with arms extended to the heavens, began with this outcry, '*Lord, have mercy upon me!*' Upon the utterance of this petition he was heard; the thick cloud instantly broke away, and an unspeakably joyful light shone in upon his soul, so that his spirit seemed to be caught up to the heavens, and he felt as though he saw God, as Moses did on the mount, face to face, and was carried forth to him with an enlargement greater than he had ever before experienced, and on every page of the Scriptures saw his Divinity inscribed in brightest colours. The result was a deep solemnity on the face of the whole congregation, and the house at the end of the prayer was a *Bochim*. He gave them the subject of his evening meditations, which was brought to his full remembrance, with an overflowing abundance of other weighty and solemn matter. The Lord blessed the discourse, so that it proved the happy means of the conversion of about thirty persons. This day he spoke of ever afterwards as his harvest-day.

' "I am, yours with esteem,

' "WILLIAM M. TENNENT."

'While on this subject, we may introduce another anecdote of this wonderful man, to show the dealings of God with him, and the deep contemplations of his mind. He was attending the duties of the Lord's day in his own congregation as usual, where the custom was to have morning and evening service, with only a half hour's intermission, to relieve the attention. He had preached in the morning, and in the intermission had walked into the woods for meditation, the weather being warm. He was reflecting on the infinite wisdom of God, as manifested in all his works, and particularly in the wonderful method of salvation, through the death and sufferings of his beloved Son. This subject suddenly opened on his mind with such a flood of light that his views of the glory and the infinite majesty of Jehovah were so inexpressibly great as entirely to overwhelm him, and he fell almost lifeless to the ground. When he had revived a little, all he could do was to raise a fervent prayer that God would withdraw himself from him, or that he must perish under a view of his ineffable glory.

When able to reflecton his situation, he could not but abhor himself as a weak and despicable worm, and seemed to be overcome with astonishment that a creature so unworthy and insufficient had ever dared to attempt the instruction of his fellow-men in the nature and attributes of so glorious a Being. Overstaying his usual time, some of his elders went in search of him, and found him prostrate on the ground, unable to rise, and incapable of informing them of the cause. They raised him up, and after some time brought him to the church, and supported him to the pulpit, which he ascended on his hands and knees, to the no small astonishment of the congregation. He remained silent a considerable time, earnestly supplicating Almighty God (as he told the writer) to hide himself from him, that he might be enabled to address his people, who were by this time lost in wonder to know what had produced this uncommon event. His prayers were heard, and he became able to stand up, by holding the desk. He now began the most affecting and pathetic address that the congregation had ever received from him. He gave a surprising account of the views he had of the infinite wisdom of God, and greatly deplored his own incapacity to speak to them concerning a Being so infinitely glorious beyond all his powers of description. He attempted to show something of what had been discovered to him of the astonishing wisdom of Jehovah of which it was impossible for human nature to form adequate conceptions. He then broke out into so fervent and expressive a prayer, as greatly to surprise the congregation, and draw tears from every eye. A sermon followed that continued the solemn scene, and made very lasting impressions on all the hearers.[1]

'The great increase of communicants in his church was a good evidence of his pastoral care and powerful preaching, as it exceeded that of most churches in the Synod. But his labours were not confined to the pulpit. He was indefatigable in his endeavours to communicate in private families a savour of the knowledge of spiritual and divine things. In his parochial visits, he used regularly

---

[1] Mr. Tennent did not confine himself to any particular length in his sermons, but regulated this very much by his feelings. The late Rev. Dr. Spring, of Newburyport, informed the editor, that he and other students of Nassau Hall walked twenty miles to hear him preach, and the sermon, measured by the watch, was no more than thirteen minutes in the delivery.

to go through his congregation in order, so as to carry the un-
searchable riches of Christ to every house. He earnestly pressed
it on the conscience of parents to instruct their children at home
by plain and easy questions, so as gradually to expand their young
minds, and prepare them for the reception of the more practical
doctrines of the Gospel. In this Mr. Tennent has presented an
excellent example to his brethren in the ministry; for certain it is
that more good may be done in a congregation by this domestic
mode of instruction than any one can imagine who has not made
the trial. Children and servants are in this way prepared for the
teachings of the sanctuary, and to reap the full benefit of the word
publicly preached. He made it a practice in all these visits to
enforce practical religion on all, high and low, rich and poor, young
and old, master and servant. To this he was particularly attentive,
it being a favourite observation with him "that he loved a religion
that a man could live by."

'Mr. Tennent carefully avoided the discussion of controversial
subjects, unless specially called to it by particular circumstances,
and then he was ever ready to assign the reason of his faith. The
following occurrence will show the general state of his mind and
feelings in regard to such subjects. A couple of young clergymen,
visiting at his house, entered into a dispute on the question, at that
time much controverted in New England, whether faith or repentance were first in order in the conversion of a sinner. Not
being able to determine the point, they agreed to make Mr.
Tennent their umpire, and to dispute the subject at length before
him. He accepted the proposal, and, after a solemn debate for
some time, his opinion being asked, he very gravely took his pipe
from his mouth, looked out of his window, pointed to a man
ploughing on a hill at some distance, and asked the young clergymen if they knew that man; on their answering in the negative,
he told them it was one of his elders, who, to his full conviction, had
been a sincere Christian for more than thirty years. "Now,"
said Mr. Tennent, "ask him whether faith or repentance came
first; what do you think he would say?" They said, they could not
tell. "Then," says he, "I will tell you; he would say that he cared
not which came first, but that he had got them both. Now, my
friends," he added, "be careful that you have both a true faith
and a sincere repentance, and do not be greatly troubled which
comes first." It is not, however, to be supposed by this, that Mr.

Tennent was unfriendly to a deep and accurate examination of all important theological doctrines. There were few men more earnest than he to have young clergymen well instructed, and thoroughly furnished for their work. This, indeed, was an object on which his heart was much set, and which he exerted himself greatly to promote.

'Mr. Tennent was remarkably distinguished for a pointed attention to the particular circumstances and situation of the afflicted, either in body or mind, and would visit them with as much care and attention as a physician, and frequently indeed proved an able one to both soul and body. But his greatest talent was that of a peace-maker, which he possessed in so eminent a degree that probably none have exceeded, and very few have equalled him in it. He was sent for far and near to settle disputes, and heal difficulties which arose in congregations; and happily for those concerned, he was generally successful. Indeed he seldom would relinquish his object till he had accomplished it.

'But while this man of God was thus successful in promoting the best interests of his fellow-creatures and advancing the glory of his Lord and Master, the great enemy of mankind was not likely to observe the destruction of his kingdom without making an effort to prevent it. As he assailed our blessed Saviour in the days of his flesh with all his art and all his power, so has he always made the faithful followers of the Redeemer the objects of his inveterate malice. If the good man of whom we write was greatly honoured by peculiar communications from on high, he was also very often the subject of the severe buffetings of that malignant and fallen spirit.

'The time of which we are now speaking was remarkable for a great revival of religion, in which Mr. Tennent was considerably instrumental, and in which a Mr. John Rowland, brought up with Mr. Tennent at the Log College, was also very remarkable for his successful preaching among all ranks of people. Possessing a commanding eloquence, as well as other estimable qualities, he became very popular, and was much celebrated throughout the country. His celebrity and success were subjects of very serious regret to many careless worldlings, who placed all their happiness in the enjoyment of temporal objects, and considered and represented Mr. Rowland and his brethren as fanatics and hypocrites. This was specially applicable to many of the great men of the

H

then province of New Jersey, and particularly to the Chief
Justice, who was well known for his disbelief of revelation. There
was at this time prowling through the country a noted man by the
name of Tom Bell, whose knowledge and understanding were
very considerable, and who greatly excelled in low art and cunning.
His mind was totally debased, and his whole conduct betrayed a
soul capable of descending to every species of iniquity. In all the
arts of theft, robbery, fraud, deception, and defamation, he was so
deeply skilled and so thoroughly practised that it is believed he
never had his equal in this country. He had been indicted in almost
every one of the middle colonies, but his ingenuity and cunning
always enabled him to escape punishment. This man unhappily
resembled Mr. Rowland in his external appearance, so as hardly
to be known from him without the most careful examination.

'It so happened that Tom Bell arrived one evening at a tavern
in Princeton, dressed in a dark, parson's gray frock. On his entering
the tavern about dusk, the late John Stockton, Esq. of that town, a
pious and respectable man, to whom Mr. Rowland was well
known, went up to Bell, and addressed him as Mr. Rowland, and
was inviting him to go home with him. Bell assured him of his
mistake. It was with some difficulty that Mr. Stockton acknowledged his error, and then informed Bell that it had arisen from
his great resemblance to Mr. Rowland. This hint was sufficient
for the prolific genius of that notorious impostor. The next day
Bell went into the county of Hunterdon, and stopped in a congregation where Mr. Rowland had formerly preached once or
twice, but where he was not intimately known. Here he met with
a member of the congregation, to whom he introduced himself as
the Rev. Mr. Rowland, who had preached to them some time
before. This gentleman immediately invited him to his house to
spend the week; and begged him, as the people were without a
minister, to preach for them on the next Sabbath, to which Bell
agreed, and notice was accordingly given to the neighbourhood.
The impostor was treated with every mark of attention and respect;
and a private room was assigned to him as a study, to prepare for
the Sabbath. The sacred day arrived, and he was invited to ride
to church with the ladies in the family wagon, and the master of the
house accompanied them on an elegant horse. When they had
arrived near the church, Bell on a sudden discovered that he had
left his notes in his study, and proposed to ride back for them on

the fine horse, by which means he should be able to return in time for the service. This proposal was instantly agreed to, and Bell mounted the horse, returned to the house, rifled the desk of his host, and made off with the horse. Wherever he stopped he called himself the Rev. John Rowland.

'At the time this event took place, Messrs. Tennent and Rowland had gone into Pennsylvania, or Maryland, with Mr. Joshua Anderson and Mr. Benjamin Stevens (both members of a church contiguous to that where Bell had practised his fraud) on business of a religious nature. Soon after their return, Mr. Rowland was charged with the above robbery; he gave bonds to appear at the court at Trenton, and the affair made a great noise throughout the colony. At the court of oyer and terminer, the judge charged the grand jury on the subject with great severity. After long consideration, the jury returned into court without finding a bill. The judge reproved them in an angry manner, and ordered them out again. They again returned without finding a bill, and were again sent out with threatening of severe punishment if they persisted in their refusal. At last they agreed, and brought in a bill for the alleged crime. On the trial, Messrs. Tennent, Anderson, and Stevens appeared as witnesses, and fully proved an *alibi* in favour of Mr. Rowland, by swearing that on the very day on which the robbery was committed they were with Mr. Rowland, and heard him preach in Pennsylvania or Maryland. The jury accordingly acquitted him without hesitation, to the great disappointment and mortification of his prosecutors and of many other enemies to the great revival of religion that had recently taken place; but to the great joy of the serious and well-disposed.

'The spirits hostile to the spread of the gospel were not, however, so easily overcome. In their view an opportunity was now presented favourable for inflicting a deep wound on the cause of Christianity; and, as if urged on by the malice of man's great enemy, they resolved that no means should be left untried, no arts unemployed, for the destruction of these distinguished servants of God. Many and various were the circumstances which still contributed to inspire them with hopes of success. The testimony of the person who had been robbed was positive that Mr. Rowland was the robber; and this testimony was corroborated by that of a number of individuals who had seen Tom Bell personating Mr. Rowland, using his name, and in possession of the horse. These sons of

Belial had been able, after great industry used for the purpose, to collect a mass of evidence of this kind, which they considered as establishing the fact; but Mr. Rowland was now out of their power by the verdict of *not guilty*. Their vengeance, therefore, was directed against the witnesses by whose testimony he had been cleared; and they were accordingly arraigned for perjury before a court of quarter sessions in the county; and the grand jury received a strict charge, the plain import of which was that these good men ought to be indicted. After an examination of the testimony on one side only, as is the custom in such cases, the grand jury did accordingly find bills of indictment against Messrs. Tennent, Anderson and Stevens for wilful and corrupt perjury. Their enemies and the enemies of the gospel now began to triumph. They gloried in the belief that an indelible stain would be fixed on the professors of religion, and of consequence on religion itself; and that this *new light*, by which they denominated all appearance of piety, would soon be extinguished for ever.

'These indictments were removed to the Supreme Court, and poor Mr. Anderson, living in the country, and conscious of his entire innocence, could not brook the idea of lying under the odium of the hateful crime of perjury; he therefore demanded a trial at the first court of oyer and terminer. This proved most seriously injurious to him, for he was pronounced guilty, and most cruelly and unjustly condemned to stand one hour on the court-house steps with a paper on his breast, whereon was written in large letters, "This is for wilful and corrupt perjury;" which sentence was executed upon him.

'Messrs Tennent and Stevens were summoned to appear at the next court, and attended accordingly, depending on the aid of Mr. John Coxe, an eminent lawyer, who had been previously employed to conduct their defence. As Mr. Tennent was wholly unacquainted with the nature of forensic litigation, and did not know of any person living who could prove his innocence (all the persons who were with him being indicted), his only resource and consolation was to commit himself to the divine will, and if he must suffer, to take it as from the hand of God, who, he well knew, could make even the wrath of man to praise him;[1] and considering it as probable that he might suffer, he had prepared a sermon to be preached

[1] 'His affectionate congregation felt deeply interested in his critical situation, and kept a day of fasting and prayer on the occasion.'

from the pillory, if that should be his fate. On his arrival at Trenton, he found the famous Mr. Smith, of New York, father of the late chief justice of Canada, one of the ablest lawyers in America, and of a religious character, who had voluntarily attended to aid in his defence; also his brother Gilbert, who was now settled in the pastoral charge of the second Presbyterian church, in Philadelphia, and who brought Mr. John Kinsey, one of the first counsellors of that city, for the same purpose. Messrs. Tennent and Stevens met these gentlemen at Mr. Coxe's the morning before the trial was to come on. Mr. Coxe requested that they would bring in their witnesses, that they might examine them previously to their going into court. Mr. Tennent answered that he did not know of any witnesses but God and his own conscience. Mr. Coxe replied, "If you have no witnesses, sir, the trial must be put off; otherwise you most certainly will be convicted. You well know the strong testimony that will be brought against you, and the exertions that are making to accomplish your ruin." Mr. Tennent replied, "I am sensible of all this, yet it never shall be said that I have delayed the trial, or been afraid to meet the justice of my country. I know my own innocence, and that God whose I am and whom I serve will never suffer me to fall by these snares of the devil, or by the wicked machinations of his agents or servants. Therefore, gentlemen, go on to the trial." Messrs. Smith and Kinsey, who were both religious men, told him that his confidence and trust in God, as a Christian minister of the gospel, was well founded, and before a heavenly tribunal would be all-important to him; but assured him it would not avail in an earthly court, and urged his consent to put off the trial. Mr. Tennent continued inflexible in his refusal; on which Mr. Coxe told him that since he was determined to go to trial, he had the satisfaction of informing him that they had discovered a flaw in the indictment which might prove favourable to him on a demurrer. He asked for an explanation, and on finding that it was to admit the fact in a legal point of view, and rest on the law arising from it, Mr. Tennent broke out with great vehemence, saying that this was another snare of the devil, and before he would consent to it he would suffer death. He assured his counsel that his confidence in God was so strong, and his assurance that he would bring about his deliverance in some way or other was so great that he did not wish to delay the trial for a moment.

'Mr. Stevens, whose faith was not of this description, and who was bowed down to the ground under the most gloomy apprehensions of suffering, as his neighbour Mr. Anderson had been, eagerly seized the opportunity of escape that was offered, and was afterwards discharged on the exception.

'Mr. Coxe still urged putting off the trial, charging Mr. Tennent with acting the part rather of a wild enthusiast than of a meek and prudent Christian; but he insisted that they should proceed, and left them in astonishment, not knowing how to act, when the bell summoned them to court.

'Mr. Tennent had not walked far in the street before he met a man and his wife, who stopped him, and asked if his name was not Tennent. He answered in the affirmative, and begged to know if they had any business with him. The man replied, "You best know." He told his name, and said that he was from a certain place (which he mentioned) in Pennsylvania or Maryland; that Messrs. Rowland, Tennent, Anderson, and Stevens, had lodged either at his house, or in a house wherein he and his wife had been servants (it is not now certain which) at a particular time, which he named; that on the following day they had heard Messrs. Tennent and Rowland preach; that some nights before they left home, he and his wife waked out of a sound sleep, and each told the other a dream which had just occurred, and which proved to be the same in substance, to wit, that he, Mr. Tennent, at Trenton, was in the greatest possible distress, and that it was in their power and theirs only to relieve him. Considering it as a remarkable dream only, they again went to sleep, and it was twice repeated precisely in the same manner to both of them. This made so deep an impression on their minds, that they set off, and here they were, and would know of him what they were to do. Mr. Tennent immediately went with them to the court house, and his counsel, on examining the man and his wife, and finding their testimony to be full to the purpose, were, as they well might be, in perfect astonishment. Before the trial began, another person of a low character called on Mr. Tennent and told him that he was so harassed in conscience for the part he had been acting in this prosecution that he could get no rest till he had determined to come and make a full confession. He sent this man to his counsel also. Soon after, Mr. Stockton from Princeton appeared, and added his testimony. In short, they went to trial, and notwithstanding the utmost exertions of the ablest counsel, who had been employed to aid the attorney-general against Mr. Tennent, the advocates on his side so traced every movement of the defendant on the Saturday, Sunday, and Monday in question, and satisfied the jury so perfectly on the subject that they did not hesitate honourably to acquit Mr. Tennent, by their unanimous verdict of *not guilty*, to the great confusion and mortification of his numerous opposers. Mr. Tennent assured the writer of this, that during the whole of this business, his spirits never failed him, and that he contemplated the possibility of his suffering so infamous a punishment as standing in the pillory without dismay, and had made preparation, and was fully determined to deliver a sermon to the people in that situation, if he should be placed in it.

'He went from Trenton to Philadelphia with his brother, and on his return as he was rising the hill at the entrance of Trenton, without reflecting on what had happened, he accidentally cast his eyes on the pillory, which suddenly so filled him with horror as completely to unman him, and it was with great difficulty that he kept himself from falling from his horse. He reached the tavern door in considerable danger, was obliged to be assisted to dismount, and it was some time before he could so get the better of his fears and confusion as to proceed on his journey. Such is the constitution of the human mind! It will often resist, with unshaken firmness the severest external pressure and violence; and sometimes it yields without reason, when it has nothing to fear. Or, should we not rather say, such is the support which God sometimes affords to his people in the time of their necessity, and such the manner in which he leaves them to feel their own weakness when that necessity is past, that all the praise may be given where alone it is due?

'The writer sincerely rejoices that though a number of the extraordinary incidents in the life of Mr. Tennent cannot be vouched by public testimony and authentic documents, yet the singular manner in which a gracious God did appear for this his faithful servant in the time of that distress which has just been noticed, is a matter of public notoriety, and capable of being verified by the most unquestionable testimony and records.

'This special instance of the interference of the righteous Judge of all the earth ought to yield consolation to pious people in seasons of great difficulty and distress, where there is none that seems able to deliver them. Yet it ought to afford no encouragement to the enthusiast, who refuses to use the means of preservation and deliverance which God puts in his power. True confidence in God is always accompanied with the use of all lawful means, and with the rejection of all that are unlawful. It consists in an unshaken belief that while right means are used God will give that issue which shall be most for his glory and his people's good. The extraordinary occurrence here recorded may also serve as a solemn warning to the enemies of God's people, and to the advocates of infidelity, not to strive by wicked and deep-laid machinations to oppose the success of the gospel, nor to attempt to injure the persons and characters of those faithful servants of the Most High, whom sooner or later he will vindicate to the unspeakable confusion of all who have persecuted and traduced them.

'Mr. Tennent was a man of the most scrupulous integrity, and though of a very grave and solemn deportment, he had a remarkably cheerful disposition, and generally communicated his instructions with so much ease and pleasantry as greatly to gain the confidence and affection of all with whom he conversed, especially of children and young people. In all his intercourse with strangers and men of the world, he so managed his conversation that, while he seldom neglected a proper opportunity to impress the mind with serious things, he always made them covet his company rather than avoid it; well knowing that there is a time for all things, and that even instruction and reproof, to be useful, must be prudently and seasonably given.

'An instance of this disposition occurred in Virginia. The late Rev. Mr. Samuel Blair and Mr. Tennent were sent by the Synod on a mission into that province. They stopped one evening at a tavern for the night, where they found a number of guests, with whom they supped in a common room. After the table was cleared, our missionaries withdrew from it. Cards were then called for, and the landlord brought in a pack, and laid them on the table. One of the gentlemen very politely asked the missionaries if they would not take a cut with them, not knowing that they were clergymen. Mr. Tennent very pleasantly answered, "With all my heart, gentlemen, if you can convince us that thereby we serve our Master's cause, or contribute any thing towards the success of our mission." This drew some smart reply from the gentlemen, when Mr. T. with solemnity added, "We are ministers of the gospel of

Jesus Christ. We profess ourselves his servants; we are sent on his business, which is to persuade mankind to repent of their sins, to turn from them, and to accept of that happiness and salvation which is offered in the gospel." This very unexpected reply, delivered in a very tender though solemn manner, and with great apparent sincerity, so engaged the gentlemen's attention that the cards were laid aside, and an opportunity was afforded and cheerfully embraced for explaining in a sociable conversation, during the rest of the evening, some of the leading and most important doctrines of the gospel, to the satisfaction and apparent edification of the hearers.

'Resignation to the will of God in all his dispensations, however dark and afflictive, was among the excellent graces that adorned the character of this man of God. He had been tried in the course of God's providence in various ways; but domestic afflictions as yet had not been laid upon him. The time, however, was now come when his character was to be brightened by a severe test of his resignation and obedience, a test attended with many peculiarly distressing circumstances. His youngest son, who was a very handsome man, had just come into public life; had commenced the practice of physic, was married and had one child. To the great distress of the parents, he discovered, though possessed of the sweetest temper and most agreeable manners, no regard to the things that belonged to his eternal peace. Wholly negligent of religion, he indulged without restraint in the gaiety and follies of the world. The pious father was incessant at the throne of grace in behalf of his dissipated son; and was continually entertaining hopes that God would, by the influences of his Spirit, arrest him in his career, and bring him into the Church of Christ, before his own summons should arrive, that he might die in peace, under the consoling hope of meeting this dear child in a better world. God, however, had determined otherwise; and the son, while engaged in inoculating a number of persons in a house he had obtained for the purpose, near his father's neighbourhood, was seized in an unusually violent manner with a raging fever. With the disorder he was brought to a sudden and alarming view of his lost condition by nature, and the grievous transgressions of his past life. His sins were all set in dread array against him. A horrible darkness and an awful dread of the eternal displeasure of Jehovah fell on him, so as to make him the dreadful example of a convicted sinner, trembling under the confounding presence of an angry God. The affectionate and pious father was constantly in prayer and supplication, that God would have mercy upon him. He seldom left the side of his bed. For many days the fever raged with unabated fury; but the immediate distresses which it occasioned were lost or forgotten in the severer pains of an awakened conscience. Such was the height to which his anguish at last arose that the bed on which he lay was shaken by the violent and united convulsions of mind and body. The parents were touched to the quick; and their unqualified submission to God, as a sovereign God, was put to the most rigorous proof. But in due time they came out of the furnace, as gold tried in the fire. God, in his infinite and condescending grace and mercy, was at last pleased, in some measure, to hear the many prayers put up by the parents and many pious friends for the relief of the poor sufferer. His views of the lost state of man by nature; of the only means of salvation, through the death and sufferings of the Saviour; of the necessity of the inward regenerating grace of the Holy Spirit became clear and consistent, and the importance of a practical acquaintance with these things was deeply and rationally impressed on his mind. He now saw that salvation, which he had deemed almost or altogether hopeless to him, was possible. His mind became calm, and he attended to religious instruction and advice. In a short time he began to give as much evidence of a change of heart as a death-bed repentance (rarely to be greatly relied on) can afford. He sent for his companions in iniquity, and notwithstanding his disorder exerted himself to the utmost to address them, which he did in the most solemn, awful, and impressive manner, as a person who, by the infinite mercy of a prayer-hearing God, had been delivered from a hell gaping to receive him. He besought them by all the terrors of everlasting destruction; by all the love they ought to bear to their own immortal souls; by the love of a crucified Jesus, who poured out his soul unto death that they might live for ever; by his own awful sufferings and terrible example, that they would repent and turn to God. This happy change was a reviving cordial to the distressed and suffering father. His soul was overjoyed, and his mouth was full of the praises of redeeming love. His mind and spirits were hereby prepared with true resignation to surrender the son of his advanced age to the God who gave him. After a few days more of severe suffering in body, but rejoicing in mind, the son was removed from time to eternity. There being no minister in the neighbourhood the father undertook to preach a funeral sermon. All the son's old companions that could be sent to were especially invited and the old gentleman preached in such a manner, with a particular address to the young men, as to astonish every hearer; and while the seriously inclined wondered and adored, the careless were confounded and greatly alarmed.

'Scarcely had Mr. Tennent got over this heavy affliction, and returned to an active and useful course of life for a few years, when God again called him to another severe and arduous struggle of the same nature. His eldest son, John, promised fair to make a distinguished figure in life; had possessed a large share in the affections of both father and mother, and was more dear to their hearts than ever since the death of his brother. It so happened that the father was called to New York to heal some differences between the members of the church there. The next morning after his arrival he went into a bookstore, when one of the ministers of the Episcopal church came in, and on being introduced to him, after the common salutations told him he condoled with him on the death of his eldest son in the West Indies. The old gentleman was at first struck dumb. With difficulty he soon inquired how the news came; being informed that it was by a circuitous route, he suddenly turned and said, "The will of the Lord be done." The clergyman observed, that it was happy for him to be able so cordially to submit to it. Mr. Tennent replied, "The Lord is my God, his will be done." On being asked by the bookseller, who was his particular friend, to retire into the house, and endeavour to settle his mind, he answered, "I am come on the Lord's business; my duty requires that I should finish it; when that is done I shall have time enough to mourn for my son." He immediately set off to attend his appointment, finished the business to his satisfaction, and the next day returned home, where he found that a letter had been received by a neighbour, containing the same information which he had before received. Thus, on the most trying occasion, he showed the same submission to the allotment of divine providence that was discoverable in all his former conduct. The following extract from a letter, written at this time to the writer of this narrative, will show the temper of his mind in his own language:

' "Freehold, March, 1776.

' "*My Dear Sir:*—Perhaps before this comes to hand you will be informed that He who gave me the honourable epithet of a father has in his wise and unerring providence written me childless.[1] My son is dead. This account I had yesterday from a letter written to a friend; the account is so straight (though not circumstantial) that I cannot doubt its truth. The tender mother has not heard it, nor do I intend she shall until authenticated. This I mention as a caution to you, in case you should write me before the matter is published. Let the dear heart have all possible ease before the load, which it is likely will try her life, falls upon her. I know her attachment to that child; his conduct has been such as greatly endeared him to us. Our pains and expense in his education have been great, but infinitely short of what God has done for him. He has, therefore, the best right to him. Should we then, were it in our power, obstruct his taking full possession of his own property? God forbid! This, sir, through God's goodness, is not only what I say, but it is the temper of my soul, for which God only deserves the honour. It is now above fifty years since my soul resigned itself to God in Jesus Christ. I had then neither son nor daughter; I was completely satisfied with Him, and, blessed be his name, I am so now. Have I then reason to cry out as if ruined? O! no; on the contrary, I have the utmost reason for thanksgiving that he has not in righteous judgment deprived me of himself, in whom all fulness dwells. My wife and myself are hastening to childhood; if spared a few years, we shall need one to lead us; and we shall look to you, under God. All the benefit you can expect from so doing will consist in the satisfaction of your own mind, that you have helped two old people through the last steps of their pilgrimage."

'Thus did this pious man turn every event of life, however afflictive, to the praise and glory of God, and he seldom omitted an opportunity of inculcating the same disposition on all his acquaintance.

'When the late Rev. George Whitefield was last in this country, Mr. Tennent paid him a visit as he was passing through New Jersey. Mr. Whitefield and a number of other clergymen, among

---

[1] 'He seems, in the depth of his distress, to have forgotten that he yet had one son left, although he was 800 miles distant from him.'

whom was Mr. Tennent, were invited to dinner by a gentleman in the neighbourhood where the late Mr. William Livingston, since governor of New Jersey resided, and who, with several other lay gentlemen, was among the guests. After dinner, in the course of an easy and pleasant conversation, Mr. Whitefield adverted to the difficulties attending the gospel ministry arising from the small success with which their labours were crowned. He greatly lamented that all their zeal-activity and fervour availed but little; said that he was weary with the burdens and fatigues of the day; declared his great consolation was that in a short time his work would be done, when he should depart and be with Christ; that the prospect of a speedy deliverance had supported his spirits, or that he should before now have sunk under his labour. He then appealed to the ministers around him, if it were not their great comfort that they should soon go to rest. They generally assented, excepting Mr. Tennent, who sat next to Mr. Whitefield in silence; and by his countenance discovered but little pleasure in the conversation. On which Mr. Whitefield, turning to him and tapping him on the knee, said, "Well! brother Tennent, you are the oldest man amongst us, do you not rejoice to think that your time is so near at hand, when you will be called home and freed from all the difficulties attending this chequered scene?" Mr. T. bluntly answered, "I have no wish about it." Mr. W. pressed him again; and Mr. T. again answered, "No, sir, it is no pleasure to me at all, and if you knew your duty it would be none to you. I have nothing to do with death; my business is to live as long as I can—as well as I can—and to serve my Lord and Master as faithfully as I can, until he shall think proper to call me home." Mr. W. still urged for an explicit answer to his question, in case the time of death were left to his own choice. Mr. Tennent, replied, "I have no choice about it; I am God's servant, and have engaged to do his business as long as he pleases to continue me therein. But now, brother, let me ask you a question. What do you think I would say if I was to send my man Tom into the field to plough, and if at noon I should go to the field and find him lounging under a tree, and complaining, 'Master, the sun is very hot, and the ploughing hard and difficult; I am tired and weary of the work you have appointed me, and am overdone with the heat and burden of the day; do, master, let me return home and be discharged from this hard service?' What would I say? Why, that he was an idle, lazy fellow; that it was his business to do the work that I had appointed him, until I, the proper judge, should think fit to call him home. Or suppose you had hired a man to serve you faithfully for a *given time* in a particular service, and he should, without any reason on your part, and before he had performed half his service, become weary of it, and upon every occasion be expressing a wish to be discharged or placed in other circumstances. Would you not call him a wicked and slothful servant, and unworthy of the privileges of your employ?" The mild, pleasant, and Christian-like manner in which this reproof was administered, rather increased the social harmony and edifying conversation of the company, who became satisfied that it was very possible to err, even in desiring with undue earnestness "to depart and be with Christ," which in itself is "far better", than to remain in this imperfect state; and that it is the duty of the Christian in this respect to say, "All the days of my appointed time will I wait till my change come."

'Among Mr. Tennent's qualifications, none were more conspicuous than his activity both of body and mind. He hated and despised sloth. He was almost always in action—never wearied in well-doing, nor in serving his friends. His integrity and independence of spirit were observable on the slightest acquaintance. He was so great a lover of truth that he could not bear the least aberration from it, even in a joke. He was remarkable for his candour and liberality of sentiment with regard to those who differed from him in opinion. His hospitality and domestic enjoyments were even proverbial. His public spirit was always conspicuous, and his attachment to what he thought the best interests of his country was ardent and inflexible. He took an early and decided part with his country in the commencement of the late revolutionary war. He was convinced that she was oppressed, and that her petitions to the sovereign of the mother country were constitutional, loyal, moderate, and reasonable; that the treatment they received was irrational, tyrannical, and intolerable. As he made it a rule, however, never to carry politics into the pulpit, he had no way to manifest his zeal for the public measures but by his private prayers and by his decided opinions delivered in private conversations. But in this way his sentiments became universally known, and he was considered as a warm friend to the American cause. Notwithstanding these political opinions, he was not blind to the errors of his countrymen, and especially to their moral and religious conduct. The following extract from a letter to the author of these sketches, dated Feb. 14, 1775, strongly marks the temper of his mind:

' "*My very dear Sir*—Your kind letter came to hand three days since. Your comforts and sorrows are mine in no small degree; I share with you in both; the tie is such as death cannot dissolve. This is a day of darkness in my view, and few are in any degree properly affected with it. I have, through grace, perhaps as little to fear for myself or mine as any living. I humbly hope we are housed in Jesus; but I am distressed for the nation and land. The ruin of both is awfully threatened; and, though now deferred, may ere long be accomplished, unless reformation takes place. It behoves every one to cry, 'Spare thy people, O Lord, and give not thine heritage to reproach.' I know God is merciful; he has, notwithstanding, disinherited a people as dear to him as ever we were, whose sins were not more aggravated than ours. The Lord can deliver, but have we reason to think he will, having told us that he will 'wound the head of his enemies, and the hairy scalps of such who go on in their trespasses?' Is there any appearance of reformation? Yea, is it not the reverse? Are not our meetings for the preservation of our liberty often abused by excessive drinking? &c. &c. Have not politics taken the place of religion in all our conversations? Is it not become unconstitutional (to use vulgar language) to mention God's name in company, unless by way of dishonouring him? Are not things sacred neglected by some, and burlesqued by others? Is not the newspaper substituted for the Bible on Lord's day, yea, at church? What will the end of these things be? Blessed be God, through Jesus Christ, He is for a sanctuary."

'Mr. Tennent was on a visit within less than twenty miles of New York, when a British frigate attempted to pass the batteries, and to proceed up the North River, while General Washington lay with the American army in that city. A very heavy cannonading took place, which was mistaken by the surrounding country for a general attack on our army. Mr. Tennent was deeply affected, and after a violent struggle within himself, he turned to a friend or two present, and said, "Come, while our fellow citizens are fighting let us retire to prayer." They, accordingly, went up into his room, where he most devoutly poured out his soul for about half an hour in the most fervent prayers, wrestling with God in behalf of his suffering country.

'In the winter of 1776–7, the British overran a great part of the state of New Jersey, and particularly the county of Monmouth, where a number of the inhabitants were in the British interests. Such was their apparent power, and the distressed situation of the American army, retreating before them, that it was generally supposed by the people in the country that the dispute was almost at an end, and that all hopes of successful opposition were nearly extinguished. A British party arose in the county, who seized their fellow-citizens and dragged them to a British provost, where they were treated in the most cruel manner, as rebels and traitors. Even citizens from other parts of the state, who had taken refuge in the county depending on the known hospitality of the inhabitants, were not respected. In this situation Mr. Tennent very justly thought himself in great danger; but having no place to flee to for safety, he remained at home, committing himself to the protection of Almighty God. In the month of Dec. 1776, a number of the inhabitants came to his house, and insisted that he should go to Princeton without delay, and take the benefit of General Howe's proclamation, offering a pardon to those who should seek it within a limited time. He refused, till he found himself in danger of being taken off and committed to a British provost, which he well knew was but another word for a lingering death. He also found that, in his present state, his usefulness as a minister of the gospel was at an end, unless he complied with the wishes of the people, most of the whigs of influence having fled. Concluding that present duty enforced the request which was thus urged upon him, he promised to go to Princeton. On his way he lodged at the house of a young clergyman, and on rising in the morning he seemed greatly oppressed in spirit. On being asked what troubled him, he answered with a heavy sigh, "I am going to do a thing for conscience sake, directly against my conscience." Soon after his return home, to the surprise of every body, the British quarters at Trenton were beaten up, and a British regiment taken at Princeton; the American army again advanced, and took a strong position at Morristown, by which the British in their turn were obliged to retreat and contract their lines to Brunswick and Amboy. The Americans again got possession of the county of Monmouth,

THE OLD TENNENT PARSONAGE.

THE OLD TENNENT CHURCH.

where the whigs returned in force. Mr. Tennent's mind was greatly oppressed with his untoward situation, and he severely blamed his untimely submission.

'About the latter end of February, or beginning of March, 1777, Mr. Tennent was suddenly seized with a fever, attended by violent symptoms. He sent for his family physician, who was in the act of setting off for the legislature of the state, of which he was a member. He called on his patient on his way, but could spend but a few minutes with him. He, however, examined carefully into Mr. Tennent's complaints, and the symptoms attending the disorder. With great candour the physician informed his patient that the attack appeared unusually violent; that the case required the best medical aid, and that it was out of his power to attend him. He feared that, at his advanced age, there was not strength of nature sufficient to overcome so severe a shock, and that his symptoms scarcely admitted of a favourable prognostic. The good old man received this news with his usual submission to the divine will; for, as he had always considered himself as bound for eternity, he had endeavoured so to live that when the summons should come he would have nothing to do but to die. He calmly replied, "I am very sensible of the violence of my disorder; that it has racked my constitution to an uncommon degree, and beyond what I have ever before experienced, and that it is accompanied with symptoms of approaching dissolution; but blessed be God, I have no wish to live if it should be his will and pleasure to call me hence." After a moment's pause he seemed to recollect himself, and varied the expression thus: "Blessed be God, I have no wish to live, if it should be his will and pleasure to call me hence, unless it should be to see a happy issue to the severe and arduous controversy my country is engaged in; but even in this, the will of the Lord be done."

'During his whole sickness, he continued perfectly resigned to the divine will, until death was swallowed up in victory on the 8th day of March, 1777. His body was buried in his own church at Freehold, a numerous concourse of people, composed not only of the members of his own congregation, but of the inhabitants of the whole adjacent country attending his funeral.

'Mr. Tennent was rather more than six feet high, of a spare, thin visage, and of an erect carriage. He had bright, piercing eyes, a long sharp nose, and a long face. His general countenance was

I

grave and solemn, but at all times cheerful and pleasant with his friends. It may be said of him with peculiar propriety that he appeared in an extraordinary manner to live above the world and all its allurements. He seemed habitually to have such clear views of spiritual and heavenly things, as afforded him much of the foretaste and enjoyment of them. His faith was really and experimentally "the substance of things hoped for, and the evidence of things unseen." Literally, his daily walk was with God, and he lived "as seeing him who is invisible." The divine presence with him was frequently manifested in his public ministrations, and in his private conduct. His ardent soul was seldom satisfied unless he was exerting himself in some way or other, in public or private, in rendering kind offices and effectual services of friendship both in spiritual and temporal things to his fellow-men. Take him in his whole demeanour and conduct, there are few of whom it might more emphatically be said, that he lived the life and died the death of the righteous.

'He was well-read in divinity, and was of sound orthodox principles. He professed himself a moderate Calvinist. The doctrines of man's depravity, the atonement of the Saviour, the absolute necessity of the all-powerful influence of the Spirit of God to renew the heart and subdue the will, all in perfect consistence with the free agency of the sinner, were among the leading articles of his faith. These doctrines, indeed, were generally interwoven in his public discourses, whatever might be the particular subject discussed. His success was often answerable to his exertions. His people loved him as a father, revered him as the pastor and bishop of their souls, obeyed him as their instructor, and delighted in his company and private conversation as a friend and brother. He carefully avoided making a difference between his doctrines publicly taught and his private practice. Attending a Synod a few years before his death, a strange clergyman, whom he never had before seen, was introduced to the Synod, and asked to preach in the evening. Mr. Tennent attended, and was much displeased with the sermon. As the congregation were going out of the church, Mr. Tennent in the crowd, coming up to the preacher, touched him on the shoulder, and said, "My brother, when I preach I take care to save myself, whatever I do with my congregation." The clergyman looked behind him with surprise, and seeing a very grave man, said, "What do you mean, sir?" Mr.

Tennent answered, "You have been sending your whole congregation, Synod and all, to perdition, and you have not even saved yourself. Whenever I preach, I make it a rule to save myself;" and then abruptly left him, without his knowing who spoke to him.

'At Mr. Tennent's death, the poor mourned for him as their patron, their comforter and support; and the rich lamented over him as their departed pastor and friend. The public at large lost in him a firm asserter of the civil and religious interests of his country. He was truly a patriot, not in words and pretences, not in condemning all who differed from him to proscription and death, but in acting in such a manner as would have rendered his country most happy if all had followed his example. He insisted on his own rights and freedom of sentiment, but he was willing to let others enjoy the same privilege; and he thought it of as much importance to live and act well, as to think and speak justly.

'To conclude these imperfect sketches,—may all who read the memoirs of this amiable and useful man, fervently and constantly beseech that God, with whom is the residue of the Spirit, that their life may be that of the righteous, so that their latter end may be like his; and that the great Head of the Church, while he removes faithful and distinguished labourers from the gospel vineyard, may raise up others, who shall possess even a double portion of their spirit, and who shall be even more successful in winning souls unto Jesus Christ, the great Bishop of souls.'

XI

Remarks on the Preceding Narrative

Mr. Tennent's trance not supernatural—The dreams of the witnesses
cannot be accounted for on natural principles—God still occasionally
gives admonitory dreams.

It must be acknowledged that some of the facts recorded in the
preceding narrative are of a marvellous nature; but we are inclined
to believe that they all may be accounted for on natural principles,
except one. The appearance of death when life is not extinguished
but only suspended has been often observed on the termination
of nervous fevers, and in epileptic and apoplectic fits. The temporary loss of memory on recovery has also been often observed.
Persons have been known to lie in one of these trances for weeks
together; and there is too much reason to fear that some persons
have been buried alive, by being prematurely carried to the grave.
This undoubtedly would have been the unhappy case of Mr.
Tennent, had not his young friend interposed. And as to the happy
state of his mind during this period and his imagining that he was
in heaven, it is all very natural, and does not require that we should
suppose the soul to have been separated from the body. We would
not deny that a man through life so highly favoured in receiving
extraordinary manifestations of God's perfections, and especially
of his love might, even when in this state of apparent death, have
been the subject of a gracious influence which filled his imagination
with the rapturous views which he enjoyed. We are disposed,
however, to admire Mr. Tennent's prudence in not being forward
to speak of his experience during this period; and we do not feel
disposed to regret that he never committed to writing an account
of his visions; or if he did, that his executor never could lay his
hands on the manuscript. When Paul was caught up to paradise,
and heard and saw the glory of the third heaven, he uttered not a
word respecting the nature of his vision; he merely said that he

'heard unspeakable things, which it is not lawful for a man to utter.' The writer would further remark that in certain states of the nervous system, when the common functions of life seem to be suspended, it is no uncommon thing for the imagination to be strongly affected.

The only thing in the foregoing history of William Tennent which cannot be accounted for upon the ordinary principles of human nature is the dreams of the man and his wife which brought them from Maryland to Trenton, and whose testimony was absolutely necessary to save this good man from an ignominious punishment. In this case, if the facts are true—concerning which there can be no reasonable doubt—there must have been a supernatural interposition. These simple people could have had no knowledge of what was transacting in New Jersey; and when they came to Trenton, they knew not for what purpose their presence was needed. In all ages of the world, suggestions and impressions have been made in dreams which have been important to the safety or interest of certain persons for whose sake the communication was made. And we learn from the Bible that dreams of this supernatural kind have not been confined to the pious, but have been granted to heathen kings and other persons who knew not the true God, as in the case of the butler and baker, of Pharaoh and Nebuchadnezzar. Such dreams are still on certain occasions granted, probably by the ministry of angels, for the admonition or direction of the people of God, or for reasons unknown to us. Although it is true, 'in the multitude of dreams there are divers vanities,' and although false prophets pretended to receive communications in dreams, and at this time, many persons are superstitiously affected by dreams, yet the truth of the fact ought not to be denied that, even in our day, dreams are sometimes admonitory, and seem to preserve certain persons from evils which they could not otherwise escape. God has nowhere informed us that this mode of communication with men should entirely cease; and if there are, however rarely, such communications to certain persons in sleep, it furnishes some proof of the existence of a world of spirits, invisible to us but near; and that we are surrounded and often guarded by kind angels, who minister unto us, and preserve us from many evils of which we are not aware. Such dreams are not properly called miraculous, nor can the persons to whom they are vouchsafed be said to be inspired. They are merely extraordinary intimations to the mind, probably as was said, by the agency of guardian angels. The only unaccountable thing in this whole business is that Mr. Tennent and his fellow-travellers had not sent off immediately to this distant place for witnesses, for there were many there who had heard him and Mr. Rowland preach. Conscious of innocence, they seem to have apprehended no danger; and when one of their number was found guilty, and actually punished for perjury, there might not have been time to bring persons from such a distance. But in regard to Mr. Tennent, he was not only conscious of innocence, but had such unshaken confidence in God that he feared nothing; being fully persuaded that he would in some way interpose by his providence for his deliverance or would overrule his unjust condemnation and punishment for his own glory. This last seems to have been especially on his mind; for we are informed that he had prepared a sermon for the occasion, to be preached while standing in the pillory.

XII

Anecdotes of the Rev. Wm. Tennent Jr.

Mr. Tennent loses some of his toes—Attempted explanation—Anecdotes supplied by Dr. Miller—Anecdotes from the Assembly's Magazine, with an account of his interview with Murray the Universalist.

We have never known a man in modern times concerning whom so many extraordinary things are related. The most important of these are contained in Dr. Boudinot's memoir of his life; but many others were omitted, either because he judged them of not sufficient importance to be recorded in such a work, or because, writing for a periodical, he was limited as to the space which the memoir was allowed to occupy. Many of these anecdotes, however, he took a pleasure in relating in conversation with his friends; and those which have been kindly furnished by my friend and colleague, the Rev. Dr. Miller, were received from him. I have been in some doubt about introducing the contents of this chapter into the volume; but as the anecdotes here given are all believed to be authentic, it was thought that they would tend to exhibit in a more distinct light the true character of this extraordinary man. Many others have been current in his vicinity, but as they have been handed down by tradition, they have not been considered as sufficiently authenticated to be inserted in this memoir; and some of them are of too ludicrous a nature to have a place in a serious narrative.

There is one remarkable thing which happened to Mr. Tennent, not recorded in the memoir written by Dr. Boudinot, which has to most appeared more inexplicable than any other event of his life. One night, as the story goes, when Mr. Tennent was asleep in his own bed, he was waked up by a sharp pain in the region of the toes of one of his feet; and upon getting a light and examining the foot, it was discovered that several of his toes had been cut entirely off, as if by some sharp instrument. But though the wounded part was bleeding, nothing was seen of the exscinded members, nor any means by which such a dismemberment could have been effected.

In the room was found no animal, rat, cat, or dog, although diligent search was made; neither could there be discovered any sharp instrument by which such a wound could have been inflicted. Mr. Tennent himself confidently believed that the injury was done by the prince of darkness, of whose power and malice he was deeply convinced. Others supposed that it must have been effected by some domestic animal, which might have made its escape before a light was obtained, as both rats and cats have been known violently to attack and wound persons while asleep. But neither of these explanations gives satisfaction. For as to Satan it cannot be doubted that his malice is great, and that it is especially directed against holy men, and particularly faithful ministers; but we have no evidence that he is now permitted to injure or wound the bodies of the saints. Our fathers were more credulous on this point than we are, and we may dismiss all further notice of this account, as an opinion properly belonging to a former age. And as to the idea that it might have been the bite of a hungry and voracious rat, or mad cat, the thing is very improbable. Neither of these animals could have with its teeth severed the toes from the foot so suddenly; and in that case the wound would have had marks of the gnawing of such an animal, whereas it was said to have had the appearance of being made by a sharp instrument. Perhaps the difficulty of accounting for the accident prevented Dr. Boudinot from inserting the story in Mr. Tennent's memoir; for there can be no doubt that he was well acquainted with the fact, and all its circumstances.

The author of this compilation has the more readily consented to record the event because he has a hypothesis by which he thinks he can account for such an accident.

Upon a survey of the circumstances of the affair, it seems highly probable that Mr. Tennent was a somnambulist, and received this injury by treading in his rambles on some sharp instrument; soon after which he returned to his bed, but did not feel the pain of the wound until he awoke. It is well known that persons in this kind of sleep are very little susceptible of the feeling of pain from any accident of this sort; and they seldom ever retain any recollection of the exercises of their minds at the time, or of the scenes through which they have passed. Many instances might be given of persons receiving bodily hurts while in this state without being awakened thereby; and apparently without any feeling of pain from wounds which would cause very acute suffering to one awake. And it may not be improper to refer for proof of this to undoubted facts, witnessed by many, in regard to persons in a mesmeric sleep, who undergo surgical operations which give intense pain in a common state, without any appearance of sensibility.

The writer recollects to have heard of an instance precisely in point which occurred in Philadelphia in relation to a son of the late Dr. Sproat, who, being a somnambulist, got out of his room at a window on a shed, and jumped on the ground, but lighting on something sharp, cut his foot; and being soon missed, was pursued by his bloody tracks on the snow, with which the ground was at the time covered. But he was not awakened from his sleep by the wound which he received. Other cases of serious injury sustained in the night by persons who could give no account how they occurred have fallen under the notice of the writer, and which can only be accounted for by this hypothesis. If it be alleged, that Mr. Wm. Tennent was not known to be a somnambulist, it may be answered that he certainly had a nervous system strung in a very peculiar manner, and many are subject to this kind of sleep who never know anything about it. And we would adduce the fact under consideration as a strong presumptive evidence of the thing supposed.

The following anecdotes of the Rev. William Tennent were kindly communicated to the author by the Rev. Doctor Miller, of Princeton.

'This remarkable man was greatly distinguished for *decision of character*. Many good men of his day had more intellectual vigour than he possessed, but few of his contemporaries possessed as much as he did of that moral courage, that fixedness of purpose, and that firmness of Christian heroism which could not be turned to the right or the left. This trait in his character was once very strongly exemplified at a meeting of the Board of Trustees of the College of New Jersey. It is well known that Mr. Tennent was one of the most active and zealous of the founders of that College; and that the great object of those worthy men, in all the labour and expense which they incurred in its establishment, was to train up a pious and learned ministry for the Presbyterian Church. For the attainment of this object, and to guard the College against every species of perversion or abuse, he was ever on the watch, and especially to promote the religious interests of the Institution.

'Soon after William Franklin (son of Benjamin) was appointed Governor of the Province of New Jersey, he took his seat according to the provision of the charter, as *ex officio* President of the Board. On one of the early occasions of his presiding in quality of governor, after coming to that office, he formed a plan of wheedling the Board into an agreement to have their charter so modified as to place the Institution more entirely in the power of the Provincial government, and to receive in exchange for this concession some inconsiderable pecuniary advantage. The Governor made this proposal in a plausible speech, and was receiving the thanks of several short-sighted and sanguine members of the Board of Trustees—when Mr. Tennent, who had been prevented by some dispensation of Providence from coming earlier, appeared in the Board and took his seat. After listening for a few minutes, and hearing from one and another of his brother trustees the nature of the Governor's plan and offer, after several of them had in his presence recognized the Governor's proposal as highly favourable and such as ought to be accepted, and praised "his Excellency's generous proposal" as what all must think well of—Mr. Tennent, looking round the Board with the sharp and piercing eye for which he was remarkable when strongly excited, rose and said: "Brethren! are you mad? I say, brethren, are you mad? Rather than accept the offer of the President, I would set fire to the College edifice at its four corners, and run away in the light of the flames." Such was the effect of this rebuff from a trustee of such known honesty, influence and decision, that little more was said. The proposal was laid on the table and never more called up.

'Mr. Tennent was full of expedients for winning souls to Christ. He was remarkably fond of horses; had a good deal of skill in the choice and management of them, and was seldom known to ride or to keep an inferior one. There was a young man in his congregation, the son of one of his church members, also distinguished for his attachment to horses and for his skill in horsemanship. Mr. Tennent was very desirous of gaining access to this young man, and of securing his confidence. But every effort to accomplish this object was disappointed; the young man, trembling at the thought of being addressed on the subject of religion, avoided his pastor with the utmost vigilance, escaped from his father's house whenever Mr. Tennent called, and in every possible way evaded an interview with him. Mr. Tennent observed this, and resorted to every contrivance in his power to overcome the young man's aversion to his company. But in vain. Things went on in this way for a considerable time. In the meanwhile Mr. Tennent's desire for an interview became more intense, from hearing that the young man had an active mind and an amiable temper, and was considered as in most respects very promising by those who knew him best. One day, when Mr. Tennent was riding out in his course of family visitation on a remarkably fleet horse, he saw this young man about a hundred yards before him, coming out from a neighbour's gate, and going toward his father's house. Mr. Tennent immediately quickened the pace of his horse for the purpose of overtaking him. The young man, looking back and seeing Mr. Tennent coming, did the same. Each spurred on his horse, until the contest became a race at full speed. After running in this manner between one and two miles, Mr. Tennent, having much the fleeter horse, overtook the young man, and on coming up to him said, in a very affable, pleasant manner, "Well, Johnny, I thought I should overtake you. I see you ride a good animal, but I had a notion that mine could beat him." He then entered into familiar conversation with the young man, adapting all his remarks to what he supposed to be his favourite pursuits and topics. After riding a mile or two together, Mr. Tennent said to him, when they were about to separate, "Johnny, come and see me. I shall be very glad to see you; I know you love a good horse. I think I have some horses and colts that will please you. It will give me real pleasure to show them to you." With this invitation, and these remarks, they parted. In a few days the young man, greatly pleased with the manner in which Mr. Tennent had treated him, accepted his invitation, and called at his house. Mr. Tennent fulfilled his promise, took him through his stables and round his farm, and entertained him greatly to his gratification, without saying one word to him of religion. The young man no longer shunned his company, but put himself in his way, not only without fear but with pleasure, whenever he had an opportunity. Mr. Tennent very soon took occasion, after gaining his confidence,

to address him on the most important of all subjects; and it was
not long before he listened with serious attention, became hopefully
the subject of renewing grace, and was soon united with the church
of Christ.

'This excellent man was remarkably skilful, discriminating, and
faithful in dealing with those who came to him, professing to be in
a state of anxiety or inquiry respecting their salvation. He was
once visited by a female advanced in life, one of his stated hearers,
who had not borne a very good character, but who now professed
to be deeply anxious concerning her eternal welfare. She wept,
acknowledged herself a great sinner, and abounded in language
of severe self-crimination, and professions of deep penitence.
Mr. Tennent thought he saw in her whole air and manner something like over-acting, which, taken in connection with her
former life, led him to suspect that her professions were not very
sincere. He therefore determined at once to put them to the test,
and said: "Mrs. ———, you speak of yourself as a great sinner;
that is just what we have always thought of you. I have no doubt
it is very much as you say." The woman, who was indeed a
hypocrite, fully expecting to be hailed with pleasure and confidence
as a genuine convert by her minister, was thrown off her guard by
this rebuff, and replied with strong resentment: "It's no such
thing. I'm not chargeable with these sins, I'm as good as you any
day," and immediately left the house; and with this interview
dismissed her serious impressions.

'At another time Mr. Tennent, in riding out, stopped opposite
the door of a small tavern in his neighbourhood to make some
inquiry. While waiting a moment to obtain the desired information,
a man evidently intoxicated with strong drink came out of the
house and accosted him by name. Finding that Mr. Tennent did
not return his salutation with the readiness and familiarity of an
acquaintance, he said: "Mr. Tennent, I believe you do not know
me; why, you converted me a few months ago." "Ah! my friend,"
said Mr. Tennent, "it's like some of my bungling work. If the
Spirit of God had converted you, we should not have seen you
in this situation."'

In the same volume of the Assembly's Missionary Magazine
which contains the biography of the Rev. William Tennent, Jr.,
we have from another hand the three following anecdotes.

'He was crossing the bay from New York to Elizabethtown in company with two gentlemen who had no great fondness for clergymen, and who cautiously avoided him for some times after getting on board the boat. As he usually spoke loudly, they overheard what he said, and finding him a cheerful companion, who could converse upon other subjects besides religion, they ventured a little nearer to him; and at length they and he engaged in a conversation upon politics. One of his congregation, who was a fellow-passenger, happening to overhear a remark he made, stepped up to him, and said, "Mr. Tennent, please to spiritualize that." "Spiritualize that!" said Mr. T., "you don't know what you are talking about." "Why, sir, there is no harm in talking religion, is there?" "Yes," replied Mr. T., "there is a great deal of harm in it; and it is such good folks as you that always lug religion in by head and shoulders, whether it is proper or not, that hurt the cause. If you want to talk religion, you know where I live, and I know where you live, and you may call at my house, or I will call at yours, and I will talk religion with you till you are tired; but this is not the time to talk religion; we are talking politics." This reply, and his conduct in other respects so much ingratiated Mr. Tennent with the two gentlemen as to furnish him with an opportunity for advantageously introducing conversation upon more important subjects; and the younger of the two was so much pleased, that on their arrival at Elizabethtown Point, he insisted upon Mr. Tennent taking his seat in a chair, and he walked from the Point to Elizabethtown through a muddy road, which, to a person of Mr. Tennent's age, would have been very inconvenient, if not impracticable.

'At New York, Mr. Tennent went to hear a sermon delivered by a transient clergyman, who was often and well spoken of, but whose manner was singular, and who frequently introduced odd conceits into his sermons, which tended to excite mirth rather than to edification. Upon leaving the church, a friend asked Mr. Tennent's opinion of the sermon. He said it made him think of a man who should take a bag, and put into it some of the very best super fine wheat flour, a greater quantity of Indian meal, and some arsenic, and mix them all together. A part of the sermon was of the very best quality, more of it was coarse, but very wholesome food, and some of it rank poison.

'Upon another occasion, he went with a friend to hear an

illiterate carpenter preach at New York; and it appeared to him
that the man denied the doctrine of the perseverance of the saints.
The next morning Mr. Tennent called upon his friend, and asked
if it appeared so to him. Upon his friend replying in the affirmative,
Mr. Tennent said, "then I must go and talk with him, and you
must go along with me." His friend begged to be excused, but
Mr. Tennent insisted upon his going, as he had heard the doctrine
denied. They found the carpenter at breakfast. Mr. Tennent asked
if he was the person who had preached last evening. He said he
was. "Then," said Mr. Tennent, "it appeared to me that you denied
the doctrine of the perseverance of the saints; did I understand
you rightly?" "Yes, sir, be sure I did," said the carpenter; "that
is a doctrine which no man in his senses can believe." "I'll tell
you," replied Mr. Tennent, "that it is the most precious doctrine
in all the book of God. I will give up my life before I will give that
up. I must talk with you about it." The man alleged that he was a
mechanic, who depended upon his trade for the support of his
family, and could not stay to *talk;* he must mind his business.
"I am glad to hear that," said Mr. Tennent, "I love to see men
diligent in their lawful callings; it is their duty; but yours is of
such a nature that you can work and talk at the same time; and I
will go with you to where your business lies, so that your time
shall not be wasted." The carpenter said he did not want to talk,
took his hat and abruptly went off. Mr. Tennent followed him.
The man walked faster. Mr. Tennent quickened his pace. At
length the man ran; so did Mr. Tennent. But the carpenter was
too fleet for his pursuer; by his speed he evaded his arguments,
and remained in error.'

The following anecdote has been handed down by tradition,
and in substance is confirmed by a one-sided account of the affair,
contained in the life of Murray, the Universalist, who is the person
concerned. Mr. Tennent's zeal for the truth and opposition to
what he viewed to be error were very strong, and were manifested
whenever an occasion occurred which called for their exercise. It
so happened that Mr. Murray, an Englishman, who had adopted
from Relly the doctrines of Universalism, was landed on the
Jersey shore not very remote from Mr. Tennent's residence.
Though he had not been a Universalist preacher in England, yet
having, while in connection with the Methodists, both in Ireland

and England, been accustomed to public speaking in the way of exhortation, he was induced, upon his landing at a place on the Jersey shore called "Good Luck," to commence preaching to the people. At first his doctrine of universal salvation was not clearly and openly announced, but rather covertly insinuated. Possessing some wit and eloquence, he attracted many hearers, and travelled about the country, addressing the people wherever he could get an opportunity. Soon after he commenced this career, he came into the congregation of Freehold, and lodged with one of Mr. Tennent's hearers. As soon as this watchful pastor heard that the wolf had entered among the sheep of his flock, taking with him some of his neighbours, he went to the house where Mr. Murray was staying, and demanded of him by what authority he had assumed the office of preacher. Murray answered him by asking by what authority he asked him such a question. An altercation ensued, Mr. Tennent continuing peremptorily to demand his authority to preach, and he as pertinaciously evading a direct answer. It does not appear, however, from Mr. Murray's account, the only written one which we have seen, that Mr. Tennent then knew that he was a Universalist, for in the interview nothing was said on that subject, nor on any other point of doctrine. It would seem that Mr. Tennent considered him as an irregular, unauthorized itinerant, who, not being in connection with any denomination of Christians, ought not to be encouraged. And this, according to Mr. Murray's own account, was the exact state of the case. He stood entirely alone, and professed to hold ecclesiastical connection with no body on earth; yet this man became the founder of a large sect in this country, for the Universalists acknowledge him as a *father*. But as the course of error is always downward, most of his followers have departed far from his opinions on other doctrinal points, as appears by his life.

XIII

Memoir of the Rev. Charles Tennent

Birth—Immigration—Education—Settlement in the ministry at White-clay Creek—Great revival under the preaching of Mr. Whitefield—Removal and death.

From an original document, a small memorandum-book, kept by the Rev. William Tennent, sen., we learn that his fourth son, Charles, was born at Coleraine, in the county of Down, on the third day of May, in the year 1711, and was baptized by the Rev. Richard Donnell. At the time of his father's emigration from Ireland, he was therefore a boy of seven years of age. He, as well as his older brothers, received his education under the paternal roof, or rather in the Log College. He appears, however, to have been less distinguished than either of his brothers; but seems to have been a respectable minister of the gospel, and was early settled in the Presbyterian congregation of Whiteclay Creek, in the state of Delaware. Soon after his settlement in this place, the great revival under the preaching of Whitefield commenced, and was very powerful in this congregation. During this remarkable season of divine influence, Mr. Whitefield spent some days with Mr. Charles Tennent, and assisted him in the administration of the Lord's Supper, preaching to vast multitudes of people every day of the solemnity, which continued four days, according to custom. This information the writer obtained many years ago from one of the subjects of the revival, Mrs. Douglass, the sister of Charles Thompson, Secretary of the Continental Congress, and grand-mother of the late Rev. James Douglass, of Fayetteville, North Carolina, so highly esteemed as a spiritual, searching, evangelical preacher. This old lady appeared to me to be as eminently pious as any person I ever knew. She informed me that while Mr. Whitefield spoke at the tables, in administering the sacrament, he poured forth such a flood of tears that his cambric handkerchief was wet as if it had been dipped in water. She spoke of that day as by far the most glorious she had ever witnessed. Her account of the Rev. Charles Tennent was that he was a plain, good preacher, but not distinguished for great abilities. I was surprised to find that this pious old lady was no longer a member of the Presbyterian church, but had long ago joined the communion of the Seceders. Upon inquiry it appeared that this change had been made by her and some others, in consequence of the union entered into with the Old Side, in 1758. The congregation of Whiteclay Creek, of which Mr. Tennent was the pastor, was situated in the neighbourhood of some congregations, the ministers and members of which opposed the revival, and represented the whole as a delusion of the devil.

The friends, and especially the subjects of the revival, could not but consider these opposers as the enemies of vital piety, and therefore felt no disposition to hold any fellowship with them. They were therefore astonished and offended when they understood that a union between the two parties had been consummated. As soon as Mr. Tennent returned from the Synod in Philadelphia where the union had been agreed on, Mrs. Douglass went to him, and expostulated with him on the subject. 'Oh! Mr. Tennent,' said she, 'how could you consent to enter into communion with those who so wickedly reviled the glorious work of God's grace in this land? As for myself, I never can and never will, until they profess repentance for their grievous sin, in speaking contemptuously of the work of the Holy Spirit.' And accordingly, she went and joined the Seceders, who had begun to form societies in several parts of Pennsylvania, and continued in their communion until her dying day. But her heart was still with the evangelical part of the Presbyterian church, and all her children entered into the communion of that church. Two of her sons, James Douglass, and Daniel Douglass, some forty years ago, were pious, intelligent, and estimable elders in the Presbyterian church in Alexandria, D.C., of which the Rev. Dr. Muir was the respected pastor. No doubt, the views of this good lady in regard to the union so happily formed between the dissentient parties in the Presbyterian church were narrow, yet they were very natural and arose from her acquaintance with the Old Side party being confined to those immediately around her, who had taken a very active part in ridiculing and maligning this blessed reformation

K

by which many sinners were converted, and turned from darkness to light and from the power of Satan unto God. The writer, in his youth, has known some people who would indulge in the most violent wrath at any favourable mention of Mr. Whitefield; and yet they professed to believe the very doctrines which he preached. A large part of those, however, who belonged to the Old Side were actuated by no such spirit, but were quiet, orderly, well-informed Christians, who were very careful in the religious instruction of their own families, and very strict and conscientious in all the duties of religion.

Some years before his death, Mr. Charles Tennent removed from Whiteclay Creek to Buckingham church, in Maryland, where he ended his days, and where, it is presumed, his remains were interred. Of his latter days, and of the circumstances of his decease, we have received no authentic information.

It may be proper, however, to observe that he had a son, the Rev. William M. Tennent, who, after receiving a finished education, entered the holy ministry, and became pastor of the Presbyterian church in Abington, in the vicinity of Philadelphia. He married a daughter of the Rev. Dr. Rodgers, of New York, and received the honorary degree of Doctor of Divinity from Yale College.

He was a man of great sweetness of temper and politeness of manners, and was distinguished for his hospitality. His house was seldom without the company of friends and acquaintances; and all who had the privilege of visiting at this pleasant retreat were delighted with their cordial reception and kind entertainment. His last sickness was long, but in it he was in a great measure exempt from pain, and was blessed with an uninterrupted assurance of the favour of God. The writer, then residing in Philadelphia, frequently saw and conversed with him; and he must say, that he never saw a person in a sweeter, calmer, happier state of mind, and it continued for many weeks. He died in the year 1811 or 1812, and had no children.

It is believed that no male descendant of any branch of the Tennent family now remains in this part of the country; though there are several in South Carolina.

XIV

Memoir of the Rev. Samuel Blair

Educated in the Log College—Licensed to preach by the New Castle
Presbytery—First settled at Shrewsbury, N.J.—Removes to New
Londonderry in Pennsylvania—Great revival in that congregation—His
letter to Mr. Prince—How far justifiable in violating rules of order—
Dr. Finley's character of him—Mr. Davies's Elegy—Publications.

The following character of Mr. Samuel Blair is given by Dr.
Finley, in his funeral sermon occasioned by the death of this
eminent servant of Jesus Christ.

'He was blessed with early piety. On his dying bed he could
recollect with delight various evidences of gracious influences in
his tender years. By this means he was happily preserved from
being ever engaged in vicious courses, and at once grew in stature
and in grace. Religion, far from being a flashy thing with him, was
rational and solid, manifesting itself in unreserved obedience to all
God's commandments.

'To a holy disposition was added a great genius, capable of the
highest improvement. He had a deep and penetrating judgment, a
clear and regular way of conceiving things, and a retentive memory.
He was an indefatigable student, a calm and impartial searcher
after truth. He thought for himself, and was determined in his
conclusions only by evidence. He had a very considerable store of
critical learning, and was especially conversant with the Scriptures
in the original languages. How great his attainments in philosophy
were was known by few; for in his last years his thirst for knowledge
did sensibly increase, and he greatly improved himself therein.
He studied several branches of the mathematics, and especially
geometry and astronomy; nor will these seem tasteless studies to
one who had such a savour of living piety, when it is considered
that he saw the glory of God in all his works, and admired and

adored him in all. He delighted to see the "invisible things of Him, even his eternal power and Godhead, manifested by the things that are made." It was edifying to him to trace the footsteps of the divine wisdom in particulars, and the infinite reach of projection in the frame and structure of the whole.

'But his critical and philosophical learning and his large acquaintance with geography and history were exceeded by his knowledge in divinity. This was the business of his life, and herein he made such proficiency as few of his standing in the ministry have attained to. Here he found what perfectly answered his refined, spiritual taste. The contemplation of redeeming love did much more elevate his soul than that of the works of creation; for therein he saw the wisdom, the power, the justice and the love of God more clearly displayed. On every subject he had a set of most accurately studied thoughts. He had often weighed in an impartial balance every theological controversy; was a solid disputant, and able to defend all necessary truth. He was a judicious casuist, and could very satisfyingly resolve dubious and perplexed cases of conscience. He was not only a proficient in systematic divinity, which is comparatively a small attainment, but a great textuary. He studied the sacred oracles above all other things, and that it was not in vain manifestly appeared from his great ability in "dividing the word of truth." He could "bring out of his treasure things new and old." How clearly and fully would he explain his subject! With what irresistible arguments confirm the truth! With what admirable dexterity accommodate it to his audience! And with what solemn pungency did he impress it on the conscience! He spoke like one who knew the worth of souls, and felt in himself the surest constraints of love to God and man.

'As to his religious principles, he was of noble and generous sentiments. He had not "so learned Christ" as to be furious in his zeal for mere circumstantial or indifferent points. He understood the nature of religion better than to place it in things in which it does not consist; and was too much exercised about "the great matters of the law," to be equally zealous for "mint, anise, and cummin." Though sacrifice be good, yet he had learned that "mercy is better." He believed, and that in accordance with the Scriptures, that the communion of saints is of much greater importance than many of those things in which Christians differ in judgment, and was, therefore, far from such narrowness as to make every principle and practice which he thought to be good and true a term of communion; and he was as far from the contrary extreme of indifference to the truth and laxness of discipline. As he was diligent in the exercise of his ministerial office to the utmost of his strength, not sparing himself, so God did very remarkably succeed his faithful ministrations to the conversion of many souls. He was the spiritual father of great numbers. I have had acquaintance with Christians in different places, where he only preached occasionally, who gave all hopeful evidences of a sacred conversion, and acknowledged him to be the instrument of it. He was strict in discipline, yet so as to be still candid; and severely just, yet so as to be still compassionate and tender. And with what wisdom and circumspection he judged in difficult cases his brethren of the Presbytery well know. We waited for his sage remarks, and heard attentively his prudent reasonings; and after his words how seldom had anyone occasion to speak again! "His speech dropped upon us, and we waited for him as for the rain." He has been eminently serviceable to the church, by assisting several promising youths in their studies for the ministry; who, becoming learned by his instructions, and formed by his example, are now wise, and useful, and faithful ministers.

'He was remarkably grave and solemn in his aspect and deportment, yet of a cheerful, even, and pleasant temper. And in conversation with his intimate friends, facetious and witty, when the season and concurring circumstances would allow him to indulge in that way; in respect of which his prudence could well direct him. He was of a generous and liberal disposition; far from being niggardly or covetous; was forward in acts of charity to the indigent according to his ability, and all his conduct discovered a noble indifference toward earthly things.

'If we consider him as a friend, he was firm and steadfast, and might as much be depended on as any I ever knew. He was remote from precarious and fickle humours: his approbation was not easily obtained, nor easily lost. Nor was he a friend only in compliment, but would cheerfully undergo hardships and suffer disadvantages, in order to do a friendly office. He was conscientiously punctual in attending ecclesiastical judicatures, presbyteries or synods. His presence might be depended on, if nothing extraordinary intervened, as certainly as the appointed day. He was not absent on every trifling inconvenience. In this respect his conduct was truly exemplary, and demonstrated his constant care for the public interests of religion. So great was his attention to matters of common concern as to incline him rather to expose himself than balk an opportunity of doing good. It is well known that his going upon an urgent call, in a weakly state of body, and in an unsettled season, to a convention of the trustees of New Jersey College, gave occasion to that fatal sickness from which he never fully recovered.

'In social life also he was worthy of imitation. As a husband, he was affectionate and kind; as a father, tender and indulgent. In him condenscension and authority were duly tempered. There was that in him that could engage love, and command reverence at the same time. Who that was acquainted with him would not be ready to say, "Happy was the family of which he was the head, and happy the congregation that enjoyed his ministry; happy the judicature of which he was a member; and happy the person who was favoured with his friendship?" He was a public blessing to the church, an honour to his people, an ornament to his profession who "magnified his office." He spoke as he believed; he practised as he preached; he lived holily, and died joyfully.

'For a long course of years, he had a habitual, unwavering assurance of his interest in the favour of God and that a blessed and glorious eternity would one day open upon him; which were his own emphatical words on his dying bed. This his assurance was solid and scriptural, arising from the many and clear experiences he had of gracious communications to his soul. He was made sensible in his early years of his guilty state by nature as well as practice; felt his inability to deliver himself; saw plainly that he lay at mercy, and that it was entirely at God's pleasure to save or reject him. This view of the case created in him a restless concern, until the way of life through Jesus Christ was graciously discovered to him. Then he saw that God could save him in consistency with all the honours of governing justice; for that the obedience and suffering of Christ, in the room of sinners, have made a sufficient atonement for sin. He saw that Christ was a Saviour every way complete and suitable for him. His soul approved the Divine and glorious plan; and freely disclaiming all dependence on his own righteousness, wisdom, and strength, most gladly accepted the offer of the gospel, that Christ should be his "wisdom, righteousness, sanctification, and redemption." Strict holiness was his choice, and it was the delightful business of his life, to do always those things which pleased his Heavenly Father. And on his dying bed he had the full approbation and testimony of his conscience, as to the general bent and tenor of his life. These particulars are the heads of what he himself told me in his last sickness, and are delivered in the same order, as near as I can possibly recollect.

'When he approached near his end he expressed most ardent desires "to depart and be with Christ;" and especially the three last days of his life were taken up in this exercise. Many gracious words he spoke, gave an affectionate farewell to his beloved, sorrowful consort, and dear children; tenderly committed them to the Divine mercy and faithfulness and fervently prayed that the blessing of the Most High might be vouchsafed to them, and rest upon them; which prayer, I hope, will be answered. His last words, a minute or two before his departure were, "the Bridegroom is come, and we shall now have all things." And thus, under a gleam of heaven, he breathed out his last."

The Rev. Samuel Davies, who had received nearly his whole education under the tuition of Samuel Blair, was deeply affected when he heard the sad tidings of the death of his revered and beloved instructor. He was then residing at Hanover, in Virginia, where he had gone to occupy an important station, as will be particularly related in another part of this work. Mr. Davies, who possessed ardent affections and a lively imagination, and frequently gave indulgence to his poetic genius, which, if it had been cultivated, might have rendered him conspicuous in that department, now invoked his sacred muse, and composed an elegy of many lines on his admired friend and tutor. The poem is more remarkable for pathos than for smooth versification. The only reason for noticing it here is to show the opinion entertained of Mr. Blair by this first of American preachers. A few extracts will be sufficient to answer our purpose.

> '—— Blair is no more—then this poor world has lost
> As rich a jewel as her stores could boast;
> Heaven, in just vengeance, has recalled again
> Its faithful envoy from the sons of men,
> Advanced him from his pious toils below,
> In raptures there, in kindred plains to glow.'

'O, had not been the mournful news divulged,
My mind had still the pleasing dream indulged—
Still fancied Blair with health and vigour blessed,
With some grand purpose labouring in his breast;
In studious thought pursuing truth divine,
Till the full demonstration round him shine;
Or, from the sacred desk proclaiming loud
His Master's message to th' attentive crowd,
While heavenly truth with bright conviction glares,
And coward error shrinks and disappears;
While quick remorse the hardy sinner feels,
And Calvary's balm the bleeding conscience heals.'

'Oh! could the Muse's languid colours paint
The man, the scholar, student, preacher, saint,
I'd place his image full in public view;
His friends should know more than before they knew.
His foes, astonished at his virtues, gaze,
Or shrink confounded from the oppressive blaze.
To trace his bright example, all should turn,
And with the bravest emulation burn.
His name should my poor lays immortalize,
Till he, t' attest his character, arise,
And the Great Judge th' encomium ratifies.'

The following lines will serve to show who were the persons, in Mr. Davies's estimation, who deserved to be handed down to posterity, as the chosen friends and faithful coadjutors of Mr. Blair in his evangelical labours. They were all alumni of the Log College, or of Mr. Blair's school at New Londonderry. And if we look at the men educated in this school, we cannot but entertain an exalted opinion of Mr. Samuel Blair, as an instructor.

'Surviving remnant of the sacred tribe,
Who knew the worth these plaintive lays describe:
TENNENTS, three worthies of immortal fame,
Brethren by office, birth, in heart and name.
FINLEY, who full enjoyed th' unbosomed friend;
RODGERS, whose soul he like his own refined,
When all attention, eager to admit

The flowing knowledge, at his reverend feet
Raptured we sat; and thou above the rest,
Brother and image of the dear deceased.
Surviving Blair! Oh, let spontaneous flow
The floods of tributary grief you owe.
And in your number—if so mean a name,
May the sad honour of chief mourner claim,
Oh! may my filial tears more copious flow,
And swell the tide of universal woe.
Oh! Blair! whom all the tenderest names commend,
My father, tutor, pastor, brother, friend!
While distance, the sad privilege denies,
O'er thy dear tomb, to vent my bursting eyes,
The Muse erects—the sole return allowed—
This humble monument of gratitude.'

As the remarkable and impressive solemnity of Samuel Blair's appearance, especially in the pulpit, has been noticed by all who have given any account of him, it will be gratifying to have the same confirmed by such a man as Samuel Davies, who himself was so distinguished for dignity and solemnity in the pulpit, that one of the most excellent laymen I ever knew told me that he went to hear Mr. Davies preach when he was just grown up, and that the sight of the man and the mere utterance of his text 'Martha, Martha,' &c. made a deeper impression on him than all the sermons he had ever heard before.

'Now, in the sacred desk, I see him rise,
And well he acts the herald of the skies.
Graceful solemnity, and striking awe
Sit in his looks, and deep attention draw.
His speaking aspect—in the bloom of youth
Renewed—declares unutterable truth.
Unthinking crowds grow solemn as they gaze,
And read his awful message in his face.'

The principal writings of the Rev. Samuel Blair were collected by his brother John after his death, and published in Philadelphia, in the year 1754.
This volume contains seven sermons, all on highly important

and practical subjects, which are treated in a very solemn and methodical manner. His style is perspicuous, but neither terse nor elegant; but the thoughts are those of a profound thinker.

To these sermons is appended an elaborate treatise on Predestination and Reprobation, evincing that the author was a thorough-going Calvinist. This treatise has been recently republished in Baltimore. This volume also contains his 'Vindication,' written by the direction of the Presbytery of New Brunswick, in answer to 'The Government of the Church,' &c., by the Rev. John Thompson.

The Rev. Samuel Blair was a native of Ireland, but came early to this country, and received his education in the Log College, under Mr. Wm. Tennent, sen., at Neshaminy. He must, indeed, have been among the first pupils of this institution. After finishing his classical and theological studies, Mr. Blair put himself under the care of the New Castle Presbytery, by which body he was in due time licensed to preach the gospel. Soon after his licensure, he was settled in the Presbyterian congregation at Shrewsbury, in New Jersey. He laboured in this field for five or six years, when he received an earnest call to settle in New Londonderry, otherwise called Fagg's Manor, in the State of Pennsylvania. Here he instituted a classical school, similar in its purpose to that of Mr. Tennent in Neshaminy, in which some of the ablest ministers of the Presbyterian church received either the whole, or the more substantial parts of their education. Among these were the Rev. Samuel Davies, the Rev. Alexander Cummings, the Rev. John Rodgers, D.D., the Rev. James Finley, and the Rev. Hugh Henry. Mr. Blair's settlement at Shrewsbury was in the year 1734, when he was only twenty-two years of age. The Presbytery of New Brunswick did not exist until the year 1738, of which Mr. Blair was one of the original members.

When he received the call from New Londonderry, in Chester county, Pennsylvania, he left it to the Presbytery to decide whether he should go or stay. After mature deliberation, they advised him to accept the call, as they were of opinion it would introduce him into a wider field of usefulness.

There are no records extant from which we can learn any particulars respecting the fruits of Mr. Blair's labours at Shrewsbury. Here he commenced his ministerial work, and as he was a faithful, able, and zealous preacher of the truth as it is in Jesus, we entertain no doubt that some of the good seed which he sowed fell into good ground and brought forth fruit. The vicissitudes of that congregation have been remarkable. For a while it was flourishing and had many respectable members, but it became apparently extinct, and the house of worship was burned; but after being dead for some years it was resuscitated; it now promises to flourish again.

Under his ministry at New Londonderry, there occurred a very remarkable revival of religion, of which he wrote a particular narrative. The congregation at Fagg's Manor consisted almost entirely of emigrants from the north of Ireland, and had been formed a number of years, but had never enjoyed the ministry of a stated pastor. His settlement among them took place in November, 1739, although he was not installed as their pastor until the month of April, 1740.

The revival referred to above commenced a short time after his settlement in the place. The following account is contained in the 'Narrative' which he wrote in a letter to the Rev. Mr. Prince, of Boston, in his 'Christian History.'

NEW LONDONDERRY IN PENNSYLVANIA, Aug, 6th, 1744.

'*Rev. Sir*—I do most gladly comply with your desire in sending you some account of the glorious appearance of God in a way of special grace for us in this congregation, and other parts of this country; and am of the same judgment with you and other pious and judicious people, that the collecting and publishing of such accounts may greatly tend to the glory of our Redeemer, and the increase of his triumphs. I much rejoice in the publication of such a collection in the Christian History, so far as it is already carried on; I think it may serve to many excellent purposes, and be a happy mean of advancing the dear interests of our glorious Redeemer's kingdom, both in the present age and the ages to come. And I cannot but look upon myself as called of God in duty, being thus invited to it by you, Rev. Sir, to put to a hand, among many others of my reverend fathers and brethren on both sides of the Atlantic, to the carrying on of the design of said history, containing accounts of the revival and propagation of religion in this remarkable day of grace. I cannot, indeed, give near so full and particular a relation of the revival of religion here as I might have done, had I had such a thing in view at the time when God was most eminently carrying on his work among us. I entirely neglected then to note down any particulars in writing, for which I have been often sorry since; so that this account must be very imperfect to what it might otherwise have been.

'That it may the more clearly appear that the Lord has indeed carried on a work of true real religion among us of late years, I conceive it will be useful to give a brief general view of the state of religion in these parts before this remarkable season. I doubt not then but there were some sincerely religious people up and down; and there were, I believe, a considerable number in the several congregations, pretty exact, according to their education, in the observance of the external forms of religion, not only as to attendance upon public ordinances on the Sabbath, but also as to the practice of family worship, and, perhaps, secret prayer too; but with these things the most part seemed to all appearance to rest contented, and to satisfy their consciences with a dead formality in religion. If they performed these duties pretty punctually in their seasons, and as they thought with a good meaning out of conscience, and not just to obtain a name for religion among men, then they were ready to conclude that they were truly and sincerely religious. A very lamentable ignorance of the main essentials of true practical religion, and the doctrines nextly relating thereunto, very generally prevailed. The nature and necessity of the new birth was but little known or thought of. The necessity of a conviction of sin and misery by the Holy Spirit opening and applying the law to the conscience, in order to a saving closure with Christ, was hardly known at all to the most. It was thought that if there was any need of a heart-distressing sight of the soul's danger, and fear of divine wrath, it was only needful for the grosser sort of sinners; and for any others to be deeply exercised this way (as there might sometimes be before some rare instances observable) this was generally looked upon to be a great evil and temptation that had befallen those persons. The common names for such soul-concern were melancholy, trouble of mind, or despair. These terms were in common, so far as I have been acquainted, indifferently used as synonymous; and trouble of mind was looked upon as a great evil, which all persons that made any sober profession and practice of religion ought carefully to avoid. There was scarcely any suspicion at all, in general, of any danger of depending upon self-righteousness, and not upon the righteousness of Christ alone for salvation. Papists and Quakers would be readily acknowledged guilty of this crime, but hardly any professed Presbyterian. The necessity of being first in Christ by a vital union, and in a justified state, before our religious services can be well-pleasing and acceptable to God was very little understood or thought of; but the common notion seemed to be that if people were aiming to be in the way of duty as well as they could, as they imagined, there was no reason to be much afraid.

'According to these principles, and this ignorance of some of the most soul-concerning truths of the gospel, people were very generally, through the land, careless at heart, and stupidly indifferent about the great concerns of eternity. There was very little appearance of any heart-engagedness in religion; and indeed the wise for the most part were in a great degree asleep with the foolish. It was sad to see with what a careless behaviour the public ordinances were attended, and how people were given to unsuitable worldly discourse on the Lord's holy day. In public companies, especially at weddings, a vain and frothy lightness was apparent in the deportment of many professors; and in some places, very extravagant follies, as horse-running, fiddling, and dancing, pretty much obtained on those occasions.

'Thus religion lay, as it were, a-dying, and ready to expire its last breath of life in this part of the visible church; and it was in the spring of 1740 when the God of salvation was pleased to visit us with the blessed effusions of his Holy Spirit in an eminent manner. The first very open and public appearance of this gracious visitation in these parts was in the congregation which God has committed to my charge. This congregation has not been erected above fourteen or fifteen years from this time; the place is a new settlement, generally settled with people from Ireland (as all our congregations in Pennsylvania, except two or three, chiefly are made up of people from that kingdom).[1] I am the first minister they have ever

[1] 'It may be convenient here to observe, that in Ireland are three different sorts of people, deriving from three several nations. 1. Those who descend from the ancient Irish; and these are generally Roman Catholics. 2. Those who descend from ancestors who came from England; and these are generally Church of England men. 3. Those who descend from ancestors who came from Scotland since the Reformation; and these are generally Presbyterians, who chiefly inhabit the northerly parts of Ireland; and these are the people who have of late years, in great numbers, removed thence into these American regions.'

had settled in the place, having been regularly liberated from my former charge, in East Jersey, above an hundred miles north-eastward from hence; the reverend presbytery of New Brunswick, of which I had the comfort of being a member, judging it to be my duty, for sundry reasons, to remove from thence. At the earnest invitation of the people here, I came to them in the beginning of November, 1739; accepted a call from them that winter, and was formally installed and settled among them as their minister in April following. There were some hopefully pious people here at my first coming, which was great encouragement and comfort to me.

'I had some view and sense of the deplorable condition of the land in general; and accordingly the scope of my preaching through that first winter after I came here was mainly calculated for persons in a natural unregenerate state. I endeavoured, as the Lord enabled me, to open up and prove from his word the truths which I judged most necessary for such as were in that state to know and believe, in order to their conviction and conversion. I endeavoured to deal searchingly and solemnly with them; and through the concurring blessing of God I had knowledge of four or five brought under deep convictions that winter.

'In the beginning of March I took a journey into East Jersey, and was abroad for two or three Sabbaths. A neighbouring minister, who seemed to be in earnest for the awakening and conversion of secure sinners, and whom I had obtained to preach a Sabbath to my people in my absence, preached to them, I think, on the first Sabbath after I left home. His subject was the dangerous and awful case of such as continue unregenerate and unfruitful under the means of grace. The text was Luke 13. 7: "Then said he to the dresser of his vineyard, Behold, these three years I come seeking fruit on this fig tree, and find none; cut it down, why cumbereth it the ground?" Under that sermon there was a visible appearance of much soul-concern among the hearers, so that some burst out with an audible noise into bitter crying; a thing not known in these parts before. After I had come home, there came a young man to my house under deep trouble about the state of his soul, whom I had looked upon as a pretty light, merry sort of a youth; he told me that he was not anything concerned about himself at the time of hearing the above-mentioned sermon, nor afterwards, till the next day that he went to his labour, which was grubbing, in order to clear some new ground. The first grub he set about was a pretty large one, with a high top, and when he had cut the roots, as it fell down, these words came instantly to his remembrance, and as a spear to his heart, "Cut it down, why cumbereth it the ground?" So, thought he, must I be cut down by the justice of God, for the burning of hell, unless I get into another state than I am now in. He thus came into very great and abiding distress, which, to all appearance, has had a happy issue, his conversation being to this day as becomes the gospel of Christ.

'The news of this very public appearance of deep soul-concern among my people met me a hundred miles from home. I was very joyful to hear of it, in hopes that God was about to carry on an extensive work of converting grace amongst them; and the first sermon I preached after my return to them was from Matthew 6. 33, "Seek ye first the kingdom of God and his righteousness." After opening up and explaining the parts of the text, when, in the improvement, I came to press the injunction in the text upon the unconverted and ungodly, and offered this as one reason among others why they should now henceforth first of all seek the kingdom and righteousness of God, viz: that they had neglected too long to do so already; this consideration seemed to come and cut like a sword upon several in the congregation; so that while I was speaking upon it, they could no longer contain, but burst out in the most bitter mourning. I desired them, as much as possible, to restrain themselves from making any noise that would hinder themselves or others from hearing what was spoken; and often afterwards I had occasion to repeat the same counsel. I still advise people to endeavour to moderate and bound their passions, but not so as to resist or stifle their conviction. The number of the awakened increased very fast; frequently under sermons there were some newly convicted and brought into deep distress of soul about their perishing estate. Our Sabbath assemblies soon became vastly large, many people, from almost all parts around, inclining very much to come where there was such appearance of the divine power and presence. I think there was scarcely a sermon or lecture preached here through that whole summer but there were manifest evidences of impressions on the hearers; and many times the impressions were very great and general; several would be overcome and fainting; others deeply sobbing, hardly able to contain; others crying in a most dolorous manner; many others more silently weeping; and a solemn concern appearing in the countenances of many others. And sometimes the soul-exercises of some (though comparatively but very few) would so far affect their bodies as to occasion some strange unusual bodily motions. I had opportunities of speaking particularly with a great many of those who afforded such outward tokens of inward soul-concern in the time of public worship and hearing of the word; indeed, many came to me of themselves in their distress for private instruction and counsel; and I found, so far as I can remember, that with by far the greater part their apparent concern in public was not a transient qualm of conscience, or merely a floating commotion of the affections; but a rational fixed conviction of their dangerous, perishing estate. They could generally offer as a convictive evidence of their being in an unconverted miserable estate that they were utter strangers to those dispositions, exercises, and experiences of soul in religion which they heard laid down from God's word as the inseparable characters of the truly regenerate people of God, even such as before had something of the form of religion; and I think the greater number were of this sort; and several had been pretty exact and punctual in the performance of outward duties; they saw they had been contenting themselves with the form without the life and power of godliness; and that they had been taking peace to their consciences from, and depending upon their own righteousness, and not the righteousness of Jesus Christ.

'In a word, they saw that true practical religion was quite another thing than they had conceived it to be, or had any true experience of. There were likewise many up and down the land brought under deep, distressing convictions that summer, who had lived very loose lives, regardless of the very externals of religion. In this congregation I believe there were very few that were not stirred up to some solemn thoughtfulness and concern more than usual about their souls. The general carriage and behaviour of people was soon very visibly altered. Those awakened were much given to reading in the Holy Scriptures, and other good books. Excellent books that had lain by much neglected were then much perused, and lent from one to another; and it was a peculiar satisfaction to people to find how exactly the doctrines they heard daily preached harmonized with the doctrines contained and taught by great and godly men in other parts and former times. The subjects of discourse almost always, when any of them were together, were the matters of religion and great concerns of their souls. All unsuitable, worldly, vain discourse on the Lord's day seemed to be laid aside among them; indeed, for anything that appeared there seemed to be almost a universal reformation in this respect in our public assemblies on the Lord's day.

'There was an earnest desire in people after opportunities for public worship and hearing the word. I appointed, in the spring, to preach every Friday through the summer, when I was at home, and those meetings were well attended; and at several of them the power of the Lord was remarkably with us. The main scope of my preaching through that summer was laying open the deplorable state of man by nature since the fall, our ruined, exposed case by the breach of the first covenant, and the awful condition of such as were not in Christ, giving the marks and characters of such as were in that condition; and, moreover, laying open the way of recovery in the new covenant, through a Mediator, with the nature and necessity of faith in Christ the Mediator, &c. I laboured much on the last-mentioned heads, that the people might have right apprehensions of the gospel-method of life and salvation. I treated much on the way of sinners closing with Christ by faith and obtaining a right peace to an awakened wounded conscience; showing that persons were not to take peace to themselves on account of their repentings, sorrows, prayers, and reformations; nor to make these things the grounds of their adventuring themselves upon Christ and his righteousness, and of their expectations of life by him; and that neither were they to obtain or seek peace in extraordinary ways, by visions, dreams, or immediate inspirations, but by an understanding view, and believing persuasion of the way of life as revealed in the gospel, through the suretyship, obedience and sufferings of Jesus Christ; with a view of the suitableness and sufficiency of that mediatorial righteousness of Christ, for the justification and life of law-condemned sinners; and thereupon freely accepting him for their Saviour, heartily consenting to and being well pleased with the way of salvation, and venturing their all upon his mediation, from the warrant and encouragement afforded of God thereunto in his words, by his free offer, authoritative command, and sure promise to those that so believe. I endeavoured to show the fruits and evidences of a true faith, &c.

'After some time, many of the convinced and distressed afforded

L

very hopeful, satisfying evidence that the Lord had brought them to a true closure with Jesus Christ; and that their distresses and fears had been in a great measure removed in a right gospel-way, by believing in the Son of God. Several of them had very remarkable and sweet deliverances this way. It was very agreeable to hear their accounts how that when they were in the deepest perplexity and darkness, distress and difficulty, seeking God as poor, condemned, hell-deserving sinners, the scheme of recovering grace through a Redeemer had been opened to their understandings with a surprising beauty and glory, so that they were enabled to believe in Christ with joy unspeakable and full of glory. It appeared that most generally the Holy Spirit improved for this purpose, and made use of some one particular passage or other of the Holy Scripture that came to their remembrance in their distress; some gospel-offer or promise, or some declaration of God directly referring to the recovery and salvation of undone sinners by the new covenant. But with some it was otherwise; they had not any one particular place of Scripture more than another in their view at the time. Those who met with such a remarkable relief, as their account of it was rational and scriptural, so they appeared to have had at the time the attendants and fruits of a true faith, particularly humility, love, and an affectionate regard to the will and honour of God; much of their exercise was in self-abasing and self-loathing, and admiring the astonishing condescension and grace of God towards such vile and despicable creatures that had been so full of enmity and disaffection to him. They freely and sweetly, with all their hearts, chose the way of his commandments; their inflamed desire was to live to him for ever, according to his will, and to the glory of his name.

'There were others that had not such remarkable relief and comfort, who yet I could not but think were savingly renewed and brought truly to accept of and rest upon Jesus Christ, though not with such a degree of liveliness and liberty, strength and joy; and some of those continued for a considerable time after, for the most part, under a very distressing suspicion and jealousy of their case. I was all along very cautious of expressing to people my judgment of the goodness of their states, except where I had pretty clear evidences from them of their being savingly changed; and yet they continued in deep distress, casting off all their evidences. Sometimes, in such cases, I have thought it needful to use greater freedom that way than ordinary; but otherwise I judged that it could be of little use, and might easily be hurtful.

'Beside those above spoken of, whose experience of a work of grace was in a good degree clear and satisfying, there were some others (though but very few in this congregation that I knew of) who, having very little knowledge or capacity, had a very obscure and improper way of representing their case. In relating how they had been exercised, they would chiefly speak of such things as were only the effects of their soul exercise upon their bodies from time to time, and some things that were purely imaginary; which obliged me to be at much pains in my inquiries before I could get any just ideas of their case. I would ask them, what were the thoughts, the views and apprehensions of their minds, and exercise of their affections, at such times when they felt, perhaps, a quivering come over them, or a faintness, or thought they saw their hearts full of some nauseous filthiness; or when they felt a heavy weight, or load at their hearts, or felt the weight again taken off, and a pleasant warmness rising from their hearts, as they would probably express themselves, which might be the occasions or causes of these things they spoke of; and then, when with some difficulty I could get them to understand me, some of them would give a pretty rational account of solemn and spiritual exercises, and after a thorough careful examination this way, I could not but conceive good hopes of some such persons.

'But there were, moreover, several others who seemed to think concerning themselves that they were under some good work, of whom yet I could have no reasonable ground to think that they were under any hopeful work of the Spirit of God. As near as I could judge of their case from all my acquaintance and conversation with them, it was much to this purpose. They believed there was a good work going on; that people were convinced, and brought into a converted state; and they desired to be converted too. They saw others weeping and fainting, and heard people mourning and lamenting, and they thought if they could be like these it would be very hopeful with them; hence, they endeavoured just to get themselves affected by sermons, and if they could come to weeping, or get their passions so raised as to incline them to vent themselves by cries, now they hoped they were got under convictions and were in a very hopeful way; and afterwards they would speak of their being in trouble, and aim at complaining of themselves, but seemed as if they knew not well how to do it, nor what to say against themselves. And then they would be looking and expecting to get some texts of Scripture applied to them for their comfort; and when any Scripture text which they thought was suitable for that purpose came to their minds, they were in hopes it was brought to them by the Spirit of God, that they might take comfort from it. And thus, much in such a way as this, some appeared to be pleasing themselves with an imaginary conversion of their own making. I endeavoured to correct and guard against all such mistakes, so far as I discovered them in the course of my ministry; and to open up the nature of a true conviction by the Spirit of God, and of a saving conversion.

'Thus I have given a very brief account of the state and progress of religion here, through that first summer after the remarkable revival of it among us. Towards the end of that summer, there seemed to be a stop put to the further progress of the work, as to conviction and awakening of sinners; and ever since there have been very few instances of persons convinced. It remains, then, that I speak something of the abiding effects and after-fruits of those awakenings and other religious exercises which people were under during the above-mentioned period. Such as were only under some slight impressions and superficial awakenings, seem in general to have lost them all again without any abiding hopeful alteration upon them. They seem to have fallen back again into their former carelessness and stupidity, and some that were under pretty great awakenings, and considerably deep convictions of their miserable state, seem also to have got peace again to their consciences without getting it by a true faith in the Lord Jesus, affording no satisfying evidence of their being savingly renewed. But, through the infinite rich grace of God (blessed be his glorious name!) there is a considerable number who afford all the evidence that can be reasonably expected and required for our satisfaction in the case of their having been the subjects of a thorough saving change. Except in some singular instances of behaviour, which alas! proceed from, and show the sad remains of original corruption even in the regenerate children of God while in this imperfect state, their walk is habitually tender and conscientious, their carriage towards their neighbours just and kind, and they appear to have an agreeable peculiar love one for another, and for all in whom appears the image of God. Their discourses of religion, their engagedness and dispositions of soul in the practice of the immediate duties and ordinances of religion all appear quite otherwise than formerly. Indeed, the liveliness of their affections in the ways of religion is much abated in general, and they are in some measure humbly sensible of this, and grieved for it, and are carefully endeavouring still to live unto God, much grieved with their imperfections and the plagues they find in their own hearts; and frequently they meet with some delightful enlivenings of soul, and particularly our sacramental solemnities for communicating in the Lord's supper, have generally been very blessed seasons of enlivening and enlargement to the people of God. There is a very evident and great increase of Christian knowledge with many of them. We enjoy in this congregation the happiness of a great degree of harmony and concord. Scarcely any have appeared with open opposition and bitterness against the work of God among us, and elsewhere up and down the land; though there are a pretty many such in several other places through the country: some indeed in this congregation, but very few have separated from us and joined with the ministers who have unhappily opposed this blessed work.

'It would have been a great advantage to this account had I been careful in time to have written down the experiences of particular persons; but this I neglected in the proper season. However, I have more lately noted down an account of some of the soul exercises and experiences of one person, which I think may be proper to make public on this occasion. The person is a single young woman, but I judge it proper to conceal her name, because she is yet living. I was very careful to be exact in the affair, both in my conversing with her, and writing the account she gave me of herself immediately after. And though I don't pretend to give her very words for the most part, yet I am well satisfied I don't misrepresent what she related. The account then is this: she was first brought to some solemn thoughtfulness and concern about her soul's case, by seeing others so much concerned about their souls. When she saw people in deep distress about the state of their souls, she thought with herself how unconcerned she was about her own. And though she thought that she had not been guilty of very great sins, yet she feared she was too little concerned about her eternal well-being; and then the sermons she heard made her still more uneasy about her case, so that she would go home on the Sabbath evenings pretty much troubled and cast down; which concern used to abide with her for a few days after, but still towards the end of the week she would become pretty easy; and then, by hearing the word on the Sabbath days, her uneasiness was always renewed for a few days again. And thus it fared with her, until one day as she was hearing a sermon preached from Heb. 3. 15: "To-day if you will hear his voice harden not your hearts," the minister in the sermon spoke to this effect: "How many of you have been hearing the gospel for a long time, and yet your hearts remain always hard, without being made better by it; the gospel is the voice of God, but you have heard it only as the voice of man, and not the voice of God, and so have not been benefited by it." These words came with power to her heart. She saw that this was her very case; and she had an awful sense of the sin of her misimprovement of the gospel, of her stupidity, hardness, and unprofitableness under the hearing of the word of God. She saw that she was hereby exposed to the sin-punishing justice of God, and so was filled with very great fear and terror; but she said there was no other sin at that time applied to her conscience, neither did she see herself as altogether without Christ.

'This deep concern, on the fore-mentioned account, stuck pretty close by her afterwards. There was a society of private Christians to meet in the neighbourhood, some day after, in the same week, for reading, prayer, and religious conference. She had not been at a society of that kind before, but she longed very much for the time of their meeting then, that she might go there; and while she was there she got an awful view of her sin and corruption, and saw that she was without Christ, and without grace; and her exercise and distress of soul was such that it made her for a while both deaf and blind; but she said she had the ordinary use of her understanding, and begged that Christ might not leave her to perish, for she saw that she was undone without him. After this she lived in bitterness of soul; and at another time she had such a view of her sinfulness, of the holiness and justice of God, and the danger she was in of eternal misery, as filled her with extreme anguish, so that had it not been that she was supported by an apprehension of God's all-sufficiency, she told me she was persuaded she should have fallen immediately into despair. She continued for some weeks in great distress of spirit, seeking and pleading for mercy without any comfort, until one Sabbath evening, in a house where she was lodged, during the time of a sacramental solemnity, while the family were singing the 84th Psalm, her soul conceived strong hopes of reconciliation with God through Jesus Christ, and she had such apprehensions of the happiness of the heavenly state that her heart was filled with joy unspeakable and full of glory. She sung with such elevation of soul as if she had sung out of herself, as she expressed it; she thought at the time, it was as if the Lord had put by the veil and showed her the open glory of heaven; she had very enlarged views of the sufficiency of Christ to save; she was clearly persuaded, to the fullest satisfaction, that there was merit enough in him to answer for the sins of the most guilty sinner; and she saw that God could well be reconciled to all elect sinners in his Son; which was a most ravishing, delightful scene of contemplation to her.

'But while she was in this frame, after some time she thought with herself that notwithstanding all this yet she could not with the full assurance of faith lay claim to the Lord Jesus as her own Saviour in particular. She could not say with such full satisfaction and certainty as she desired, that he would be a Saviour in particular to her; and hence, for want of thoroughly understanding wherein the very essence of saving faith consists, she had some jealous fear that she was not yet brought truly to believe in Christ. However, she was pretty free from her former terrors after this sweet interview. But after some time, she grew more disconsolate, and more sensibly afraid of her state, on the forementioned account. She heard that sinners in closing with Christ by faith, received him for their Saviour, which she thought included in it a persuasion that he was theirs in particular, and she could not clearly say that this had ever been her case; and so she came awfully to suspect herself to be as yet an unbeliever; and though she came in time to that sweet plerophory and full assurance of faith, yet she has since seen her mistake in that matter about the nature of a true and saving faith. She continued very much under those grievous dejections for about two years, and yet enjoyed considerable sweetness and comfort at times. She often came to hear sermons with a desire to get clearly convinced of her being yet in a Christless state, and with a formed resolution to take and apply to herself what might be said in the sermon to the unconverted; but most commonly she returned very agreeably disappointed. She would generally hear some mark of grace, some evidence of a real Christian laid down, which she could lay claim to, and could not deny; and thus she was supported and comforted from time to time. During these two years, it was still with much fear and perplexity that she adventured to communicate in the Lord's supper, but she could not omit it; and she always found some refreshing and sweetness by that ordinance.

'After she had been so long under an almost alternate succession of troubles and supports, the Sun of Righteousness at last broke out upon her, to the clear satisfaction and unspeakable ravishment of her soul, at a communion table. There her mind was let into the glorious mysteries of redemption with great enlargement. While she meditated on the sufferings of the Lord Jesus, she thought with herself, he was not merely a man who suffered so for sinners, but infinitely more than man, even the most high God, the eternal Son, equal with the Father; and she saw his being God put an infinite lustre and value upon his sufferings as man; her heart was filled with a most unutterable admiration of his person, his merit, and his love; she was enabled to believe in him with a strong self-evidencing faith; she believed that he had suffered for her sins; that she was the very person who by her sins had occasioned his sufferings, and brought agony and pain upon him. The consideration of this filled her with the deepest abhorrence of her sins, and most bitter grief for them; she said she could have desired with all her heart to have melted and dissolved her body quite away in that very place, in lamentation and mourning over her sins. After this enjoyment, her soul was generally delighting in God, and she had much of the light of his countenance with her; and oh! her great concern still was how she might live to the Lord, how she might do anything for him and give honour to him. The Lord condescended to be much with her by his enlivening and comforting presence, and especially sacramental seasons were blessed and precious seasons to her. At one of those occasions she was in a sweet frame, meditating on the blood and water that issued from the wound made by the spear in her Saviour's side. She thought as water is of a purifying cleansing nature so there was sanctifying virtue as well as justifying merit in the Lord Jesus; and that she could no more be without the water, his sanctifying grace to cleanse her very polluted soul, than she could be without his blood to do away her guilt; and her heart was much taken up with the beauty and excellency of sanctification. At another time, a communion solemnity likewise, she was very full of delight and wonder with the thoughts of electing love; how that God had provided and determined so great things for her before ever she had a being. And a very memorable enjoyment she had at another time, on Monday after a communion Sabbath, when these words came to her mind, "The Spirit and the bride say, Come, and let him that is athirst come, and whosoever will let him take the water of life freely." The glory and delight let in upon her soul by these words was so great that it quite overcame her bodily frame. She said it seemed to her that she was almost all spirit, and that the body was quite laid by; and she was sometimes in hopes that the union would actually break, and the soul get quite away. She saw much at that time into the meaning of her Lord in those words, "Because I live ye shall live also."

'Respecting a time of sickness she had, concerning which I inquired of her, she told me she expected pretty much to die then and was very joyful at the near prospect of her change and sensibly grieved to find herself recover again, chiefly because that while she lived here she was so frail and sinful and could do so little for the Lord's honour. I was with her in the time of that sickness and indeed I scarcely ever saw one appearing to be so fully and sweetly satisfied under the afflicting hand of God; she manifestly appeared to lie under it with a peaceful serenity and divine sweetness in her whole soul. In a word, her whole deportment in the world bespeaks much humility and heavenliness of spirit.

'One of our Christian friends, a man about fifty years of age, was removed from us by death in the beginning of May last, of whom I can give some broken imperfect account, which perhaps may be of some use. His name was Hans Kirkpatrick; he was a man of pretty good understanding, and had been, I believe, a sober professor for many years, though he had not been very long in America. After the work of religion began so powerfully amongst us, I found, in conversation with him, that he believed it to be a good work but seemed very unwilling to give up his good opinion of his own case. He told me of some concern and trouble he had been in about his soul in his younger years; but yet the case looked suspicious that he had got ease in a legal way, upon an outward form of religion. At another time, being at his house and taking up a little book that lay by me on the table, which I found to be

Mr. Mather's "Dead Faith Anatomized, and Self-justiciary Convicted," he said to me that was indeed a strange book as ever he saw, and that according to that author it was a great thing indeed to have a right faith that was true and saving, another thing than it was generally supposed to be; or to this purpose. He seemed to me at that time to be under more fears about his own case than I had observed in him before. Not long after this, as he was hearing a sermon one day, the word was applied with irresistible evidence and power to his heart, so that he saw himself as yet in a perishing, undone case; whereupon the distress and exercise of his soul was so great that he fell off the seat on which he was sitting and wept and cried very bitterly. A little after this he went to Philadelphia, at the time of the meeting of the Synod, in hopes that perhaps he might meet with some benefit to his soul by hearing the ministers preach there, or by conversing with some of them. He told me afterwards that while he was there, and as he walked the streets, he was unspeakably distressed with the view of his miserable condition, so that he could hardly keep his distress from being publicly discerned upon him; and that he seemed sometimes to be even in a manner afraid that the streets would open and swallow up such a wretched creature. He told me of his trouble, and his very sweet relief out of it, in a most moving manner, under a very fresh sense and impression of both; but the particulars of his relief I have quite forgot.

'He was afterwards chosen and set apart for a ruling elder in the congregation. He died of an imposthume, and gradually wasted away for a long time before his death, and was for about two months entirely confined to his bed. He told me that for some time before he was laid bedfast he had been full of very distressing fears and jealousies about his soul's state, and was altogether unsatisfied about his interest in Christ; but that soon after he was confined to his bed the Lord afforded him his comforting presence, cleared up his interest, and removed his fears. After this he continued still clear and peaceful in his soul, and sweetly and wholly resigned to the Lord's will until death. While he had strength to speak much, he was free and forward to discourse of God and divine things. One time, as two other of our elders were with him, he exhorted them to continue steadfast and faithful to God's truths and cause, for, he said, if he had a thousand souls he could freely venture them all upon the doctrines which had been taught them in this congregation. One time when I took leave of him he burst out into tears saying, "I had been the messenger of the Lord of hosts to him, that the Lord had sent to call him out of the broad way of destruction." For some days before his decease he could speak but very little, but to all appearance with a great deal of serenity and sweetness of soul he fell asleep in Jesus.

'There have been very comfortable instances of little children among us. Two sisters, the one being about seven, the other about nine years of age, were hopefully converted that summer, when religion was so much revived here. I discoursed with them both very lately, and from their own account, and the account of their parents, there appears to have been a lasting and thorough change wrought in them. They speak of their soul experiences with a very becoming gravity and apparent impression of the things they speak of.

'The youngest was awakened by hearing the word preached; she told me she heard in sermons that except persons were convinced and converted, they would surely go to hell; and she knew she was not converted. This set her to praying with great earnestness, with tears and cries; yet her fears and distress continued for several days until one time as she was praying, her heart, she said, was drawn out in great love to God; and as she thought of heaven and being with God she was filled with sweetness and delight. I could not find by her that she had at that time any explicit particular thoughts about Christ as a Redeemer, but she said she knew then that Christ had died for sinners. She told me she often found such delight and love to God since, as she did then, and at such times she was very willing to die that she might be with God; but she said she was sometimes afraid yet of going to hell. I asked her, "If she was troubled at any time when she was not afraid of going to hell?" She said, "Yes." I asked her "what she was troubled for, then?" she said, "because she had done ill to God;" meaning that she had done evil, and sinned against God. Some time after she first found comfort, one night when her father and all the rest of the family but her mother and herself were gone to a private society, she said to her mother, "that the people were singing and praying where her father was gone," and desired her mother to do the same with her; and after they were gone to bed, "she desired her mother to sing some psalms which she had by heart," for she said she did not want to go to sleep.

'Her sister was brought into trouble about her soul that same summer, by sickness. It continued with her some time after her recovery; until one day, coming home from meeting, as she heard some people speaking about Christ and heaven her heart was inflamed with love to Christ. She says that "when she has Christ's presence with her, she does not know what to do to get away and be with God." Their parents told me that for a long time they seemed to be almost wholly taken up in religion; that no weather, through the extremity of winter, would hinder them from going out daily to by-places for secret prayer; and if anything came in the way that they could not get out for prayer at such times as they inclined and thought most proper they would weep and cry. Their parents say they are very obedient children, and strict observers of the Sabbath.

'There are likewise other young ones in the place of whom I know nothing to the contrary, but that they continue hopeful and religious to this day.

'This blessed shower of divine influences spread very much through this province that summer; and was likewise considerable in some other places bordering upon it. The accounts of some ministers being something distinguished by their searching, awakening doctrine, and solemn, pathetic manner of address, and the news of the effects of their preaching upon their hearers seemed in some measure to awaken people through the country to consider their careless and formal way of going on in religion, and very much excited their desires to hear those ministers. There were several vacant congregations without any settled pastors, which earnestly begged for their visits; and several ministers who did not appear heartily to put their shoulder to help in carrying on the same work, yet then yielded to the pressing importunities of their people, in inviting those brethren to preach in their pulpits; so that they were very much called abroad, and employed in incessant labours, and the Lord wrought with them mightily. Very great assemblies would ordinarily meet to hear them on any day of the week; and oftentimes a surprising power accompanying their preaching was visible among the multitudes of their hearers. It was a very comfortable, enlivening time to God's people; and great numbers of secure, careless professors, and many loose, irreligious persons through the land were deeply convinced of their miserable, perishing estates; and there is abundant reason to believe and be satisfied that many of them were, in the issue, savingly converted to God. I, myself, have had occasion to converse with a great many up and down, who have given a most agreeable account of very precious and clear experiences of the grace of God. Several, even in Baltimore, a county in the province of Maryland, who were brought up almost in a state of heathenism, without almost any knowledge of the true doctrines of Christianity, afford very satisfying evidences of being brought to a saving acquaintance with God in Christ Jesus.

'Thus, sir, I have endeavoured to give a brief account of the revival of religion among us in these parts; in which I have endeavoured, all along, to be conscientiously exact in relating things according to the naked truth; knowing that I must not speak wickedly, even for God, nor talk deceitfully for him.

'And, upon the whole, I must say it is beyond all dispute with me, and I think it is beyond all reasonable contradiction, that God has carried on a great and glorious work of his grace among us.

'I am, Rev. sir,

'Your very respectful son and servant,

'SAMUEL BLAIR.'

'REV SIR:—Having an opportunity of obtaining these attestations before sending my letter to you, I send them also along; if you please they may be inserted in the Christian History at the end of my account.

S.B.

'NEW LONDONDERRY, August, 7th, 1744.

'We the subscribers, ruling elders in the congregation of New Londonderry, do give our testimony and attestation to the above account of the revival of religion in this congregation and other parts of this country, so far as the said account relates to things that were open to public observation, and such things as we have had opportunity of being acquainted with. Particularly, we testify that there has been a great and very general awakening among the people, whereby they have been stirred up to an earnest uncommon concern and diligence about their eternal salvation, according to the above account of it; and that many give very comfortable evidence by their knowledge, declaration of experience, and conscientious practice of their being savingly changed and turned to God.

JAMES COCHRAN,	JOHN SMITH,
JOHN RAMSAY,	JOHN SIMSON,
JOHN LOVE,	WM. BOYD.'

Mr. Samuel Blair was truly a burning and a shining light; but like many others of this description, while he warmed and enlightened others, he himself was consumed. Though his life was protracted beyond the age attained by Davies and Brainerd, yet he may be said to have died young, for from the inscription on his tomb it appears that he was only thirty-nine years and twenty-one days old when he was taken away. His remains lie in the burying ground of Fagg's Manor, where his tomb may yet be seen. The whole inscription is:

'Here lieth the body of
The REV. SAMUEL BLAIR,
Who departed this life,
The 5th day of July, 1751.
Aged 39 years and 21 days.'

'In yonder sacred house I spent my breath,
Now silent, mouldering, here I lie in death;
These lips shall wake again and yet declare
A dread amen to truths they published there.'

Mr. Blair was one of the most learned and profound, as well as pious, excellent, and venerable men of his day. His deep and clear views as a theologian are sufficiently evident from his treatise on 'Predestination,' where this awful and mysterious doctrine is treated with the hand of a master.

As a preacher, Mr. Blair was very eminent. There was a solemnity in his very appearance which struck his hearers with awe before he opened his mouth. And his manner of preaching, while it was truly evangelical and instructive, was exceedingly impressive. He spoke as in the view of eternity, as in the immediate presence of God. The opinion which Mr. Davies entertained of Mr. Blair as a preacher, may be learned from an anecdote received from Dr.

Rodgers by the late Rev. Dr. S. Miller: 'When the Rev. Samuel Davies returned from Europe, his friends were curious to learn his opinion of the celebrated preachers whom he had heard in England and Scotland. After dealing out liberal commendations on such as he had most admired, he concluded by saying that he had heard no one who, in his judgment, was superior to his former teacher, the Rev. Samuel Blair.'

Mr. Blair was intimately associated with Mr. Gilbert Tennent in all his controversies with the Synod of Philadelphia. He concurred in all the proceedings of the New Brunswick Presbytery in which they acted in opposition to the rule of the Synod requiring candidates to be examined by a committee of their appointment, and in preaching within the bounds of settled congregations, where the people requested it. He also united with Mr. Tennent in presenting to the Synod complaints against the members of that body, by which proceedings the minds of the majority of the Synod were so exasperated that they introduced a solemn protest against the New Brunswick brethren, which led to an immediate separation of the parties, a schism which continued seventeen years before it could be healed, as has been already related. To ascertain at this time which of the parties were most to blame in these unhappy controversies and divisions is not easy. Faults undoubtedly there were on both sides. The Old Side were much to blame in setting themselves in opposition to the revival of religion which had so gloriously commenced. By doing so, they incurred a fearful responsibility. That Tennent and Blair transgressed the rules of order cannot be denied. They disobeyed the Synod, and entered into the congregations of their brethren without their consent. Whether in these things they were excusable will depend upon the true state of the churches at that time. Our Saviour and his apostles disregarded the orders of the priests and of the synagogue. And Luther and the other reformers did not feel themselves bound by the authority of the popish magistracy and priesthood. Every minister holds a commission to preach the gospel to every creature to whom he can gain access, and if a certain number of people who are anxious to hear the gospel happen by human arrangements to be circumscribed within the limits of a parish over which another has charge; and if this nominal pastor is believed not so to preach the gospel as to lead the people in the way of salvation, why may not the faithful preacher disregard these human arrangements intended to promote order, and carry the gospel to those who are thirsting for the word of life? No doubt the principle is liable to great abuse, and may occasion great disorder, and result in much more evil than good. The question in regard to these devoted men is whether the people in the congregations of their opponents were really in such a perishing condition as would authorize them to overleap the fence which, for the sake of order, had been set up. And this is the point which, in my opinion, we are incapable of deciding. Men may continue to maintain in theory an orthodox creed, and yet may manifest such deadly hostility to vital piety that they must be considered the enemies of the cause of God and the work of the Spirit. That the opposers of the revival at that time did exhibit such a character cannot be asserted universally, for some of them appear to have been in the main sincere Christians, and only meant to set themselves in opposition to those opinions and practices connected with the revival which were reprehensible.

But that many of those of the Old Side manifested a malignity of spirit against the revival which was wicked in the extreme I entertain no doubt. I have heard so much from aged persons who were living in the midst of the revival; and even the subjects of it have given me such accounts of the malign spirit with which the whole work was ridiculed and opposed by many, that I cannot doubt that, in a good degree, the contest between the parties was between the friends and the enemies of true religion. And something of the same spirit of hostility to revivals was handed down to our own times. I have known men of high standing in the church and undoubted learning who derided every account of revivals and sudden conversions as fanatical and foolish. It is, therefore, my deliberate opinion that in the general, the Tennents and Blairs and their coadjutors were men approved of God, and greatly honoured as the instruments of winning many souls to Christ, while their opponents were for the most part unfriendly to vital piety.

But while I consider the ministers of the New Brunswick Presbytery and their coadjutors as the real friends and successful promoters of true religion in this land, I do not mean to exonerate them from all blame. They were men, and liable to human imperfections. Some of them were men of ardent temperament and somewhat overbearing disposition; and under the influence of a fervid zeal, they did and said many unadvisable things. When the state of the church became more settled, and the warmth of their feelings had subsided, they themselves viewed matters in a very different light from what they had done in the heat of the controversy.

M

XV

Memoir of the Rev. John Blair

Education—First settlement—Driven away by the Indians—Is called to
Fagg's Manor—Continues the school—Elected Professor of Theology
in Nassau Hall—Resigns on the arrival of Dr. Witherspoon—Removes
to Orange County, N.Y.—His end—The family of the Blairs.

The Rev. John Blair was a younger brother of the person whose
memoir is given in the preceding chapter. He was also an alumnus
of the Log College, and as a theologian was not inferior to any
man in the Presbyterian church in his day. He was first settled
in Pennsylvania, at Big Spring (now Newville) in the Cumberland
Valley, in the vicinity of Carlisle. But by reason of the hostile
incursion of the Indians, his people were obliged to leave their
rude habitations on the frontier, and to retreat into the more
densely populated part of the colony. Mr. Blair, it would seem,
never returned to the place whence he had been driven by the
invasion of the savages, but upon the decease of his brother
Samuel he received and accepted a call to be his successor at
Fagg's Manor; and that not only as pastor of the church, but also
as the teacher of the school which his brother had instituted in
that place. In this important station he continued for nine years;
and though not equal to his brother as an impressive preacher, as
a scholar and as a theologian he was not inferior.

New Jersey College having been founded for the very purpose
of giving a complete education to candidates for the ministry,
these academies, which had done so much for the church, no
longer had the same importance as when no such institution existed.
Accordingly, not only did the Log College, at Neshaminy, which
was the mother institution, cease as soon as the college was
erected, but the celebrated school at Nottingham was not continued after Dr. Finley was chosen president of Nassau Hall.
And when Dr. Finley died, a sum of money having been left for

the support of a professor of divinity, Mr. John Blair was elected professor of theology in the College of New Jersey. This invitation he accepted, and removed to Princeton. He was also appointed Vice-President of the college, and until the arrival of Dr. Witherspoon performed all the duties of President.

The funds of the college not being adequate to support a professor of theology distinct from the President, and it being known that Dr. Witherspoon was an orthodox and eminent theologian, who could consistently with his other duties teach theology, Mr. Blair judged it would be expedient for him to resign. Upon this he received a call to settle as pastor of a Presbyterian congregation in Wallkill, Orange county, New York. Here he continued to labour in the duties of the ministry until he was called away from the field by death, which occurred Dec. 8, 1771, in his 52nd year.*

The character of Mr. John Blair is thus drawn by a writer of a sketch of his life in the Assembly's Magazine:

'John Blair, an eminent minister of Pennsylvania, was ordained to the pastoral charge of three congregations in Cumberland county as early as 1742. These were frontier settlements and exposed to the depredation of the Indians, with whom a state of war then existed, and he was obliged to remove. He accepted a call from Fagg's Manor in 1757. The congregation had been favoured with the ministry of his brother, Samuel Blair. And here he continued about nine years; and besides discharging the duties of the ministry, he superintended also a flourishing grammar-school, and prepared many young men for the ministry. When the presidency of New Jersey College became vacant by the death of Dr. Finley, he was chosen professor of divinity, and had for

---

* The following is the inscription on his tomb-stone:

'Here lie interred the remains of the Rev. Mr. John Blair, A.M., who departed this life December 6, 1771, in the 52nd year of his age.

'He was a gentleman of a masterly genius. A good scholar, an excellent divine. A very judicious, instructive, and solemn preacher. A laborious and successful minister of Christ. An eminent Christian. A man of great prudence—and a bright example of every social virtue.

'He was some time Vice-President of Nassau Hall, and Professor of Divinity in the College of New Jersey, which places he filled with fidelity and reputation. He lived greatly beloved, and died universally lamented.'

some time the charge of that seminary before the arrival of Dr. Witherspoon.

'He was a judicious and persuasive preacher, and through his exertions sinners were converted and the children of God edified. Fully convinced of the truth of the doctrines of grace, he addressed immortal souls with that warmth and power which left a witness in every bosom. Though he sometimes wrote his sermons in full, yet his common mode of preaching was by short notes comprising the general outlines. His labours were too abundant to admit of more; and no more was necessary to a mind so richly stored with the great truths of religion. For his large family he amassed no fortune, but he left them what was infinitely better, a religious education, a holy example, and prayers which have been remarkably answered. His disposition was uncommonly patient, placid, benevolent, disinterested and cheerful. He was too mild to indulge bitterness or severity; and he thought that the truth required little else but to be fairly stated and properly understood. Those who could not relish the savour of his piety loved him as an amiable, and revered him as a great man. Though no bigot he firmly believed that the Presbyterian form of government is most Scriptural, and the most favourable to religion and happiness.

'In his last sickness, he imparted his advice to the congregation, and represented to his family the necessity of an interest in Christ. A few nights before he died, he said, "Directly I am going to glory—my Master calls me, I must be gone." '

Mr. John Blair left behind him a treatise on Regeneration, which is ably written and entirely orthodox. He also published a treatise on the Scriptural terms of admission to the Lord's Supper, in which he maintains that ministers and church officers have no more authority to debar from the Lord's table those who desire to attend than from any other duty of God's worship. This piece the late Rev. J. O. Wilson, D.D., pastor of the first Presbyterian church, Philadelphia, had republished in a small selection of treatises on the Lord's Supper; from which it may be inferred that he approved the sentiments which it contains.

It is always gratifying to a laudable curiosity to learn something respecting the families and descendants of men once eminent in the church, although in the pursuit of this knowledge we often meet with mortifying instances of a sad degeneracy. But when it is otherwise, it is always pleasing to the pious mind to be able to trace eminent piety and talents descending from generation to generation. Two of the sisters of Samuel and John Blair were married to distinguished ministers of the Presbyterian church; the one to the Rev. John Carmichael, pastor of the church at the Forks of Brandywine, who was also an eminent patriot in the struggle of this country for independence. The other was married to the Rev. Robert Smith, D.D., of Pequea, the father of three ministers who were eminent in the Presbyterian church, and two of them distinguished presidents of literary institutions. The Rev. Doctor Samuel S. Smith was the first President of Hampden Sidney College in Virginia, and then the immediate successor of Dr. Witherspoon as President of New Jersey College. The other, the Rev. John B. Smith, D.D., succeeded his brother as President of Hampden Sidney, and was afterwards the first President of Union College in Schenectady. He was an eloquent, evangelical, and successful minister. Under his ministry in Virginia commenced a powerful and extensive revival, the influence of which extended far and wide through the state, and also to North Carolina and Kentucky. Mr. William Smith, the third son, was a pious, judicious minister, less distinguished than either of his brothers; but his good old father was wont to say that though William was inferior to his brothers in learning and eloquence, yet to comfort and edify the plain Christian he was equal to either of them. The Rev. Samuel Blair, of Fagg's Manor, had a son of the same name, who was considered the most accomplished and promising young minister in the Presbyterian church. He, at an early age, received a call to be colleague with the Rev. Mr. Sewall, in the old South church, Boston. Before he was licensed, he had for some time acted as a tutor in his alma mater. The estimation in which he was held by the trustees of the college may be learned from the fact that after Dr. Witherspoon had declined the first invitation of the board, young Mr. Blair was elected President, before he was thirty years of age. But soon after his election, intelligence was received from Scotland that if the call were repeated, Dr. Witherspoon would in all probability accept the invitation. As soon as this was known to Mr. Blair, he immediately wrote to the President of the board, declining the office. This prompt and generous decision freed the trustees from all the embarrassment in which otherwise they might have been involved.

Of course, the election of Mr. Blair could not have been known to Dr. Witherspoon when he signified his willingness to accept the appointment; and when he understood from what motives Mr. Blair had declined the office, he was much affected with the disinterestedness of the young man, and often spoke of it with admiration.

But though the morning of Mr. Blair's life was so bright, and promised so much to the church, the sanguine hopes of his friends were far from being realized in his future usefulness. By being shipwrecked on his way to Boston, he was much exposed, and to this was attributed the decline of his health and spirits. He also lost at this time the whole of his manuscript sermons, a loss which could not be suddenly repaired and which affected his spirits not a little. He therefore did not remain long in Boston, but returned to Pennsylvania, where he resided at the house of his father-in-law, Dr. Shippen, in Germantown, and was very little engaged in the duties of his office afterwards, although his life was protracted to a good old age.

The writer, having spent several summers in Germantown before Dr. Blair's decease, had the opportunity of becoming well acquainted with him, and found him to be a man of great refinement of mind, mild and amiable in disposition, and friendly to evangelical doctrine and practical piety.

From the history of this popular young man it may be inferred that too much applause is a dangerous thing to a young minister. Another remark which may be made is that for a young man to form a connection by marriage with a rich and fashionable family seldom works well for his usefulness in the ministry, especially if his partner is of a gay and worldly disposition. And lastly, that speculation on deep points of theology, when the mind is not under a decided spiritual influence, is always attended with evil even to those who at bottom are sincerely pious.

One of the daughters of Samuel Blair, sen. was married to a young minister from Virginia, the Rev. David Rice, and became the mother of a numerous progeny, who are now scattered through Virginia and Kentucky, to which last-mentioned place Mr. Rice removed, and on the rising population of which his evangelical labours and holy example left a lasting impression.

Another daughter was married to the Rev. William Foster, who was Pastor of the Presbyterian Congregations at Octarara and

Doe Run, in Chester county, (Pa.). Mr. Foster died at the age of thirty-eight years in the year 1780, leaving a large family; his widow died in Mercer, (Pa.). Their descendants reside in Western Pennsylvania.

Mr. John Blair also had a son educated at Princeton, New Jersey, who became a minister of the gospel. He graduated in the year 1775, soon after which he went to the county of Hanover, in Virginia, and became the Principal of an academy which had been established by the Rev. Daniel McCalla. While in this office he applied himself to the study of theology without any instructor, and having passed the usual trials, to the approbation of the Presbytery of Hanover, he was licensed to preach the gospel. The academy not prospering according to his wishes, Mr. Blair removed from Hanover to the city of Richmond, where he taught a classical school at his own house, and preached alternately at Hanover meeting-house, and in the capitol in Richmond. At this time there was no Presbyterian church in Richmond; but before Mr. Blair's death, and after Dr. Rice had collected a congregation and erected a church in the lower part of the city, Mr. Blair's hearers made an exertion and built a handsome church on Shockoe Hill. He was a sensible, pleasant man, and much respected by all the leading characters in the city of Richmond; he possessed but a moderate degree of religious zeal, and no considerable fruits attended his ministry, as far as has come to our knowledge.

Another son of the Rev. John Blair, also educated at Princeton, went to Kentucky, where it is understood that he was a respectable lawyer. He was the father of Mr. Blair, the well-known editor of a leading political paper in Washington city.

XVI

Memoir of the Rev. Samuel Finley

Birth in Ireland—Emigration to America—Education at the Log College
—Becomes a popular Preacher—A successful Itinerant—Settles at
Nottingham, Maryland—Institutes a Classical School—Eminent as a
Teacher—Distinguished Scholar—Elected President of New Jersey
College—Continues in this station five years—Seized with a Liver
Complaint—Goes to Philadelphia to consult Physicians—Dies there
in the triumph of Faith—Burial—Writings.

Dr. Finley was born in the county of Armagh, in the province
of Ulster, Ireland, in the year 1715, and was one of seven sons, who
were all esteemed pious. One of his brothers, the Rev. James
Finley, was an esteemed minister in the Presbyterian church; and
although his talents were very inferior to those of his brother
Samuel, yet he was reckoned to be eminently pious, and continued
laboriously to preach the gospel until an advanced period of life.
His latter years he spent in the western part of Pennsylvania, where
he died some years before the close of the last century. The writer
remembers to have seen him at a meeting of the Virginia Synod, in
Lexington, in the year 1789. He was one of the pioneers who,
amidst many hardships and privations, carried the gospel to the
settlers in the country round about Pittsburgh; and was the
companion and coadjutor of such men as McMillan, Joseph
Smith, Power, Patterson, Dod, Dunlap, &c.

The parents of Dr. Finley were of Scotch descent, and were
distinguished for their piety. Finding their son to be of quick
capacity, and fond of learning, they resolved to give him the best
education which their circumstances would admit; and after he
had obtained the rudiments of an English education, he was sent
abroad some distance from home to prosecute his studies. In this
school he distinguished himself by his assiduity and his proficiency
in learning.

When he was in his nineteenth year, he emigrated from his
native country, and came to America. He arrived in Philadelphia

on the 28th of September, in the year 1734. He appears to have become a subject of divine grace at a very early age. He has been heard to say that when only six years old he heard a sermon which made a deep impression on his mind, the text of which he never forgot. From that day he was seized with an ardent desire to become a minister of the gospel. As he grew up, this desire continued to ripen and increase; so that his purpose was early formed to devote his life to the service of God. Upon his coming to America, he steadily pursued his studies with a view to the holy ministry. As he arrived in Philadelphia at the very time when Mr. Tennent's school was flourishing at Neshaminy, and as there was then no other institution in the Presbyterian church where young men were trained for the ministry, there is the stongest probability that he was a student at the Log College. This probability is strengthened by the fact that he put himself under the care of the New Brunswick Presbytery, most of the members of which were educated in this school. His licensing took place on the 5th of August, in the year 1740. Having received authority to preach, he itinerated extensively; and as his pulpit talents were of a high order of excellence, he was greatly instrumental in carrying on the work of the Lord, which at that time prevailed in almost every part of the land.

His labours in the gospel were greatly blessed in West Jersey— in Deerfield, Greenwich, and Cape May. He preached also for six months with great acceptance in the congregation to which Gilbert Tennent was afterwards called in Philadelphia. His ordination took place on the 13th of October, in the year 1742. He was probably ordained as an evangelist, and continued to visit the places destitute of the stated means of grace for several years; and all accounts agree in ascribing much success to his itinerant labours. It was, probably, during this period that he made a preaching excursion into Connecticut. But so rigid were the laws of this land of steady habits that Mr. Finley, for preaching in a congregation in New Haven, was seized as a vagrant by the civil authority, and carried beyond the limits of the colony. He does not appear to have been permanently settled as a pastor until June, 1744, when he accepted a call from Nottingham, Maryland. In this place he remained for seventeen years.[1]

[1] In Allen's American Biography, his continuance here is made to be only seven years; but he went there in 1744, and removed in 1761.

In this place he instituted an academy, with the view, chiefly, of preparing young men for the gospel ministry. This school was conducted with admirable wisdom and success, and acquired a higher reputation than any other in the middle colonies, so that students from a distance were attracted to it. Some of the most distinguished men in our country laid the foundations of their eminence and usefulness in this academy. At one time, there was a cluster of such young men, who all were afterwards distinguished, and some of them among the very first men in the country, as the following names well show: Governor Martin, of North Carolina; Dr. Benjamin Rush, of Philadelphia, and his brother, Jacob Rush, an eminent and pious judge; Ebenezer Hazard, Esq. of Philadelphia; Rev. James Waddel, D.D., of Virginia; Rev. Dr. McWhorter, of Newark, N.J.; Col. John Bayard, speaker of the House of Representatives; Governor Henry, of Maryland, and the Rev. William M. Tennent, of Abington, Pa. It would not be easy, in any country, to find such a constellation in one school at the same time. That Dr. Finley was an accomplished scholar and a skilful teacher was universally admitted. Perhaps this country has not had better classical scholars formed anywhere, than in this school. The method of instruction in the Latin and Greek languages was thorough and accurate. The scholars were carefully drilled in the application of the rules of syntax, and in the prosody of these languages. Dr. Finley boarded most of his pupils in his own house, and when they were met at meals, he was in the habit of relaxing from the severity of the pedagogue, and indulging in facetious remarks; saying that nothing more helped digestion than a hearty laugh. His own temper was remarkably benignant and sweet, and his manners affable and polite.

Dr. Finley had been seriously thought of before Mr. Davies was called to the presidency of Nassau Hall, and when Mr. Davies at first declined the invitation, he strongly recommended Dr. Finley. It cannot be denied that both in scholarship and skill in teaching the latter was far superior. Dr. Finley too was a much older man and had been several years longer in the ministry. But Davies was a man of much more genius and eloquence, and his acquaintance with English literature was far more perfect.

The premature decease of so many presidents of New Jersey College brought forward a succession of illustrious men who have ever since reflected honour on that literary institution. Dickinson,

Burr, Edwards, Davies, and Finley all filled the presidential chair within five or six years. Dr. Finley was elected President in the year 1761, and immediately entered on the duties of the office, and the trustees were not disappointed in their expectations of his wisdom and efficiency. As he was permitted to remain five years in office, he had the opportunity of carrying into effect plans for the improvement of the institution, so that its reputation was greatly extended. Dr. Finley held correspondence with some of the learned men of Europe, among whom was Dr. Samuel Chandler of London, who, as appears by his letters, entertained a high esteem and indeed affectionate friendship for his distant correspondent. It was through the influence of this learned dissenter that without the knowledge of Mr. Finley, the degree of doctor of divinity was bestowed upon him by the University of Glasgow, which seems to have been the first instance of any Presbyterian minister in America receiving that honorary distinction. But if genius and theological learning could have commanded it, Dickinson, Burr, Edwards, and Davies would all have been distinguished in the same way. But they need no such appendage to their names; their works have secured to them a much higher honour in the estimation of posterity. And it must be a mortification to many modest men who bear the title of *doctor* that divines to whom they are conscious that they are not fit to be compared, lived and died without having their names distinguished by any such title. The disease by which Dr. Finley's constitution was attacked, an obstruction of the liver, was supposed to have been contracted by too great assiduity in his studies and too constant occupation in the public duties of his office. He did not die at home, but in the city of Philadelphia, whither he had gone to consult physicians respecting his disease. When informed by the physician who attended him that nothing could be done to remove his malady, and that it must soon prove mortal, he expressed an entire resignation to the divine will, and from that time was engaged in setting his house in order. He said, 'If my work is done, I am ready; I do not desire to live a day longer than I can work for God.' At that time, however, he did not apprehend that his end was so near as it proved to be. His disease made rapid progress; and he was informed by one of his physicians that he had but a few days to live, on which, lifting up his eyes to heaven, he exclaimed, 'Then, welcome, Lord Jesus.'

On the Sabbath preceding his death he was informed by Dr.

Clarkson, his brother-in-law, that he perceived a manifest alteration in his appearance and that evidently his end was near. 'Then,' said he, 'may the Lord bring me near himself! I have been waiting with a Canaan hunger for the promised land. I have often wondered that God suffered me to live. I have more wondered that he ever called me to be a minister of his word. He has often afforded me much strength, which, though I have often abused, he returned in mercy. Oh! faithful are the promises of God! O that I could see him as I have seen him in the sanctuary! Although I have earnestly desired death, as the hireling pants for the evening shade, yet will I wait all the days of my appointed time. I have often struggled with principalities and powers, and have been brought almost to despair—Lord, let it suffice!' Here he sat up, and closing his eyes he prayed fervently that God would show him his glory before he should depart hence—that he would enable him to endure patiently to the end, and particularly, that he might be kept from dishonouring the ministry. He then resumed his discourse, and spoke as follows, 'I can truly say, I have loved the service of God. I know not in what language to speak of my own unworthiness; I have been undutiful; I have honestly endeavoured to act for God, but with much weakness and corruption.' He then lay down, but continued to speak in broken sentences. 'A Christian's death,' said he, 'is the best part of his experience. The Lord has made provision for the whole way; provision for the soul and for the body. O, that I could recollect Sabbath blessings! The Lord has given me many souls as crowns of my rejoicing. Blessed be God, eternal rest is at hand. Eternity is but long enough to enjoy my God. This has animated me in my secret studies. I was ashamed to take rest here. O, that I could be filled with the fulness of God! that fulness which fills heaven.' Being asked whether he would choose to live or die, he replied, 'to die—though I cannot but say, I feel the same strait that Paul did, that he knew not which to choose, "for to me to live is Christ, but to die is gain." But should God by a miracle prolong my life, I would still continue to serve him. His service has ever been sweet to me. I have loved it much. I have tried my Master's yoke, and will never shrink my neck from it. "His yoke is easy and his burden light." ' One said to him, 'You are more cheerful and vigorous, sir.' 'Yes. I rise or fall as eternal life seems nearer, or further off.' It being remarked that he always used the expression, 'dear Lord,' in his prayers, he answered, 'O, he is very dear—very precious, indeed. How pretty is it for a minister to die on the Sabbath—I expect to spend the remainder of this Sabbath in heaven.' One of the company said, 'You will soon be joined to the blessed society of heaven; you will for ever hold intercourse with Abraham, Isaac, and Jacob, and with the spirits of the just made perfect—with old friends, and many old-fashioned people.' 'Yes, sir,' he replied with a smile, 'but they are a most polite people *now*.' He expressed great gratitude to friends around him, and said, 'May the Lord repay you—may he bless you abundantly, not only with temporal, but with spiritual blessings!' Turning to his wife, he said, 'I expect, my dear, to see you shortly in glory.'[1] Dr. Finley seeing a member of the Second Presbyterian church present said, 'I have often preached and prayed among you, my dear sir, and the doctrines I preached to you are now my support, and blessed be God they are without a flaw. May the Lord bless and prosper your church. He designs good for it yet, I trust.'

To a person from Princeton, he said, 'Give my love to the people of Princeton, and tell them that I am going to die, and that I am not afraid to die.' He would sometimes cry out, 'The Lord Jesus will take care of his cause in this world!' Upon awaking the next morning, he exclaimed, 'Oh what a disappointment I have met with—I expected this morning to have been in heaven!' On account of extreme weakness, he was unable to speak much during this day, but what he did say was the language of triumph. The next morning with a pleasing smile on his countenance, he cried out, 'O I shall triumph over every foe. The Lord hath given me the victory. I exult—I triumph. O that I could see untainted purity! Now I know that it is impossible that faith should not triumph over earth and hell. I think I have nothing to do but to die. Yet, perhaps I have—Lord show me my task.' He then said, 'Lord Jesus, into thy hands I commend my spirit—I do it with confidence; I do it with full assurance. I know that thou wilt keep that which I have committed to thee. I have been dreaming too fast of the

[1] This hope, however, was not realized, for Mrs. Finley continued to live many years after her husband's decease. She was a long time completely blind; but under this privation, manifested a pious and contented disposition, being entirely resigned to the will of her Heavenly Father. It was an edifying and refreshing thing for any person to pay a visit to her and her companion, Mrs. Hodge, with whom she lived. Their conversation was indeed in heaven.

time of my departure, for I find it does not come; but the Lord is faithful, and will not tarry beyond the appointed time.'

In the afternoon of this day, the Rev. Elihu Spencer called to see him and said, 'I have come, dear sir, to see you confirm by facts the gospel you have been preaching. Pray, sir, how do you feel?' To which he replied, 'Full of triumph—I triumph through Christ. Nothing clips my wings but the thoughts of my dissolution being prolonged. O that it were to-night! My very soul thirsts for eternal rest.' Mr. Spencer asked him what he saw in eternity to excite such vehement desires. 'I see,' said he, 'the eternal love and goodness of God. I see the fulness of the Mediator. I see the love of Jesus. . . . O to be dissolved, and to be with him! I long to be clothed with the complete righteousness of Christ.' He then desired Mr. Spencer to pray with him before they parted, and said, 'I have gained the victory over the devil. Pray to God to preserve me from evil—to keep me from dishonouring his great name in this critical hour, and to support me with his presence in my passage through the valley of the shadow of death.'

The remainder of the evening he spent in taking leave of his friends, and blessing and exhorting such of his children as were present. He would frequently cry out, 'Why move the tardy hours so slow?' The next day terminated the conflict. He was no longer able to speak, but a friend having desired him to give a token by which it might be known whether he still continued to triumph, he lifted up his hand and uttered the word, 'YES.' About nine o'clock he fell into a profound sleep, and appeared to be much more free from pain than he had been for many days before. He continued to sleep without changing his position, till about one o'clock, when he expired without a sigh or a groan. During his whole sickness he was never heard to utter a repining word, and in taking leave of his dearest friends he was never seen to shed a tear or to exhibit any sign of sorrow. His death occurred on the 16th of July, 1766, in the fifty-first year of his age.

It was the purpose of Dr. Finley's friends to have his remains removed to Princeton and buried with his illustrious predecessors, who lie interred in the cemetery of that place; but the heat of the weather rendered it inconvenient to carry the body so far, and therefore he was buried by the side of his dear friend, Gilbert Tennent, within the Second Presbyterian church. When this church was enlarged, the remains of both these venerable men were removed to the common burying-ground of the congregation. Agreeably to his dying request, his body was carried to the grave by eight members of the senior class of the College of New Jersey. The Trustees of the College, to show their respect for the deceased, caused a cenotaph to be erected in the cemetery of Princeton, in a line with the tombs of the other Presidents whose remains are there entombed.

Dr. Finley was a person of low stature, and of a round and ruddy countenance. In the pulpit he was solemn, sensible, and sententious, and sometimes glowed with fervid animation. He was remarkable for sweetness of temper, and politeness, and generosity. He was also distinguished for diligence and punctuality in the performance of all his duties. His sermons were solid rather than brilliant; not hasty productions, but composed with care, and while they were in a style pleasing to the cultivated mind, they were at the same time intelligible by the illiterate.

Dr. Finley was twice married; first to Sarah Hall, by whom he had eight children. She died in the year 1760, before he left Nottingham. His second wife was Ann Clarkson, daughter of Mr. Clarkson, merchant of New York, who was a lineal descendant of the Rev. David Clarkson, B.D., one of the two thousand ministers ejected for non-conformity in England in the year 1662. His second wife survived him forty-one years. His son, Ebenezer Finley, was a physician in Charleston, South Carolina, where his descendants still dwell, and are respectable, and generally pious. One of his daughters was married to Samuel Breeze, Esq., of Shrewsbury, New Jersey, and was the mother of the wife of the Rev. Jedediah Morse, D.D.

Dr. Finley wrote no work of any considerable size; but published several sermons and essays which, however, are nearly out of print. In 1741 he published a sermon on Matthew 12. 28, entitled 'Christ Triumphing and Satan Raging.' In 1743, 'A Refutation of Mr. Thompson's Sermon on Conviction;' and in the same year, a treatise against the Moravians, entitled 'Satan Stripped of his Evangelical Robe.' In 1747, a treatise against the Anti-pædobaptism of Abel Morgan, entitled 'A Plea for the Speechless.' And in 1749 he published a sermon, preached at the ordination of the Rev. Dr. Rodgers, at St. George's, March, 1749; also, a 'Sermon on the Death of the Rev. Samuel Davies,' his predecessor in the college, which is prefixed to most editions of Davies's Sermons; to which may be added, 'A Sermon occasioned by the Death of the Rev. Gilbert Tennent,' preached in the Second Presbyterian Church, Philadelphia.

It would be desirable, if we had the materials, to give a history of the flourishing and important academical institutions which arose out of the Log College, and which were conducted on the same principles, and with the same views, by men who had received their education in that school. And it would be gratifying to our readers, we doubt not, if we were to annex some biographical account of the eminent men who proceeded from these academies prior to the erection of the College of New Jersey. Such, for example, as the Rev. Samuel Davies, the Rev. John Rodgers, D.D., the Rev. Dr. McWhorter, the Rev. Mr. Cumming, and the Rev. Dr. Waddel; but this would carry us much beyond our prescribed limits, and in regard to several of the most distinguished of the persons mentioned would lead us over ground which has already been occupied by abler hands.

XVII

Memoir of the Rev. Wm. Robinson

An Englishman—Occasion of his Emigration—Teaches in New Jersey
and in Delaware—Is converted—Joins the Presbyterians—Studies at
the Log College—Seeks out the Destitute—Taken up in Virginia—
Visits Cub Creek—Conversion of David Austin—Sent for to Hanover
—Extraordinary religious awakening—Success of his labours—Mr.
Davies's Letter to Mr. Bellamy—Preaches in New York with his
wonted success—Also in Maryland—Died early.

Concerning the early history of this successful evangelist very
little is known. The only account which the writer has met with, is
that found in a note in the 'Life of the Rev. Dr. Rodgers,' by the
Rev. Dr. Miller.[1] It is here stated that Mr. Robinson was the
son of a wealthy Quaker in England. Being permitted to pay a visit
of a few weeks to an aunt in the city of London, from whom he
had considerable expectations, he greatly overstayed the time
which had been allowed him; and becoming deeply involved in
the dissipations of the town, he incurred large debts, which he
knew his father would never pay, and which his aunt refused to
discharge. In this situation, fearing to return home, and unable to
remain longer in London, he determined to quit his native country,
and seek his fortune in America. In this determination his aunt
reluctantly acquiesced and furnished him with a small sum of
money for the purpose. Soon after his arrival in America he had
recourse for subsistence to teaching a school in New Jersey, in the
bounds of the Presbytery of New Brunswick. He had been for
some time engaged in this business without any practical sense of
religion, when it pleased God to bring him to a knowledge of
himself and the way of salvation in a remarkable manner. He was
riding at a late hour one evening, when the moon and stars shone
with unusual brightness, and when every thing around him was
calculated to excite reflection. While he was meditating on the

[1] Published by the Presbyterian Board of Publication.

beauty and grandeur of the scene which the firmament presented, and was saying to himself, 'How transcendently glorious must be the Author of all this beauty and grandeur!', the thought struck him with the suddenness and force of lightning, 'But what do I know of this God? Have I ever sought his favour, or made him my Friend?' This happy impression, which proved by its permanency and its effects, to have come from the best of all sources, never left him until he took refuge in Christ as the hope and life of his soul.

It appears from some circumstances of the life of the Rev. Samuel Davies that Mr. Robinson also taught a classical school in the state of Delaware; for it is mentioned that Mr. Davies, when a boy, was one of his pupils; and his parents, we know, resided in the state of Delaware.

After Mr. Robinson's conversion he determined to devote his life to the service of God in the work of the holy ministry; and having fallen in with the Presbyterians, he connected himself with that church; and the uncontradicted tradition is that he pursued a course of preparation for the ministry in the Log College; and, after the usual trials, was licensed to preach the gospel by the Presbytery of New Brunswick; and, after some probation, was ordained by them as an evangelist.

Mr. Robinson, soon after his ordination, determined to go and visit the 'lost sheep of the house of Israel,' that is, the distant and dispersed settlements of Presbyterians in the states south of New Jersey. The Presbyterians from the north of Ireland, between the years 1720 and 1730, had come over to America in large numbers. They generally landed at New Castle, or Philadelphia, and then proceeded to the interior of the country. On the frontier of Pennsylvania they were greatly infested by the hostile incursions of the Indians, which induced them to turn their attention to the western parts of Virginia and North Carolina. In some instances whole congregations, driven from their homes by the savages, removed in a body with their ministers to a region less exposed to the incursions of their murderous foes.

The valley between the Blue Ridge and the North mountain— a fine lime-stone farming country—was first occupied by these Irish Presbyterians; the Germans, who now possess a large part of this fertile region, came in afterwards. In many places, all along the frontier, were small groups of Presbyterians, who were

entirely destitute of the public means of grace. To these scattered
sheep Mr. Robinson directed his benevolent attention. Feeling
something of the zeal which actuated Paul, he did not wish to build
on another man's foundation, but to preach Christ where he had
not been named. In another respect he resembled Paul, for he
went forward, fearless of danger, and as it would seem, without
even inquiring whether the laws of the colonies into which he was
going would allow itinerant preachers to pass through the land.
Accordingly, he had penetrated but a short day's journey into the
Old Dominion, and reached the town of Winchester, when he was
apprehended by the civil authorities; and it appearing that he had
transgressed the laws of the colony, a mittimus was made out by
the magistrate to send him to Williamsburg, the then seat of
government, for they were at a loss what disposal to make of him.
The sheriff to whom he was committed, having set off on the
journey, began to think that it would be a useless thing to conduct
his prisoner to a place so distant, and finding that he was a sensible,
well-disposed man, he assumed the responsibility of letting him
go on his missionary tour. Mr. Robinson proceeded along the
valley, everywhere finding new settlements of Presbyterians, until
he reached the waters of James river. The writer has heard an
old man who was among the first settlers of the country round about
Lexington, then called the Forks, say that he had heard Mr.
Robinson preach in that settlement soon after it was formed. But
the inhabitants in the valley not extending any further to the
south-west, he returned, and crossing the Blue Ridge at Rock-fish
Gap, proceeded to the south, across the country, until he reached
Cub Creek, then in Lunenburg, now Charlotte. Here he found a
pretty large settlement of Presbyterians, where he stopped and
preached; and here, as in all other places, his ministry was
attended by the Spirit of God; sinners were awakened and converted, and the people of God were greatly strengthened and
comforted. I have conversed with an old man, when I was young,
who was living in this settlement at the time, and was afterwards
an elder in the church organized there. His name was Robert
Weakly, born in Pennsylvania; and though brought up among the
opposers of the revival, he was led by curiosity to hear the
Rev. Samuel Blair preach, and was brought under deep conviction,
and after many trials, he hoped, to a sound conversion. From this
time he connected himself with the 'New Lights,' as they were

called. This man, late in life, having removed into Halifax county, where he had no opportunity of attending on the Lord's supper in his own church, and being debarred from the communion by the Baptists among whom he lived unless he would submit to be immersed, was at length induced to go down with them under the water; but though thus nominally a Baptist, his heart was as truly Presbyterian as ever. He was a man of eminent and long-tried piety, and had a good report from all of every name, whether in the church or out of it.

This man informed me that under Mr. Robinson's first sermon, a remarkable conversion of a half-breed Indian, one of the wickedest of men, had taken place under unusual circumstances. When notice was given to his family of a sermon at the stand, by a travelling preacher, his wife wished to go, but he positively forbade her, but said he would go himself. His name was David Austin. When the congregation had collected, he was seen lying outside the assembly under a tree asleep. And thus he lay until the preacher took his text, which he uttered in a thundering voice, 'Awake, thou that sleepest.' Austin sprang to his feet as if pierced with a dart, and fixing his eyes on the preacher, never removed them, but drew nigher and nigher to the stand, until at the close he was observed standing at the preacher's feet, and the tears streaming from his eyes. After a few days of pungent conviction, he received comfort by faith in Christ, and became one of the most eminent Christians in all the land. His talent for administering consolation to distressed consciences was so well known that he has been sent for as far as thirty miles, to converse with a lady under spiritual darkness and distress of mind. I have heard a pious old mother in Israel say that she had heard Mr. Davies, and Dr. Waddel, and the Smiths converse on religion, but she never heard anyone whom she found so much comfort in hearing as old David Austin.

A remarkable attention to religion in the county of Hanover existed at this time, without the aid of the ministry. Some persons from that place being on a visit to Cub Creek, when Mr. Robinson, on his way to Carolina, visited that settlement, then called 'The Caldwell Settlement, ' gave an account upon their return of the preacher they had heard. Upon hearing this account, the serious people of Hanover inquired at what time Mr. Robinson expected to return from Carolina to Cub Creek, and they immediately resolved to send two of their number to meet him at the time specified. It so happened, however, that the information received was not correct, for when the messengers arrived at Cub Creek, they found to their disappointment that he had passed several days before. Determined, however, not to go back without him, they pursued after him through a very rugged, mountainous country, and overtook him at Rock-fish, at the foot of the Blue Ridge. Mr. Robinson, upon hearing the state of things in Hanover, did not hesitate to go with the men, but in order to reach the place before the Sabbath it became necessary to ride one whole night; and when he arrived the leaders of the dissenting congregation were much perplexed and concerned lest his doctrines should not accord with those which from books they had imbibed. Therefore, before he was introduced to the congregation, they took him into a private room, and asked him what was his opinion of such works as Luther on the Galatians, Boston, Bunyan, &c., and when he expressed the warmest approbation, they were delighted above measure. But as it will be gratifying to the reader to see the whole of the letter which Mr. Davies wrote to Mr. Bellamy, in which the narrative of Mr. Robinson's visit to Hanover is contained, it shall be here inserted.

Letter from Mr. Davies, minister of Hanover, Virginia, to Mr. Bellamy of Bethlehem in New England:

'*June 28, 1751.*

'REV. AND DEAR SIR:—If the publication of a narrative of the rise, progress, and present situation of religion in Virginia, may not only gratify good people, but (as you give me reason to hope) animate their prayers for us, and also encourage preachers to come into these parts, I should charge myself with a criminal neglect if I refused to publish the marvellous works of the Lord among us. I hope I may observe without the umbrage of calumny what is but too evident to serious people of all denominations among us, that religion has been and in most parts of the colony still is in a very low state. A surprising negligence in attending public worship, and an equal surprising levity and unconcernedness in those that attend. Family religion a rarity, and a solemn concern about eternal things, a greater. Vices of various kinds triumphant, and even a form of godliness not common. But universal fame makes it needless for me to enlarge on this disagreeable subject. Before the revival in 1743, there were a few who were awakened, as they have told me, either by their own serious reflections, suggested and enforced by divine energy, or on reading some authors of the last century, particularly Bolton, Baxter, Flavel, Bunyan. There was one Mr. Samuel Morris who had for some time been very anxious about his own salvation, who, after obtaining blessed relief in Christ, became zealous for the salvation of his neighbours, and very earnest to use means to awaken them. This was the tendency of his conversation; and he also read to them such authors as had been most useful to himself, particularly Luther on the Galatians, and his Table Discourses, and several pieces of honest Bunyan's. By these means some of his neighbours were made more thoughtful about their souls; but the concern was not very extensive. I have prevailed on my good friend just now named, who was the principal private instrument of promoting the late work, and therefore well acquainted with it, to write me a narrative of its rise and progress, and this, together with what he and others have told me, I shall present to you without any material alterations.

' "In the year 1740, Mr. Whitefield had preached at Williamsburgh, at the invitation of Mr. Blair, our late commissary. But we being fifty miles distant from Williamsburgh, he left the colony before we had an opportunity of hearing him. But in the year 1743, a young man from Scotland had got a book of his sermons preached in Glasgow, and taken from his mouth in short hand, which, after I had read with great benefit, I invited my neighbours to come and hear it; and the plainness and fervency of these discourses being attended with the power of the Lord, many were convinced of their undone condition, and constrained to seek deliverance with the greatest solicitude. A considerable number met to hear these sermons every Sabbath, and frequently on week days. The concern of some was so passionate and violent, that they could not avoid crying out, weeping bitterly, &c. And that when such indications of religious concern were so strange and ridiculous that they could not be occasioned by example or sympathy, and the affectation of them would be so unprofitable an instance of hypocrisy that none could be tempted to it. My dwelling-house at length was too small to contain the people, whereupon we determined to build a meeting-house merely for reading. And having never been used to social extempore prayer, none of us durst attempt it. By this single means several were awakened, and their conduct ever since is a proof of the continuance and happy issue of their impressions. When the report was spread abroad I was invited to several places to read these sermons, at a considerable distance, and by this means the concern was propagated. About this time our absenting ourselves from the established Church, contrary as was alleged, to the laws of the land, was taken notice of, and we were called upon by the court to assign our reasons for it, and to declare what denomination we were of. As we knew but little of any denomination of dissenters except Quakers, we were at a loss what name to assume. At length, recollecting that Luther was a noted reformer, and that his books had been of especial service to us, we declared ourselves Lutherans; and thus we continued, until Providence sent us the Rev. Mr. William Robinson. This Mr. Robinson was a zealous, laborious minister of Christ, who, by the permission of the Presbytery, took a journey through the new settlements in Pennsylvania, Virginia, and North Carolina. He founded a congregation at Lunenburg.[1] In Amelia,[2] also, a county somewhat nearer us than the former, his labours were extensively blest; and while he was there, some of our people sent him an invitation to come and preach at our reading house. Being satisfied about the soundness of his principles, and being informed that the method of his preaching was awakening, we were very eager to hear him. On the 6th of July, 1743, he preached his first sermon to us from Luke 13. 3, and continued with us preaching four days successively. The congregation was large the first day, and vastly increased the three ensuing. 'Tis hard for the liveliest imagination to form an image of the condition of the assembly, on these glorious days of the Son of Man. Such of us as had been hungering for the word before were lost in an agreeable surprise and astonishment, and some could not refrain from publicly declaring their transport. We were overwhelmed with the thoughts of the unexpected goodness of God in allowing us to hear the gospel preached in a manner that surpassed our hopes. Many that came through curiosity were pricked to the heart, and but few in the numerous assemblies on these four days appeared unaffected. They returned alarmed with apprehensions of their dangerous condition, convinced of their former entire ignorance of religion, and anxiously inquiring what

[1] Now Charlotte.   [2] Now Cumberland.

they should do to be saved. And there is reason to believe there was as much good done by these four sermons as by all the sermons preached in these parts before or since. Before Mr. Robinson left us he successfully endeavoured to correct some of our mistakes, and to bring us to carry on the worship of God more regularly at our meetings. After this we met to read good sermons, and began and concluded with prayer and singing of psalms, which till then we had omitted. The blessing of God remarkably attended these more private means, and it was really astonishing to observe the solemn impressions begun or continued in many by hearing good discourses read. I had repeated invitations to come to many places round, some of them thirty or forty miles distant, to read. Considerable numbers attended with eager attention and awful solemnity, and several were in a judgment of charity turned to God, and thereupon erected meeting-houses and chose readers among themselves, by which the work was more extensively carried on.

' "Soon after Mr. Robinson left us, the Rev. Mr. John Blair paid us a visit, and truly he came to us in the fulness of the gospel of Christ. Former impressions were ripened, and new ones made on many hearts. One night in particular a whole house full of people was quite overcome with the power of the word, particularly of one pungent sentence, and they could hardly sit or stand or keep their passions under proper restraint. So general was the concern during his stay with us and so ignorant were we of the danger of apostasy that we pleased ourselves with the thoughts of more being brought to Christ at that time than now appears to have been; though there is still the greatest reason to hope that several bound themselves to the Lord in an everlasting covenant never to be forgotten. Some time after this the Rev. Mr. Roan was sent us by the Presbytery of New Castle. He continued with us a longer time than any of the former, and the happy effects of his ministrations are still apparent. He was instrumental in beginning and promoting the religious concern in several places where there was little appearance of it before. This, together with his speaking pretty freely about the degeneracy of the clergy in this colony gave a general alarm, and some measures were concerted to suppress us. To incense the indignation of the government the more, a perfidious wretch deponed he heard Mr. Roan utter blasphemous expressions in his sermon. An indictment was thereupon drawn up against Mr. Roan (though by that time he had departed the colony), and some who had invited him to preach at their houses were cited to appear before the general court, and two of them were fined. While my cause was upon trial I had reason to rejoice that the throne of grace is accessible in all places, and that helpless creatures can send up their desires unseen in the midst of a crowd. Six witnesses were cited to prove the indictment against Mr. Roan, but their depositions were in his favour, and the witness who accused him of blasphemy, when he heard of the arrival of Messrs. Tennent and Finley fled, and has not returned since, so that the indictment was dropped. But I had reason to fear being banished the colony, and all circumstances seemed to threaten the extirpation of religion among the dissenters in these parts. In these difficulties, having no person of a public character to appear in our favour, we were determined to acquaint the Synod of New York with our case. Accordingly four of us went to the Synod, May, 1745, when the Lord favoured us with success. The Synod drew up an address to our governor, the honourable Sir William Gooch, and sent it with Messrs. Tennent and Finley, who were received by the governor with respect, who gave them liberty to preach among us. By this means the dreadful cloud was scattered for a while, and our languid hopes revived. They continued with us about a week, and though the deluge of a passion in which we were at first overwhelmed was by this time somewhat abated, yet much good was done by their ministry. The people of God were refreshed, and several careless sinners were awakened. Some that had trusted before in their moral conduct and religious duties, were convinced of the depravity of their nature, and the necessity of regeneration, though indeed there were but few unregenerate persons among us at that time, that could claim so regular a character, the most part indulging themselves in criminal liberties, and being remiss in the duties of religion, which alas is too commonly the case still in such parts of the colony as the late revival did not extend to.

' "After they left us, we continued vacant for a considerable time, and kept up our meetings for reading and praying in several places, and the Lord favoured us with his presence. I was again repeatedly presented and fined in court for absenting myself from church, and keeping up unlawful meetings (as they were called), but the bush flourished in the flames. The next that were ap-

pointed to supply us were the Rev. Messrs. William Tennent and
Samuel Blair. They administered the Lord's supper among us, and
we have reason ever to remember it as a most glorious day of the
Son of Man. The assembly was large, and the novelty of the
manner of the administration did peculiarly engage their attention.
It appeared as one of the days of heaven to some of us, and we
could hardly help wishing we could with Joshua have delayed the
revolutions of the heavens to prolong it. After Messrs. Tennent
and Blair were gone, Mr. Whitefield came and preached four or
five days, which was the happy means of giving us further
encouragement and engaging others to the Lord, especially among
the church people, who received the gospel more readily from him
than from ministers of the Presbyterian denomination. After his
departure we were destitute of a minister, and followed our usual
method of reading and prayer at our meetings, till the Rev. Mr.
Davies, our present pastor, was sent us by the Presbytery to supply
us a few weeks in the spring, 1747, when our discouragements
from the government were renewed and multiplied; for upon a
Lord's day a proclamation was set up at our meeting house,
strictly requiring all magistrates to suppress and prohibit, as far
as they lawfully could, all itinerant preachers, &c., which occasioned us to forbear reading that day till we had time to deliberate
and consult what was expedient to do. But how joyfully were we
surprised before the next Sabbath when we unexpectedly heard
that Mr. Davies was come to preach so long among us, and
especially that he had qualified himself according to law, and
obtained the licensing of four meeting houses among us, which
had never been done before. Thus man's extremity is the Lord's
opportunity. For this seasonable interposition of Divine Providence
we desire to offer our grateful praises, and we importune the friends
of Zion to concur with us."

'Thus far Mr. Morris's narrative. Then the Rev. Mr. Davies
proceeds to given an account of the state of their affairs since he
came among them in April, 1747. "Upon my arrival I petitioned
the general court to grant me a license to officiate in and about
Hanover, at four meeting-houses, which, after some delay, was
granted, upon my qualifying according to the act of toleration. I
preached frequently in Hanover, and some of the adjacent
counties; and though the fervour of the late work was considerably
abated, and my labours were not blessed with success equal to those

of my brethren, yet I have reason to hope they were of service in several instances. The importunities they used with me to settle with them were invincible, and upon my departure they sent a call for me to the Presbytery. After I returned from Virginia I spent a year under melancholy and consumptive languishments, expecting death. In the spring of 1748, I began slowly to recover, though I then looked on it only as the intermission of a disorder that would finally prove mortal. But upon the arrival of a messenger from Hanover I put my life in my hand, and determined to accept of their call, hoping I might live to prepare the way for some more useful successor, and willing to expire under the fatigues of duty rather than in voluntary negligence. The Hon. Sir Wm. Gooch, our late governor, always discovered a ready disposition to allow us all claimable privileges, and the greatest aversion to persecuting measures; but, considering the shocking reports spread abroad concerning us by officious malignants, it was no great wonder that the council discovered considerable reluctance to tolerate us. Had it not been for this I persuade myself they would have shown themselves the guardians of our legal privileges, as well as generous patriots to their country, which is the character generally given them. In October, 1748, besides the four meeting-houses already mentioned, the people petitioned for the licensing of three more, which with great difficulty was obtained. Among these seven I have hitherto divided my time. Three of them lay in Hanover county, the other four in the counties of Henrico, Carolina, Louisa, and Goochland. The nearest are twelve or fifteen miles distant from each other, and the extremes about forty. My congregation is very much dispersed, and notwithstanding the number of the meeting-houses some live twenty, some thirty, and a few forty miles from the nearest. Were they all compactly situated in one county they would be sufficient to form three distinct congregations. Many of the church people also attend when there is sermon at any of these houses. This I looked upon at first as mere curiosity after novelty, but as it continues and in some places seems to increase, I cannot but look upon it as a happy token of their being at length thoroughly engaged. And I have the greater reason to hope so now, as experience has confirmed my former hopes. Fifty or sixty familes having thus been happily entangled in the net of the gospel by their own curiosity or some such motive. There are about three hundred communicants in my congregation, of whom the greater number are in the judgment of rational charity real Christians; besides some who through excessive scrupulousness do not seek admission to the Lord's table. There is also a number of negroes. Sometimes I see an hundred and more among my hearers (Psa. 68. 31). I have baptized about forty of them within these three years upon such a profession of faith as I then judged credible. Some of them, I fear, have apostatized; but others, I trust, will persevere to the end. I have had as satisfying evidences of sincere piety from several of them as I ever had from any person in my life, and their artless simplicity, their passionate aspirations after Christ, their incessant endeavours to know and do the will of God have charmed me. But alas! while my charge is so extensive I cannot take sufficient pains with them for their instruction, which often oppresses my heart.

' "There have been instances of unhappy apostasy among us; but, blessed be God, not many in proportion to the number brought under concern. At present there are a few under promising impressions, but in general a lamentable security prevails. Oh, for a little reviving in our bondage! I might have given you a particular account of the conversion of some persons here, as indeed there are some uncommon instances of it, but I shall only observe in general that abstracting from particular circumstances, the work of conversion has been carried on in such steps as are described by experimental divines, as Alleine, Shepard, Stoddard, Flavel, &c. And nothing confirms me more in the truth of their opinions concerning experimental piety than this agreement and uniformity as to the substance in the exercises of those that can make the fairest claim to saving grace. There is one Isaac Oliver here, whose history, could I write it intelligibly to you, would be very entertaining. He has been deaf and dumb from his birth, and yet I have the utmost reason to believe he is truly gracious, and also acquainted with most of the doctrines, and many of the historical facts of the Bible. I have seen him represent the crucifixion of Christ in such significant signs that I could not but understand them. Those that live in the house with him can hold conversation with him very readily. There is so much of the devout ardour of his soul discovered at times as is really affecting, and I have seen converse in signs about the love and sufferings of Christ till he has been transported into earnestness, and dissolved in tears. The above Mr. Morris, with whom he lives, has told me that eight years ago he appeared remarkably changed, and ever since is very conscientious in the whole of his behaviour; generally delights to attend both public and family worship, though he cannot hear a word; and is observed sometimes to retire to secret prayer, though he signifies that he is praying with his heart when about his business or in company, which is peculiarly practicable to him, as in all places he enjoys retirement. I could relate several peculiarities about him, but as they are unintelligible to myself, or might seem incredible to those that are unacquainted with him, I omit them. So much, however, I know of him that I cannot but look upon him as a miraculous monument of Almighty grace, that can perform its purposes on men notwithstanding the greatest natural or moral impediments; and I submit it to the judgment of others whether a person so incapable of external instructions could be brought to know the mysteries of the kingdom of heaven any other way than by immediate revelation. Besides the people here, several of my brethren who have been here, particularly Messrs. Samuel Blair and John Roan, can attest this relation. I forgot to inform you, in its proper place, that the Rev. Mr. Davenport was sent by the Synod to Hanover last summer, and continued here about two months, and, blessed be God, did not labour in vain. Some were brought under concern, and many of the Lord's people much revived, who can never forget the instrument of it.

' "Thus, dear sir, I have given you a brief account of what I am persuaded you will readily own to be the work of the Lord. We claim no infallibility, but we must not fall into scepticism. If we could form no judgment of such a work, why should we pretend to promote the conversion of men, if we cannot have any satisfying knowledge of it when it appears? Indeed, the evidence of its divinity here is so irresistible that it has extorted an acknowledgment from some from whom it could hardly be expected. Were you sir, a narrow bigot, you would, no doubt, rejoice to hear that there are now some hundreds of dissenters in a place where, a few years ago, there were not ten; but I assure myself of your congratulations on a nobler account, because a considerable number of perishing sinners are gained to the blessed Redeemer, with whom, though you never see them here, you may spend a blissful eternity. After all, poor Virginia demands your compassion, for religion at present is but like the cloud which Elijah's servant saw. Oh that it may spread and cover the land!"

'As to other counties where dissenters are settled. There are two congregations, one in Albemarle, and one in Augusta county, belonging to the Synod of Philadelphia, that have ministers settled among them; but those that have put themselves under the care of the New Castle Presbytery (which are vastly more numerous), notwithstanding their repeated endeavours are still destitute of ministers. There are as many of them as would form five distinct congregations, three at least in Augusta, one in Frederick, and one at least in Lunenburg and Amelia.[1] Notwithstanding the supplies our Presbytery have sent them, some of them, particularly Lunenburg, have been both a year together without one sermon. I hope one of them may soon be provided by a pious young man, Mr. Todd, sent by New Brunswick Presbytery, but I have no prospect as to the rest; for I can now count up at least six or seven vacant congregations in Pennsylvania, and two or three in Maryland, besides the five mentioned in the frontier counties of Virginia, and a part of my own congregation, which I would willingly declare vacant, had they opportunity of obtaining another minister. And there are but twelve members in New Castle Presbytery, and two or three candidates that are pre-engaged to vacancies in Pennsylvania. We have indeed, of late, licensed several pious youths, but our vacancies increase almost as fast as our ministers by the settlement of new places or the breaking out of religious concern in places where there was little before; and some of our most useful members are lately called home by death, such as Messrs. Robinson and Dean, and now Mr. Samuel Blair. May the Lord induce faithful ministers from New England, or wherever they might be spared, to come and help us! While these congregations have been destitute of settled pastors, itinerant preaching among them has, by the blessing of God, been very useful. Mr. Robinson underwent great hardships in North Carolina without much success, by reason of the fewness and savage ignorance of the inhabitants; but the case is now happily altered. A new congregation, I think upon Pee-dee river, sent a petition lately to our Presbytery for a minister. Besides this, I hear of several other places in North Carolina that are ripening very fast for the gospel. O that the Lord would send forth faithful

[1] Now Charlotte and Cumberland.

labourers into his harvest! Mr. Robinson was the instrument of awakening several in Lunenburg and Amelia, with whom I lately spent a fortnight at their earnest desire; and there is a prospect of doing much service were they furnished with a faithful minister. I met with most encouragement in a part of Amelia county where very few had heard any of my brethren. The assemblies were large even on week days, and sometimes there appeared much solemnity and affection among them. There appears great probability of success if they had a faithful minister. It was really afflicting to me that the necessity of my own congregation constrained me to leave them so soon. In Augusta there is a great number of solid, lively Christians. There was a pretty general awakening there some years ago, under the ministry of Messrs. Dean and Byram. I believe three ministers might live very comfortably among them. In Frederick county, there has also been (as I am informed by my brethren who have been there) a considerable awakening some years ago, which has had a blessed issue in many, and the congregation have been seeking a minister these several years. In Maryland also there has been a considerable revival (shall I call it?) or first plantation of religion in Baltimore county, where I am informed Mr. Whittlesey is likely to settle. In Kent county, and Queen Anne's, a number of careless sinners have been awakened and hopefully brought to Christ. The work was begun and chiefly carried on by the instrumentality of that favoured man, Mr. Robinson, whose success, whenever I reflect upon it, astonishes me. Oh! he did much in a little time, and who would not choose such an expeditious pilgrimage through this world? There is in these places a considerable congregation, and they have made repeated essays to obtain a settled minister.

'There was a great stir about religion in Buckingham, a place on the sea-shore, about four years ago, which has since spread and issued in a hopeful conversion in several instances. They also want a minister. But the most glorious display of divine grace in Maryland has been in and about Somerset county. It began, I think, in 1745, by the ministry of Mr. Robinson, and was afterwards carried on by several ministers that preached transiently there. I was there about two months, when the work was at its height, and I never saw such deep and spreading concern; the assemblies were numerous, though in the extremity of a cold winter, and unwearied in attending the word; and frequently there were very few among them that did not give some plain indications of distress or joy. Oh! these were the happiest days that ever my eyes saw. Since that, the harvest seems over there, though considerable gleanings, I hear, are still gathered. They have of late got Mr. Henry for their minister, a young man who I trust will be an extensive blessing to that part of the colony. I shall prize it, dear sir, as a great blessing, if you and others of the Lord's servants and people in distant parts favour us with your prayers, and shall be glad to correspond with them. Our acquaintance with the various parts of the church qualifies us to adapt our prayers to their state. May your divine Master bless you and succeed your ministrations, and pour out his Spirit on the land where you reside."[1]

Not only in Hanover, but in all the places where Mr. Robinson preached, there were permanent fruits of his labours. The writer has seen and conversed with a number of persons who were brought to serious consideration under the ministry of this successful evangelist. Old John White, who resided near Charlestown, in Jefferson county, and who was the father of Judge White of Winchester, was one of Mr. Robinson's great admirers, and I believe brought to the experimental knowledge of the truth under

[1] 'May 22nd, 1745, Mr. Gilbert Tennent and Mr. Davies being at Edinburgh, as agents for the trustees of the college of New Jersey (an institution that promises well, if the Lord vouchsafe it his blessing, for the success of the gospel), Mr. Davies informs that one Mr. Brown is lately ordained in Augusta county, where there were sundry congregations vacant ever since their first settlement; that he has the care of two meetings, and as he is a youth of piety, prudence, and zeal, there is reason to expect that his labours will be of service in that wilderness, not only in his own more peculiar charge, but in the neighbouring places that have no minister of their own. Also, that Mr. John Wright, who supplies Mr. Davies's charge in his absence, has wrote that since he has officiated in his place there are considerable appearances of success in Carolina and Henrico, where Mr. Davies was apprehensive he laboured much in vain. When Mr. Davies left Virginia in August last, there was a hopeful appearance of a greater spread of religious concern among the negroes. A few weeks before he left home he baptized in one day fifteen negroes after they had been catechized for some months, and given credible evidence of their sincerely embracing the gospel. He also says that Isaac Oliver the dumb man mentioned in his letter above, has behaved as one would expect from such promising beginnings, his conduct such as becomes the profession of the gospel.'

his ministry. Old Mr. Hoge, the father of the Rev. Dr. Moses Hoge, who was a seceder, informed the writer that he often heard Robinson when he preached at Opekin and Cedar Creek, in Frederick county, and while he admitted that he preached the gospel faithfully and with great zeal, yet he said there was a want of method in his discourses. After Mr. Robinson's return from this interesting tour, he laboured in the state of New York with his usual success, and also in some congregations in Maryland, where there was a blessed work of grace under his ministry.

Probably Mr. Robinson, during the short period of his life, was the instrument in the conversion of as many souls as any minister who ever lived in this country. The only circumstance relating to his person which has come down is, that he was blind of one eye; so that by some he was called 'the one-eyed Robinson.'

We are also entirely ignorant of the circumstances of his death. This event we know occurred before the year 1751, in which Mr. Davies wrote his letter to Mr. Bellamy, for it is mentioned with grief in that communication. If we mistake not, Mr. Davies has celebrated the labours and successes of this servant of God in one of his poems, and Mr. Tennent somewhere speaks of him as 'that wonderful man.' Mr. Robinson was never married, and had, it is believed, no relatives in this country, and as far as appears never printed anything nor left any of his writings to be a memorial to posterity of his fervent piety and evangelical spirit. It is not even known where his body rests; but his glorious Master whom he served so faithfully in the gospel will know where to find it when he shall come to resuscitate the bodies of his saints.

XVIII

Memoir of the Rev. John Rowland

Mr. Rowland received by the New Brunswick Presbytery at its first
meeting, in violation of the rule of Synod—His trials—Speedy
licensure—Accepts a call to Maidenhead and Hopewell—Great revival—
His letter to Mr. Prince—Removal to Pennsylvania—Revival at New
Providence—Close of life unknown.

Of Mr. Rowland nothing is known prior to the time when he was
taken under the care of the New Brunswick Presbytery, at its
first meeting in August, 1738. It is certain, indeed, that he was
an alumnus of the Log College, where probably he received the
principal part of his education.

In receiving him under their care, the Presbytery deliberately
violated a standing rule of the Synod, which required that every
candidate, before being taken on trials by any Presbytery, should
submit himself to an examination on his classical and scientific
attainments by a committee of the Synod. This rule the Presbytery
of New Brunswick believed to be arbitrary and an undue infringe-
ment on the rights of Presbyteries, and therefore determined to
disregard it. This was undoubtedly a rash and disorderly pro-
ceeding. Even if their opinion about the rights of Presbyteries had
been correct, they should first have remonstrated against the
Synod's rule and endeavoured to have it repealed. But the members
of this new Presbytery, having been the principal supporters of the
Log College, considered the rule of the Synod as particularly
directed against that institution and on this account were disposed
to resist it. Hence arose the violent dissension between this
Presbytery and the Synod which issued in a division of the body
into two parts, the Old and the New Side; of which an account
has already been given.

At the first meeting of the New Brunswick Presbytery, the
following ministers and elders were present, viz., Gilbert Tennent,
John Cross, William Tennent, Eleazer Wales, and Samuel Blair.
The elders were James McCoy, John Henry, William Moor,

Robert Cunningham, and Thomas Davis. As none in the minutes are marked as absent, it would seem that this first meeting of the Presbytery set an example deserving the imitation of their successors. All the ministers were in their places, and an equal number of ruling elders, so that there was no delinquency on their part. The first business, after they were regularly constituted, was the receiving of Mr. John Rowland as a candidate under their care. And in regard to the rule of Synod, after much discussion they adopted the following resolution:

'That in point of conscience, they were not restrained from using the liberty and power which Presbyteries all along have hitherto enjoyed; but that it was their duty to take the said Mr. Rowland on trials, for which conclusion they conceive they have many weighty and sufficient reasons.'

The Presbytery then proceeded to the examination of Mr. Rowland, 'on the several parts of learning, and on his experience of a work of converting grace in his soul, which he sustained to their satisfaction.'

The trials of Mr. Rowland were carried through as rapidly as was consistent with the usage in such cases. The Presbytery met again on the 1st day of September of the same year, when he read a Latin exegesis and a sermon on Psalm 87. 5. With these trials the Presbytery expressed themselves well pleased, and assigned him as the subject of a popular sermon, Romans 3. 24, and adjourned to meet the following week at Freehold, when Mr. Rowland preached at the opening of the Presbytery, who having taken the sermon under consideration, it was highly and unanimously approved.

The candidate having now gone through all the prescribed trials, after adopting the Westminster Confession of Faith as the confession of his faith, was licensed to preach the gospel of Christ. His licensure took place exactly one month after he was taken under the care of the Presbytery. There is no reason to lead us to conclude that Mr. Rowland was deficient in the qualifications requisite for the office of the ministry. From the record it appears that the Presbytery were well satisfied with all the parts of his trials; and it is known that he was a popular and an awakening preacher, and that his ministry was attended with much success.

As might have been expected, this act of the Presbytery brought down upon them the censure of the Synod; and the Presbytery not being disposed to submit to a rule which they considered arbitrary and inconsistent with their rights, relations grew worse and worse until the parties separated. Before this event, however, the Synod absolutely refused to consider Mr. Rowland as a member of their body. They did not deny that he was a minister of the gospel, but alleged that having been brought in contrary to their rules, he could not be recognized as a member. It appears from Mr. Rowland's letter to the Rev. Mr. Prince of Boston that on the very day of his being licensed to preach the gospel an application was made to the Presbytery for his services by the united congregations of Maidenhead (Lawrence) and Hopewell (Pennington). And it was not long after this that he was artfully personated by Tom Bell, when he was absent on a preaching tour in Maryland, in company with the Rev. William Tennent. On his return, as has been related in the life of Mr. William Tennent, he was indicted for horse-stealing and robbery, and was cleared by the testimony of Mr. Tennent and two others, who swore that he was at the time in a distant part of the country. But the impression on the public mind was so strong, that he was the person seen by many in the possession of the stolen horse, that the three witnesses, including Mr. Tennent, were indicted for perjury, and one of them actually suffered the penalty of the law for his crime. How wonderfully Mr. Tennent was delivered from an ignominious punishment may be seen in the memoir which we have published of this extraordinary man.

Mr. Rowland accepted the invitation of the congregations before mentioned, and his labours among them were attended with an extraordinary blessing, in a great revival of religion in both these congregations. But as Mr. Rowland himself has given a narrative of this work of grace in a letter to the Rev. Mr. Prince, of Boston, we think it most expedient to publish his own account in his own words.

The letter is as follows:

'REV. SIR:—In answer to yours, &c.—I was sent forth to preach the gospel of Christ by the Presbytery of New Brunswick, on September 7th, 1738, on which day the congregations of Maidenhead and Hopewell put in a supplication for me to the Presbytery, and accordingly I complied therewith. In process of time, we had the privilege of Maidenhead meeting-house, and my people built a meeting-house in Hopewell; but before this, we were constrained to keep our meetings in barns in both towns; and though we thus appeared as poor, despised creatures, yet the congregation that attended my ministry was so numerous that the largest barns among us were chosen to worship God in. It was some discouragement to me at first that I and my people had no better places for divine worship; but at that time I thought on these things, which proved some support to me, viz., that our Lord and Saviour was born in a mean place, and likewise preached in the ship and on the mountain, as well as in the synagogues, and that it had been the frequent lot of his people to betake themselves to worship him in places attended with many inconveniences. There is another town lying contiguous to Hopewell, which is called Amwell; the people there were something numerous likewise, and having none to labour among them in the word they petitioned for a part of my time, viz., one Sabbath in three, and it was granted unto them; so that my labours among these three towns for the most part of the time that I lived in the Jerseys were equally divided. There was a small number in Hopewell and Maidenhead truly acquainted with vital religion, as far as I could judge, before I came among them, and they seemed so earnest in prayer night and day to have the gospel in power among them, as if they would take no denial. But of them who became my congregation in Amwell there were but very few that knew the Lord Jesus when I came among them; yet in many ways they were a very agreeable people, so that I was much encouraged to labour among them.

'The subjects which I chiefly insisted on for about six months were conviction and conversion, and usually I made choice of the most rousing and awakening texts to set forth the nature of these doctrines; and I have reason to hope that the Lord began to accompany his word in a measure from the very first. Some began to be convinced that they were in the way to misery and unacquainted with the way to the kingdom of heaven. But then, let it be observed, that but one or two were taken with convictions at a time, or under one sermon. For many months together[1] their

---

[1] 'Let none suppose that because I speak of convictions being still carried on, that I mean that sinners must be convinced to some high degree before they can be converted; I only mean that this was the way which the Lord observed in carrying on his work, to keep sinners for a long time under conviction before he manifested his love to them.'

convictions were still increased, and the number of the convinced was still multiplied. I commonly preached in the night as well as in the day, and frequently on week days also; so that they had hardly any opportunity to cast their convictions out of their thoughts, the Lord continuing to co-operate with his word. The frequent opportunities which I took to examine them were made very beneficial, through the Divine blessing, to preserve their convictions alive until the time of grace, of which I shall speak afterwards. The attention of all in general was awakened; fathers, mothers, and the youth; some negroes, also, seemed very earnest after the word, and were convinced thereby of their sin and misery, and that Christ they must have, or perish for ever.

'The people of God were much enlivened to see poor sinners convinced of the perishing nature of their state, and their absolute need of Christ. Their supplications to God were mostly bent for the conversion of sinners; and their conversation, whenever they met together, as far as I observed it (and frequent opportunities I had to observe it), savoured exceedingly of the things of God, so that I cannot say that I ever saw those pious people given to worldliness in their conversation, or to lightness and vanity in their discourses. Great was the love they bore to one another, and sweet was the peace which subsisted among themselves, so that I was not interrupted from my work by making up differences among them.

'In the month of May, 1739, I began to think that the most inviting and encouraging subjects would be the most agreeable to convinced souls, and accordingly I began with these words, John 11. 28, 29: "The Master is come, and calleth for thee. As soon as she heard that, she rose quickly, and came unto him." The discourse upon this subject was brought home, through the divine influence, upon the souls of many. Solemn weeping and deep concern appeared through the congregation. I had hopes that the hearts of some had been knit close to Jesus our Lord, which afterwards appeared to be so; of which more hereafter. I was still encouraged to go on in inviting convinced sinners to come and embrace the person and purchase of the dear Lord Jesus. Then I made choice of that word in Matthew 22. 4:—"And all things are ready: come unto the marriage." This was also blessed to poor convinced souls. They were brought under a full persuasion that Jesus, the Son of God, was ready and willing to embrace them with his everlasting favour, and to pardon their sins and transgressions; but then they found more of their own hardness, and had a clearer view of their own unwillingness to come unto the Lord Jesus Christ, which increased their mourning and sorrow, and made them press forward with more living earnestness in search after Jesus Christ. A variety of other engaging subjects I made use of for a considerable time, to press them to a full closure with Jesus Christ. At length by frequent converse among them, and inquiring strictly into the nature of the views they had of Christ, and the outgoings of their souls after him, and their willingness to be ruled by Jesus Christ, in their whole hearts and lives, I could not but be favourable in my thoughts of such as persons favoured of the Lord.

'I find, by reading what accounts I kept by me of the blessed work of grace which hath been in these towns, that there was much good done by visiting, by which means I found out many that had been touched, of whom I had not well heard how it was with them, which gave me an opportunity to offer such things unto them as might tend to fix these beginnings in their souls, and increase them. So, likewise, many were convinced of their lost state by nature. By particular examinations I found, likewise, that private examination of persons, as to their state and condition, is an excellent means to lay them open to conviction under the public word; and thus were some convinced in these towns.

'The divine influence of the Spirit of God was very evidently afforded with his word, though not in every opportunity, yet in several, until May 1740, in which time many more were added unto the Lord's people. Some of these opportunities, for clearness sake, I shall mention. One was on October 6th, 1739, in a night meeting; but the people not having been warned with sufficient care, there met but about fifteen persons, eleven of whom were deeply convinced of their misery, and some of them cried out so very awfully that I was constrained to conclude. After sermon I took an opportunity to inquire of those persons what was the real cause of their crying out in such a manner. Some of them answered me, "that they saw hell opening before them, and themselves ready to fall into it." Others answered me, "that they were struck with such a sense of their sinfulness, that they were afraid the Lord would never have mercy on them." Another of these opportunities was on December 30th, 1739. As to myself, I felt exceedingly poor in the frame of my soul; so that I thought I might well say, as in the words of the text I preached on that day, Isa. 40. 6, "What shall I cry?" But the Lord was pleased to manifest his grace and power exceedingly through the whole service. The people of God were much enlarged in love to see that whatever gracious word was sent with power into their hearts was sent from God; for the man knoweth not what to cry, without being guided by the word and Spirit. Some hardened creatures, who thought not much of religion, as if there was no reality in it, were deeply convinced of the truth, reality, and beauty of religion. Others who knew not well which way to walk, or what to choose, opposers I cannot call them though they had not joined with our side; such I say, as far as we could judge the tree by the fruit, were also convinced and converted under that discourse. Many youths also were wrought upon, so that I cannot say truly that any remained untouched. Some of these persons were pleased to tell me that they never would forget this day, in which God had been so gracious unto them. As to backsliders from convictions who were not converted, I shall afterwards speak of them. The night of the same day being spent in public worship (viz. the first part thereof) was attended with the same divine influence. Another of these opportunities was on April 6th, 1740, in Maidenhead. The subject that was insisted on was the GOSPEL-NET, from Matt. 13. Many who were not acquainted with the spiritual nature of the gospel in the least degree, as far as I found, were greatly bowed down, and brought to own that it was the Lord's work which was carried on. The people, in general, through the whole assembly, seemed as if they were humbled before the Lord, which afterwards proved itself to be so. Without controversy, many of these slipped out of the net as fast as they could; yet many, blessed be God, were held in it by almighty power.

'I come next to speak of the times of most remarkable power that I witnessed in these towns. It began on this wise: there had been a week-day's meeting in Maidenhead, on July 24th, 1740. Worship seemed to be attended with much warmth of affection, which gave much encouragement to the minister again; for lukewarmness at this time had prevailed very much among the people, and the affections of some were much removed from others of their fellow-members, neither did they seem to have such a thirst for the word of God as formerly. Things had come to this pass in about two months; but how astonishing it is to consider what sweet methods the Lord observed to remove them! for, as the people were passing homewards through the town after worship, some inclined to stop at one of the Christian houses; and the stopping of some occasioned others to stop till the number was about forty; and when they were all set in the house, that the time might be profitably spent, the first part of the fiftieth psalm was sung, which seemed to be performed with unusual quickening. When singing was over, the same verses were explained at some length, and the Spirit of the Lord was pleased to work by it upon all that were present, as far as we could discern by the outward man, and much converse that was spent among them all in particular. In about an hour afterwards, the love of God's people that were present was uncommonly inflamed to Jesus Christ; their views of his majesty and glory were much enlarged, their longings after him much stirred up, and their fear of him graciously increased; their zeal for God's glory was kindled anew, and their concern for the cause of God seemed to receive much growth; and as to the unconverted that were present we could not find otherwise but that they had received very clear discoveries of their undone state by nature.

'This was followed with the mighty power of God in a sermon next evening to a large congregation in the same town. And in Amwell, July 27th, and in Maidenhead again on August 3rd, God was pleased to magnify his grace in visiting many poor sinners. In these opportunities he opened their eyes to see themselves without Christ, and without hope in the world; their convictions were attended with great horror and trembling, and loud weeping, which I supposed could not be stopped so easily as some do imagine; for I observed that many did continue crying in the most doleful manner along the road in their way home, and it was not in the power of man to prevail with them to refrain, for the word of the Lord remained like fire upon their hearts. Furthermore, the Lord was pleased to add many more to my people, who used not to walk with them, who still continue in communion with them, of whom I hope it may be said that they are growing in grace, and in the knowledge of Jesus Christ. The seed of the word was dropped into the hearts of others, who bore not much regard to the doctrine of the new-birth which was preached among us, and did not spring up visibly until near three years after.

'As to the issue of these convictions which I have last mentioned,

I think it must be owned that many of them were followed with a sound conversion, or else we must give up speaking any thing as to any grace in this life. Many backslided and became stiff-necked again, though I must say that I have not seen such backslidings in these towns as I have seen in many others; the instances are but few in them in comparison to what I have seen in most other places that I have been acquainted with. One great means to prevent backsliding from convictions in Amwell was this: when the husband was taken, the wife was also taken, or when the wife was visited, the husband was also, so that they were ever stirring up each other. Many such instances are in the town of Amwell, upon which account that congregation appears to me peculiarly beautiful; and as to Maidenhead and Hopewell, I believe that one great means that the Lord used there to prevent backsliding was the care and diligence of some of the Christian people in conversing with the convinced; for several of the Christians were so engaged in deep concern for the work of God that they could not rest satisfied until they had reason to hope that the souls that were convinced from one time to another were also brought through to sound conversion.

'Respecting the nature of this work which I have been speaking of, it will appear yet more distinct by giving some account of their experiences. And first, I would speak something more of their convictions; they can give a very different account of sin, both original and actual; their views of heart corruption, their distance from God, and their having lived so long without him were very clear and affecting; their hardness and unbelief, their ignorance and blindness pressed very close upon them; their need of Christ and his Spirit was such, in their apprehension, that there was no rest nor contentment to be taken in any thing here below, until they did obtain an interest in Jesus Christ, and receive his Spirit to purify and sanctify their hearts. There are a few among them whose convictions were not attended with any considerable degree of horror; they were very watchful over themselves lest they should receive false comfort, and so rest in ungrounded hopes; their hunger after Jesus Christ, his righteousness, and all his fulness, was very earnest, and their experience of it very clear; therefore they wanted the word preached often, and they would sit under it with great affection, waiting on the Lord. Their views of the Lord Jesus, in his person, nature and offices, were very clear, and their acquaintance with the actings of their faith on him, together with the out-going of their souls in love towards him. They can give a satisfying account of those things according to the holy Scriptures. Their experience of a saving closure with Jesus Christ, and the sweet manifestations they had of him at the time of spiritual marriage, were very glorious, and their affections have been often stirred afresh towards Jesus Christ in meditating on and speaking of their espousals. They are careful to maintain a holy communion with God in the general course of their lives. I have seen some of them in considerable agonies when they have been under the hidings of God's face, so that they could take no rest by any means until the gracious Lord would be pleased to shine again upon them with the light of his countenance. They are properly diligent in the things of this life, yet they are ready to attend on the word of God on any opportunity that offers to them on week-days.

'They still continue zealous for God and his truth; their walk is steady in the ways of God, and not unconstant and uneven. And that I may conclude with Hopewell and Maidenhead, I would say, that Jesus Christ has gathered for himself a blessed flock there; and however they may be vilified and scorned by those who have their portion in this life, yet I hope no less but that they are precious with God, and shall be satisfied with the pleasures of his right hand for evermore. Amen.'

After some time, Mr. Rowland removed from New Jersey into Pennsylvania, where he had charge of a congregation in what is called 'the Great Valley,' and also of Providence, near to Norristown. Much of his time, however, seems to have been spent in itinerating and preaching from place to place during the great awakening with which the churches were then visited.

The only account which we have of Mr. Rowland's labours and success in Pennsylvania is given by himself in his narrative sent to Mr. Prince.

'In the year 174–,' says he, 'I came and lived in Charlestown, Pennsylvania, and have continued according to the order of the Presbytery, preaching among them, and the people of New Providence. But as my ministry has been chiefly successful at the latter place since I came into these parts, I shall only speak of what I have observed of the work of God in New Providence.

'The people of this place before I came were but an ignorant sort of people, unacquainted with religion, both as to principle and practice; and though they would pretend, some to be of one denomination, and some of another, yet a vain name was all. Looseness prevailed much in the place, and there was not one to speak to another in a suitable manner, neither of the vileness, deformity, and unprofitableness of the ways of sin, nor of the glory and excellency and profitableness of the ways of God. I know not that any of them observed family prayer, or even asked a blessing on their food. This was the case among them, as they told me at several times, and again since I began to write this narrative. The conviction and conversion of the people of New Providence occurred within about two months of one another. It was the time of my travelling among them that the Lord chose to bless for their ingathering to Jesus Christ; and since I have laboured statedly among them, it has been as much my endeavour to build up those who were called into the fellowship of God as to convince sinners of their misery, and to this end my labours were blessed again among them throughout the year 174–. As to their conviction and conversion unto God, I may say, they are capable to give a scriptural account of these things. I forbear to speak of many extraordinary appearances, such as some scores crying out at one instant, and of others falling down and fainting.

'These people are still increasing, and blessed be the Lord, they are endeavouring to walk in communion with God, and with one another. And for this end, they meet in society, in the meeting house, two or three hours at a time, for prayer and praise; and they find this an excellent means to prepare them for the holy Sabbath. They are careful to maintain the worship of God in their families, and to use all agreeable [proper] means to increase their own knowledge in the things of God.

'I choose to say no more, though I may truly say that what I have spoken of the glorious work of God in this place, and in the towns of Amwell, Hopewell, and Maidenhead, is but a very little to what I might have said.'

There is one circumstance connected with this revival in New Providence which in a peculiar manner interests the writer. His own grandfather and grandmother, then residing on the Schuylkill above Norristown, were subjects of this revival, and members of this church, although they were awakened under the preaching of Mr. Whitefield, at White Clay Creek.

Though Mr. Rowland filled a considerable space in the church while he lived, as he was a Boanerges in denouncing the terrors of the law against impenitent sinners, insomuch that he acquired among the irreligious the title so often given to faithful preachers, 'the hell-fire Rowland,' yet no word or memorial of the close of his life remains. He seems not to have been married, and to have died early.

Here we may remark that none of the distinguished ministers of that period, except William Tennent, sen., reached the age of seventy; and some of the most able and successful among them did not even arrive at the age of forty. Among these we reckon Samuel Blair, Samuel Davies, Wm. Robinson, and John Rowland. These men may be said to have lived fast. They did much for their Lord in a short time. Being burning as well as shining lights, they were themselves consumed while they gave light to others. Oh that a race of ministers, like-minded, burning with a consuming zeal, might be raised up among us!

XIX

Memoir of the Rev. Charles Beatty

Rev. Charles Beatty—Birth and education—Acts as a pedlar—Converses
in Latin with the Founder of the Log College—Becomes a student in
the Institution—Is licensed to preach—Settles at Neshaminy—A missionary to the Indians—An agent for the Widows' Fund—For the
College of New Jersey—Goes to Barbadoes and dies there—Mr. Treat.

The Rev. Charles Beatty was another of the pupils of the Log
College whose name should be rescued from oblivion.

Mr. Beatty was a native of the north of Ireland, where he had
enjoyed the privilege of a pretty good classical education, but
being of an adventurous and enterprising spirit, when quite
young he determined to emigrate from the land of his nativity, and
seek his fortune in America. Being destitute of property, he adopted
the plan of making his living in the capacity of a pedlar or travelling
merchant. One day, in the prosecution of his business he called at
the Log College, and astonished Mr. Tennent, the principal, by
addressing him in correct Latin, and appeared to be familiar with
that language. After much conversation, in which Mr. Beatty
manifested fervent piety, and considerable religious knowledge,
as well as a good education in other respects, Mr. Tennent said to
him, 'Go and sell the contents of your pack, and return immediately
and study with me. It will be a sin for you to continue a pedlar,
when you can be so much more useful in another profession.'
He accepted Mr. Tennent's offer, and in due time became an
eminent minister. This account is no doubt authentic, as it is taken
from Dr. Miller's 'Life of Dr. Rodgers,' who had long been
intimately acquainted with Mr. Beatty.

After Mr. Beatty had finished his studies at the Log College,
he was licensed to preach the gospel by the Presbytery of New
Brunswick; and in a short time afterwards, was settled as pastor
of the church at Neshaminy, left vacant by the death of the
venerable founder of the Log College. About this time, in con-

sequence of the publication of Brainerd's journal of missionary labours among the Indians, a missionary spirit seems to have been enkindled among the ministers of the Presbyterian church in connection with the Synod of New York and New Jersey. Under this influence, both Mr. Beatty of Neshaminy and Mr. Treat of Abington left their congregations, and went on a mission to the Indians. In Allen's 'American Biographical Dictionary, it is stated that Mr. Beatty was engaged in missionary work from 1740 to 1765, a period of twenty-five years. This must be a great mistake; Mr. Beatty was not in the ministry so early as 1740, and his service as a missionary did not continue one-sixth of the time specified.[1]

Mr. Beatty was an able, evangelical preacher, and was much esteemed for his private virtues and public labours. He seems to have possessed much of a public spirit, and a popular address; for he was twice employed as an agent, first in behalf of the Widows' Fund, established for the benefit of the families of poor Presbyterian ministers. This agency was performed by the appointment of the Synod, and occurred about the year 1761, so that he could not then have been on a mission to the Indians. Afterwards he was appointed to collect funds for New Jersey College, and in pursuance of this object he went to the island of Barbadoes, where he was taken sick, and died on the 13th of August, 1772. He had been appointed a trustee of the College in 1763, and continued its ardent friend until the day of his death; and indeed, he sacrificed his life in endeavouring to promote its prosperity.

It appears from the college records, that Dr. Witherspoon himself had been appointed to visit the West Indies to collect funds for the college, but finding it inconvenient to go he recommended his son, James Witherspoon, to the Board; upon which this gentleman was commissioned, and also the Rev. Charles Beatty to accompany him. The death of Mr. Beatty frustrated the scheme, as upon his death Mr. Witherspoon returned home. In regard to Mr. Beatty's death, the only thing on record in the minutes of the trustees, in whose service he was employed, is the following, viz: 'It appearing that Mr. Edward Ireland, in Barbadoes, had showed particular kindness to Mr. Beatty, ordered that W. P. Smith, Esq., write a letter of thanks to him in the name of the Board.'

[1] See Appendix IV.

As Mr. Treat, minister of Abington, though not educated at the Log College, was closely associated with the members of the New Brunswick Presbytery, and sympathized with them in all their measures, and was one of those cast out by the protest of the majority of the members of the Synod of Philadelphia, it may be proper to say of him that he was highly esteemed as a preacher and as a man, and was an active and zealous promoter of the revival. He and Mr. Beatty were neighbours in their fields of labour, and were men of a like spirit. They both went as missionaries to the Indians, and were devotedly attached to the Rev. David Brainerd; an evidence of which we have recorded in his journal. When they understood that he was about to leave the work on account of increasing ill-health, they travelled all the way to Princeton to see him before he left New Jersey.

Mr. Treat is mentioned by Mr. Whitefield in his journal as a minister who had been preaching several years without any acquaintance with experimental religion, but was brought under deep concern for his soul by hearing Mr. Whitefield preach. And having, as he believed, experienced at this time a change of heart, he became very zealous in preaching the doctrines of grace, and warning professors against the delusion of resting on a mere form of religion.

Appendix I

MR. WILLIAM TENNENT'S LETTER

February 27, 1757.

'MY DEAR BROTHER:—Yours of the 14th of January I received last night. It was precious to me, as it seemed to inflame an affection which I trust shall continue throughout eternity. How sweet is love to the brethren! How refreshing to feel that what we have is no further our own than as it serves to glorify God and benefit his people! I never questioned, though I wondered at your regard for me. But to pass to something of greater importance. I went to college last Monday, having heard that God had begun a work of the Spirit there, and saw as astonishing a display of God's power and grace as I ever beheld or heard of in the conviction of sinners. Not one member in the house missed it in a greater or lesser degree. The whole house was a Bochim. A sense of God's holiness was so impressed on the hearts of its inhabitants that there were only two who were esteemed to be religious, that I know of, whose hopes were not greatly shaken. The glorious ray reached the Latin school, and much affected the master and a number of the scholars. Nor was it confined to the students only; some others were awakened. I spoke with all the members personally, except one that I providentially found, the most of whom inquired with anxious solicitude what they should do to be saved, according to the example of the trembling jailor. . . . I never saw any in that case who had more clear views of God, themselves, their duty, defects, their impotence and misery, than they had in general. Every room had mourning inhabitants; their *studies* witnessed to their prayers. You will want to know how they behaved. I answer, as solemn mourners at the funeral of a dear friend. It pleased the Lord so to order it that there were no public outcries. I believe there never was in any house more genuine sorrow for sin and longing for Jesus. The work so far exceeded my most enlarged expectations that I was lost in surprise, and constrained

P

often to say, "Is it so? Can it be true?" Nor is my being eye and ear witness from Monday to Friday at two o'clock, able to recover me from my astonishment. I felt as the apostles when it was told them the Lord had risen. They could not believe through fear and great joy. Surely the good, the great Jehovah is wise in counsel and wonderful in working. I can truly say that my reverend brethren and myself felt no small degree of that pleasing surprise that possessed the Israelities in their return from the Babylonish captivity, mentioned in Psalm 126: "When the Lord turned again the captivity of Zion, we were like them that dream. The Lord hath done great things for us, whereof we are glad."

'This glorious work was gradual, like the increasing light of the morning. It was not begun by the ordinary means of preaching nor have any alarming methods been used to promote this religious concern, yet so great was the distress that I did not think proper to use any arguments of terror in public, lest some should sink under the weight of their distress. Notwithstanding, I found by conversing with them that a wise and gracious Providence had brought about a concurrence of different incidents, which tended to engage them to a serious thoughtfulness about their souls. These things considered in connection, I humbly conceive, manifest singularly the finger of God, the freeness of which grace will equally appear by considering that a little before this gracious, never-to-be-forgotten visitation, some of the youth had given a greater loose to their corruptions than was common among them—a spirit of pride and contention, to the great grief and almost discouragement of the worthy President. There was little or no motion of the passions in the preachers during their public performances, nor any public discourses in the hours allotted for study, but at the morning and evening prayers, and these brief, consisting of plain scriptural directions, proper to persons under spiritual trouble. The President never shone in my eyes as he does now. His good judgment and humility, his zeal and integrity greatly endeared him to me. Before I came away, several received something like the spirit of adoption, being tenderly affected with a sense of redeeming love, and thereby disposed and determined to endeavour after holiness in all things.

'I cannot fully represent the glorious work. It will bear your most enlarged apprehensions of a work of grace. Let God have all the glory. My poor children, through free grace, partook of the shower of blessing. Eternally praised be my God and Father, who has herein pitied the low estate of his most mean and worthless servant, in graciously granting me my desire. This to me is a tree of life; yea, it is to my soul as if I had seen the face of God. I left them in distress. They are in the hands of a gracious God, to whom I have long since devoted them with all my heart and soul. Seeing you desire to know their names, they are John and William. Perhaps a few lines from you, dear brother, might be blessed to them. Praying our sincerest affection to Mrs. Finley, I greatly need your prayers, that I may be thankful and faithful unto death.

I am yours,

'WM., TENNENT, JR.'

Appendix II

THE REV. WILLIAM TENNENT'S LETTER

The Rev. William Tennent's Letter to the Rev. Mr. Prince, of Boston, giving the character of the revival at Freehold, N.J.

The following letter gives an interesting account of the fruits of the ministry of the Rev. John Tennent. It is taken from Prince's Christian History.

Freehold, October 11th, 1744.

'REV. AND DEAR SIR—I desire to notice thankfully the late rich display of our glorious Emmanuel's grace, in subduing by his word and Spirit multitudes of sinners to himself, both in this and other lands. O may he go on "conquering and to conquer," until he has subdued all things unto himself! Neither can I think but that the writing of a history of the great things our Lord has done among us has a tendency to, and will, by the blessing of God upon it, excite generations yet unborn to praise his glorious name, and thereby his honour will be advanced and his triumphs increased. Most gladly, therefore, do I comply with your request, and herewith send such an account as I can of what the Lord has done among us. But herein, as I must be very general, having never made any memorandum in writing of the Lord's work here, so I trust I shall be strictly true, for the Lord hates a false witness.

'This place lies southwest from New York, and is distant from it about fifty miles. It was the first in the East Jersey, on the west side of the Raritan river, which was settled with a gospel ministry. This was owing, under God, to the agency of some Scotch people that came to it; among whom there was none so painful in this blessed undertaking as one Walter Ker, who, in the year 1685, for his faithful and conscientious adherence to God and his truth, as professed by the Church of Scotland, was there apprehended and sent to this country under a sentence of perpetual banishment.

By which it appears that the devil and his instruments lost their aim in sending him from home, where it is unlikely he could ever have been so serviceable to Christ's kingdom as he has been here. He is yet alive, and blessed be God he is flourishing in his old age, being in his 88th year.

'But to return; the public means of grace dispensed here were at first, for a season, too much like a miscarrying womb and dry breasts, so that the major part of the congregation could not be said to have so much as a name to live. Family prayer was unpractised by all, a very few excepted; ignorance so overshadowed their minds that the doctrine of the new birth, when clearly explained and powerfully pressed upon them as absolutely necessary to salvation (by that faithful preacher of God's word, Mr. Theodorus Jacobus Frelinghuysen, a Low Dutch minister, and some other English ministers who were occasionally here) was made a common game of; so that not only the preachers but professors of that truth were called in derision *newborn*, and looked upon as holders forth of some new and false doctrine. And, indeed, their practice was as bad as their principles, viz. loose and profane.

'In the year 1729, their minister removed from them, and they were so grievously divided among themselves that it appeared improbable they would ever agree in the settlement of another. In this miserable, helpless, and almost hopeless condition they lay, and few among them had either eyes to see or hearts to bewail their woeful, wretched circumstances. Thus they seemed to be cast out, as the prophet Ezekiel represents it in the 16th chapter of his book, and 5th verse. But the Lord, who is rich in mercy, of his unexpected and unmerited love passed by them lying in their blood, and said unto many of them since that day, *Live:* and live they shall to all eternity.

'About this time, my dear brother John (who is now with Jesus) was licensed as a candidate for the sacred ministry, a youth whom the Author of every good gift had uncommonly furnished for that important trust. To him application was made by some of the congregation, entreating that he would supply them for a time, to which, with the leave of the Presbytery, he consented. But ere he went, he often told me that he was heartily sorry he had engaged to go among them, for it seemed to him that they were a people whom God had given up for their abuse of the gospel. But the Lord's thoughts are not our thoughts, nor his ways our ways, for

when he had preached four or five Sabbaths in the place, which
was the whole time he tarried among them at first, the Lord so
blessed his labours, engaging people to attend to the things which
were spoken, and in stirring them up to search the Scriptures
whether these things were so or not, and withal enabling him to
preach to them with such uncommon freedom and earnestness,
that he told me he was fully persuaded Christ Jesus had a large
harvest to bring home there; so that, though they were a poor
broken people, yet if they called him he would settle among them,
albeit he should be put to beg his bread by so doing. April the
15th, 1730, the congregation unanimously called him; which he
accepting of, was ordained the 19th of November following, and
continued with them until April 23rd, 1732, and was then
translated to glory.

'During this short time his labours were greatly blessed, so that
the place of public worship was usually crowded with people of
all ranks and orders as well as professions that obtained in that
part of the country, and they seemed to hear generally as for their
lives; yea, such as were wont to go to those places for their
diversion, viz. to hear news or speak to their tradesmen, &c., even
on the Lord's day, as they themselves have since confessed, were
taken in the gospel net. A solemn awe of God's majesty possessed
many, so that they behaved themselves as at his bar while in his
house. Many tears were usually shed when he preached, and sometimes the body of the congregation was moved or affected. I can
say, and let the Lord alone have the glory of it, that I have seen
both minister and people wet with their tears, as with a bedewing
rain. It was no uncommon thing to see persons in the time of hearing,
sobbing as if their hearts would break, but without any public
outcry, and some have been carried out of the assembly (being
overcome) as if they had been dead.

'Religion was then the general subject of discourse, though they
did not all approve the power of it. The holy Bible was searched
by people on both sides of the question, and knowledge surprisingly
increased. The terror of God fell generally upon the inhabitants
of this place, so that wickedness as ashamed in a great measure
hid itself; frolicking, dancing, horse-racing, with other profane
meetings, were broken up. Some of the jolly companions of both
sexes were constrained by their consciences to meet together, the
men by themselves, and the women by themselves, to confess

privately their abominations before God, and beg the pardon of them.

'Before my brother's death, by reason of his bodily weakness and inability on that account to officiate publicly, I preached here about six months; in which time many came inquiring what they should do to be saved, and some to tell what the Lord had done for their souls. But the blessing on his labours to the conviction and conversion of souls was more discernible some months after his death than at any time in his life. Almost in every neighbourhood, I cannot say in every house, there were sin-sick souls longing for and seeking after the dear physician, Jesus Christ; several of whom, I no ways doubt, have since that time sincerely closed with him, and are healed; glory, glory to his holy name be given, for ever and ever, Amen!

'Some time after my brother's decease, the congregation called me to labour among them statedly, which I accepted, and was ordained October 25th, 1733. Thus my Lord sent me to reap that on which I had bestowed but little labour. May this consideration be blessed to make me thankful and humble while I live.

'I must further declare, to the honour of God, that he has not yet left us, although awfully provoked by our crying crimes; but ever since that more remarkable outpouring of his Spirit has continued to bless his own ordinances, to the conviction, conversion and consolation of precious souls, so that every year some, more or less, have been in a judgment of charity added (savingly) to his mystical body; to his holy name be all the glory. In the meantime, I would have it observed, that two or three years last past have afforded fewer instances of this kind than formerly. However, through grace some have been lately awakened who are even now seeking Jesus sorrowing. What the number is of those who have tasted the sweet fruits of the Redeemer's purchase in a saving manner, in this congregation, I cannot tell. It is my comfort that the Lord will reckon them, for he knows who are his; and indeed none but the omniscient God is equal to the difficult province of determining certainly concerning the internal states of men. Yet I may be bold to say that to all appearance, both old and young, males and females, have been renewed, though none so young as I have heard of in some other places. Some negroes, I trust, are made free in Christ, and more seem to be unfeignedly seeking after it. But after all that the Lord has been pleased to do among us, I am persuaded that the greater number by far are yet in the gall of bitterness and bond of iniquity. This makes me sometimes ready to wish that I had in the wilderness the lodging-place of a wayfaring man, that I might leave my people and go from them; or rather that my head were waters, and mine eyes a fountain of tears, that I might weep day and night for them! Such as have been converted were every one of them prepared for it by a sharp law-work of conviction, discovering to them in a heart-affecting manner their sinfulness both by nature and practice, as well as their liableness to damnation for their original and actual transgressions. Neither could they see any way in themselves by which they could escape the Divine vengeance, for that their whole life past was not only a continued act of rebellion against God, but their present endeavours to better it, such as prayers, &c., were so imperfect that they could not endure them, and much less they concluded would a holy God. They all confessed the justice of God in their eternal perdition, and thus have been shut up to the blessed necessity of seeking relief by faith in Christ alone. It would be endless to mention the evils they complained of, viz., ignorance, unbelief, hardness of heart, hatred against God, his laws and people, worldliness, wandering of heart in duty, pride, sensuality, sloth, &c. With what grief, shame, and self-loathing have I heard them bewail their loss of time and neglect of the great gospel salvation. Those that were communicants before their awakening have with trembling declared that their unworthy partaking grieved them more than anything ever they did, for hereby they had as it were murdered the Lord. It is almost incredible to relate the indignation that such awakened sinners expressed against themselves, on the account of their sinfulness. They looked upon themselves to be mere monsters of nature, and that none were worse, if any so bad. Others signified that they could not find their pictures out of hell, and that they were just fit companions for the damned, and none else. Let it be here noted that some who have expressed themselves in the manner I have mentioned were before taken for believers both by themselves and others, being sober and regular in their walk.

'The sorrows of the convinced were not all alike, either in degree or continuance. Some have not thought it possible for them to be saved if God would vindicate the honour of his justice; but these thoughts continued not long at a time, blessed be God. Others thought it was possible, but not very probable, because of their vileness. The greatest degree of hope which any had under a conviction that issued well was a may-be; 'peradventure, or may-be, God will have mercy on me.' said the sinner. Some, in coming to Jesus, have been much rent with blasphemous and other horrible temptations, which have turned their moisture into the drought of summer, who now through pure grace serve God without such distractions in gladness and singleness of heart. The conviction of some has been instantaneous; by the Holy Spirit's applying the law to the conscience, and discovering to the eye of the understanding, as it were, all their heart deceits very speedily, by which they have been stabbed as with a sword. But the conviction of others has been in a more progressive way. They have had discovered to them one abomination after another in life, and from thence were led to behold the fountain of all corruption in the heart; and thus they were constrained to despair of life by the law, and consequently to flee to Jesus as the only door of hope, and so rest entirely on his merit for salvation.

'After the aforesaid sorrowful exercises, such as were reconciled to God have been blessed with the Spirit of adoption, enabling them to cry Abba, Father. But some have had greater degrees of consolation than others, in proportion to the clearness of the evidences of their sonship. The Lord has drawn some out of the horrible pit of distress and darkness, and brought them into the light of his countenance. He has filled their hearts with joy, and their mouths with praises; yea, given them the full assurance of faith. Others have been brought to peace in believing, but have not had so great a *plerophory* of joy, yet they go on in a religious course, trusting in the Lord. The way they have been comforted is either by the application of some particular promise of holy Scripture, or by a soul-affecting view of the way of salvation by Christ, as free, without money and without price. They were enabled to behold the valuable mercies of the covenant of grace, freely tendered to the vilest transgressors, that were poor in their own eyes, sin-sick, weary and wounded, together with the ability and willingness of the Lord Jesus to relieve them from all the evils they either feared or felt. With this way of salvation their souls were well pleased, and thereupon have ventured their case into his hands, expecting help from him only who has given them both peace and rest; yea, filled some of them with joy unspeakable and full of glory. I remember not of any that received their first comforts otherwise. Some few have retained their confidence in God ever since, without any considerable questionings of their state, although they have not always tasted the comforts of it. But the most by far have questioned all, and doubted it was a delusion. This I suppose is generally owing to the remains of corruption, which blot the evidences of grace in good men, so that they can hardly read them, and particularly to the awful sin of unbelief; together with the prevalence of a legal spirit, which presses them to perfect holiness on pain of death, and because they cannot obtain that, they conclude they are unsanctified and have no right to Christ. I might add the ignorance of sanctification; they seem to think that in the justified sin is killed in its being as well as governing power; and therefore, because they feel their old sins sometimes stirring in them, they conclude that all is wrong; nay, although they hate the doctrine of perfection as held by some, yet because they are not perfect they think they have no grace. But however distressing it is to them to feel their imperfections, it helps to persuade me that they are regenerate, else it would not be so; sin would not be their chief burden in a general way.

'However, our Lord, who comforts those that are cast down, even the Wonderful Counsellor, teaches them that he not only saves those who have been sinners before conversion, but even such as after it find a law in their members warring against the law of their minds, which too often causes them to do the things they would not; and enables them to reflect upon what they have and do daily experience, and compare it with the evidences of grace in the word of God. The blessed God does likewise give them renewed tastes of his love, even after mis-steps; and thus they are established in faith and hope, so that they have a prevailing persuasion of their interest in Christ, except it be in times of desertion and temptation, with which some are more exercised than others, for reasons best known to a sovereign God.

'Doubtless, sir, you will desire to know what effects this work produces on the minds and manners of its subjects. I answer, they are not only made to know, but heartily to approve of the great doctrines of the gospel, which they were before either ignorant of or averse to (at least some of them), so that they do harmonize sweetly in exalting free, special, and sovereign grace, through the

Redeemer Jesus Christ, being willing to glory only in the Lord,
who has loved them and given himself for them, an offering and a
sacrifice of a sweet-smelling savour.

'I cannot express with what satisfaction I have heard them speak
of the new covenant method of salvation. They have spoken
with such affection and clearness as I have thought was sufficient
to convince an atheist that the Lord was their teacher. The alteration in some, from almost gross ignorance to such clear gospel
light, and in others from such corrupt principles as the Papists
and Quakers hold, to the believing acknowledgment of the truth,
none but he that made the understanding could effect. They
approve of the law of God after the inward man as holy, just and
good, and prize it above gold, yea, much fine gold. They judge it
their duty as well as privilege to wait on God in all the ordinances
of his own institution, although they expect to merit nothing
thereby. A reverence for God's commanding authority and
gratitude for his love conspire to incite and constrain them to a
willing, unfeigned, universal and unfainting obedience to his
laws; yet they declare that in everything they come sadly short of
what they ought to do, and bitterly bewail their defects. But
blessed be God, they are not discouraged in their endeavours to
reach forward, if by any means they may apprehend that for
which they are apprehended of God; and in all things they
acknowledge that they ought to look to Jesus as the author and
finisher of faith, whose alone it is to work all good in them and for
them, to whom be glory for ever. They are not unmolested in their
way by enemies, both from within and from without. Yet they
profess that the comforts which they receive do more than com-
pensate all their labour, were there no good to be expected hereafter; and surely, as the psalmist observes, "in keeping God's
commands there is a great reward." But to proceed:

'They have not all made a like proficiency in the Christian
course, neither are they all equal in religious endeavours, nor
are they at all times alike lively. They are sometimes obstructed in
their religious progress by coldness and deadness; but this the
blessed Jesus removes at times by the influence of his Holy Spirit;
then, O then, their hearts are enlarged, and they run the sweet
way of God's commandments with alacrity and delight; they love
all such as they have reason to think from their principles,
experience and practice are truly godly, though they differ from

them in sentiment in lesser things, and look on them to be the excellent of the earth. They rejoice in Zion's prosperity, glorifying God on that account, and feel a sympathy in her sorrows. They do prefer one another before themselves in love, except under temptation, which they are ready to confess and bewail, when they are themselves generally accounting that they are the meanest of the family of God, and unworthy of the blessing; yea, the most so of any living, all things considered. In a word the sapless formalist is become spiritual in his conversation; the proud and haughty are made humble and affable; the wanton and vile, sober and temperate; the swearer honours that venerable name he was wont to profane, and blesses instead of curses; the sabbath-breaker is brought to be a strict observer of holy time; the worldling now seeks treasures in the heavens; the extortioner now deals justly, and the formerly malicious forgives injuries; the prayerless are earnest and incessant in acts of devotion, and the sneaking self-seeker endeavours the advancement of God's glory and the salvation of immortal souls.

'Through God's mercy we have been quite free from enthusiasm; our people have followed the holy law of God, the sure word of prophecy, and not the impulses of their own minds. There have not been that I know of among us any visions, except such as are by faith, namely, clear and affecting views of the new and living way to the Father through his dear Son Jesus Christ; nor any revelations but what have been long since written in the sacred volume; nor any trances but such as all men now living shall meet with, for it is appointed for all men once to die.

'It may not be amiss to inform you that many who have been awakened, and seemed for a time to set out for Zion are turned back. Yea, of those who have been esteemed converts, some have made shipwreck of faith and a good conscience; though, glory to God, there have not been many such, yet some of them who have thus awfully apostatized were highly esteemed in the church. By this, our good and gracious God has given check to too high an esteem of our own judgment concerning the spiritual states of others (an evil which is too common among young converts) and awfully warned all that stand to take heed lest they fall. Many, I have cause to fear, have been hardened in their impieties and unreasonable prejudices against vital religion by the backslidings of some professors. "Woe to the world, because of offences!"

But in the mean time, blessed be God, wisdom is and will be justified of her children.

'This sir, is as particular an account as I can at present give of the Lord's work in this place. If my Lord will accept it as a testimony for him, it will be a greater honour than ever I deserved. I need your prayers, and earnestly desire them. O beg of God that I may be faithful to the death, and wise to win souls. I am with all due respects, yours in the dearest Jesus,

WM. TENNENT.'

'ATTESTATION *to the preceding Account by the Ruling Elders and Deacons of the Congregation of Freehold.*

'We the subscribers, Ruling Elders and Deacons of the Presbyterian congregation of Freehold, having had perfect knowledge of the circumstances of this place, some of us from the first settling of it, and others of a long time, do give our testimony to the truth in general of the above letter of our Rev. pastor. May the Lord make the same of use for the carrying on his glorious work begun in these lands, and make the name of the dearest Jesus glorious from the rising to the setting sun.

WALTER KER,	ROBERT CUMMING,
DAVID RHEA,	JOHN HENDERSON,
WILLIAM KER,	SAMUEL KER.

Freehold, in New Jersey, October 11th, 1744.'

Appendix III

MR. DICKINSON'S LETTER

ADDRESSED TO THE REV. MR. FOXCROFT, OF LONDON

'Elizabethtown, Aug. 23rd, 1743.

'In these towns, religion was in a very low state; professors generally lifeless, and the body of our people careless, carnal and secure, till some time in August, 1739, the summer before Mr. Whitefield came first into these parts, when there was a remarkable revival at Newark, especially among the rising generation, many of whom were now brought under convictions, and instead of frequenting vain company as usual, were flocking to their minister with that important inquiry, 'What shall we do to be saved?' This concern increased for a considerable time among the young (though not wholly confined to them), and in November, December and January following it, became more remarkable as well as more general. There was an apparent reformation among the youth of the town; their customary tavern-haunting, frolicking, and other youthful extravagancies were now laid aside; a new face of things appeared in the town; all occasions of religious conversation were improved with delight; a seriousness, solemnity, and devout attention appeared in their public assemblies, and a solemn concern about their eternal welfare was visible in the very countenances of many. This revival of religion was chiefly observable among the younger people till the following March, when the whole town in general was brought under an uncommon concern about their eternal interests, and the congregation appeared universally affected under some sermons that were then preached to them; and there is good reason to conclude that there was a considerable number who experienced a saving change about that time. The summer following, this awakening concern sensibly abated, though it did not wholly die away; and nothing remarkable occurred till February, 1740–41, when they were again visited with the special and manifest effusions of the Spirit of God. A plain, familiar sermon then preached, without any peculiar terror, fervour, or affectionate manner of address, was set home with power. Many were brought to see and feel that till then they had no more than a name to live; and professors in general were put upon serious and solemn inquiries into the foundation of their hope. There seemed to be very few in the whole congregation but who felt more or less the power of God at this happy season, though the greatest concern now appeared among the rising generation. There is good reason to conclude that there were a greater number now brought home to Christ than in the former gracious visitation. It was remarkable at this season that as sinners were generally under an awakening, distressing sense of their guilt and danger, so the children of God were greatly refreshed and comforted; their souls were magnifying the Lord, and rejoicing in God their Saviour, while others, in distressing agony, were crying out, "Men and brethren, what shall we do?"

'In the summer following, this religious concern sensibly decayed; though the sincere converts now held fast their profession without wavering, yet there were too many who had been under convictions that grew careless and secure; and all endeavours proved ineffectual to give new life to their former solicitude about their eternal welfare. What seemed greatly to contribute to this (now growing) security among these was the pride, false and rash zeal, and censoriousness, which appeared among some few at this time who made high pretences to religion. This opened the mouths of many against the whole work, and raised that opposition which was not before heard of; almost every body seeming to acknowledge the finger of God in these wonderful appearances, till this handle was given to their opposition. And the dreadful scandals of Mr. C——, which came to light about this time, proved a means to still further harden many in their declension and apostasy. That unhappy gentleman having made so high pretensions to extraordinary piety and zeal, his scandals gave the deeper wound to vital and experimental godliness. Thus, sir, I have faithfully given you a narrative, in some brief and general hints, of the late revival of religion at Newark, and shall now proceed to give you a brief view of the like manifestations of the Divine grace at Elizabethtown.

'The Rev. Mr. Whitefield preached a sermon here in the fall of the year 1739 to a numerous and attentive auditory; but I could observe no further influence upon our people by that address than a general thoughtfulness about religion, and a promptitude to make the extraordinary zeal and diligence of that gentleman the common and turning topic of their conversation. I do not know that there was any one person brought under conviction, or any new and special concern about their salvation by that sermon; nor more than one by any endeavours that were used with them that fall, or the succeeding winter. Though there was such a shaking among the dry bones so near to us as is above represented, and we had continual accounts from Newark of the growing distress among their people (their young people especially), our congregation remained yet secure and careless, and could not be awakened out of their sleep. You will easily conceive that this must needs be an afflicting and discouraging consideration to me; that when from other places we had the joyful news of so many flying to Christ as a cloud, and as doves to their windows, I had yet cause to complain that I laboured in vain and spent my strength for nought. But, notwithstanding all these discouraging appearances, I could not but entertain an uncommon concern, particularly for the young people of my charge, during that winter and the ensuing spring, which not only animated my addresses to the throne of grace on their behalf, but my endeavours to excite in them, if possible, some affecting sense of their misery, danger, and necessity of a Saviour. To that end, there were frequent lectures appointed for the young people in particular, but without any visible success until some time in June, 1740, when we had a remarkable manifestation of the Divine presence with us.

'Having at that time invited the young people to hear a sermon, there was a numerous congregation convened, which consisted chiefly of our youth, though there were many others with them. I preached to them a plain, practical sermon, without any special liveliness or vigour, for I was then in a remarkably dead and dull frame, till enlivened by a sudden and deep impression, which visibly appeared upon the congregation in general. There was no crying out or falling down, as elsewhere has happened, but the inward distress and concern of the audience discovered itself by their tears, and by an audible sobbing and sighing in almost all parts of the assembly. There appeared such tokens of a solemn and deep concern as I never before saw in any congregation whatsoever. From this time we heard no more of our young people's meeting together for frolics and extravagant diversions, as had been usual among them, but instead thereof private meetings for religious exercises were by them set up in several parts of the town. All our opportunities of public worship were carefully and constantly attended by our people in general, and a serious and solemn attention to the ministry of the word was observable in their very countenances. Numbers were almost daily repairing to me for assistance in their eternal concerns. There were then probably more came to me in one day on that errand than usually in half a year's space before.[1] In a word, the face of the congregation was quite altered, and religion became the common subject of conversation among a great part of the people.

'Though this work was begun among our young people, and the most of those with whom we have reason to conclude it became effectual were of the younger sort, yet there were some who lived a careless and sensual life to an advanced age who were under convictions, and I hope savingly brought home to Christ at this blessed time of the effusion of his Holy Spirit. Though there were so many brought under conviction at once, we had very little appearance of those irregular heats among us which are so loudly complained of in some other parts of the land. I do not remember to have heard of above two or three instances of any thing of that nature, in this congregation, and those were easily and speedily regulated. It is observable that this work was substantially the same in all the different subjects of it, though some passed through much greater degrees of distress and terror than others; and this distress lasted much longer with some than with others, and yet all were brought under a deep sense of their sin, guilt, and danger, and none that I know of obtained satisfying discoveries of safety in Christ, till they were first brought to despair of help from themselves or any of their own refuges, and to see and feel that they lay at mercy.

'We had no instances among us of such sudden conversions as I

[1] 'Agreeable to this, the Rev. Mr. Dickinson, in another letter, written about that time to the Rev. Mr. Foxcroft, viz: September 4th, 1740, has these remarkable passages: 'I have still the comfortable news to inform you of, that there is yet a great revival of religion in these parts. I have had more young people address me for direction in their spiritual concerns within these three months than in thirty years before." '

Q

have heard of elsewhere; but our new converts were all for a considerable time under a law work before they were brought to any satisfying views of their interest in Christ and the favour of God. Nor had we many instances of those ecstatic, rapturous joys that were so frequent in some other places. It was remarkable that they who were formerly eminent for religion were now quickened and revived, and some of them had now such joyful manifestations of God's love to their souls as they had never before experienced. It was also remarkable that as this work began among us in a time of greatest health and prosperity, so the concern began sensibly to wear off in one of the greatest mortalities that had ever been known in the town, which makes it appear more evidently to be the work of God himself. Though there were some of those who were then under special convictions that have worn off their impressions and are become secure and careless, yet I do not know of any two persons who gave reasonable hopes of a real change at that time but who have hitherto by their conversation confirmed our hopes of their saving conversion to God.

'I would be very cautious of any confident determinations with respect to the conversion of particular persons; but if we may judge the tree by its fruits, which we have now had so long a time to observe, we have reason to suppose that near about sixty persons have received a saving change in this congregation only, and a number in the parish next adjoining to us, though I dare not pretend to guess how many since the beginning of this work. The general concern which, as I have observed, appeared upon the face of the congregation has gradually worn off, and a great part of those who came short of the effectual and saving influences of the blessed Spirit are returned to their former security and insensibility, and again appear like a valley of dry bones. Though there be yet a considerable number that do not give satisfying evidences of a regenerate state, who have not worn off their serious impressions.

'I entreat your prayers for us, that he with whom is the residue of the Spirit would again revive his work among us, and have compassion upon the many poor souls who are yet in the paths of destruction and death. And be pleased particularly to remember at the throne of grace.

Yours, &c.,
JONATHAN DICKINSON.'

Appendix IV

MR. BEATTY'S JOURNAL

The following account of a missionary tour of two months, in company with the Rev. George Duffield is taken from Mr. Beatty's Journal, published in London, in 1768. It was, probably, never published in this country. It consists of eighty-two pages.

'Being appointed by the Synod of New York and Philadelphia to visit the frontier inhabitants, and likewise to visit the Indians, in case it could be done with safety, to know whether they were inclined to receive the gospel, I set out on my journey, August 12th, 1766, accompanied by Joseph Peepy, a Christian Indian, as an interpreter. After arriving at Carlisle, Pennsylvania, I met with Mr. Duffield, who was appointed to accompany me.

On Monday, the 18th, after riding about six miles, we came to the North Mountain, which is high and steep. The day being warm, we were obliged to walk or rather climb it the greatest part of the way, so that then we reached the top we were much fatigued. After passing four miles into Sherman's Valley, we lodged at night at Thomas Ross's.

'*Tuesday* 19*th.*—Rode five miles, and preached to a small auditory, notice not having been generally spread. Lodged at Mr. Fergus's.

'*Wednesday* 20*th.*—Crossed the Tuscarora mountain, which is very high and difficult to pass. Preached after crossing the mountain to a few people who were convened, and lodged at the house of William Graham.

'*Thursday* 21*st.*—Mr. Duffield preached at a place where a house of worship had been commenced, but was discontinued on account of the war. In this valley of Tuscarora, thirty miles long and six or seven in breadth, we found that the inhabitants had suffered much from the invasion of the Indians. The number of families in the valley about thirty-four. Here we met with one

Levi Hicks, who had been a captive with the Indians from his youth. He gave us some interesting information respecting the situation of their towns, one hundred miles west of Fort Pitt.

'*Friday 22nd.*—Preached in the woods, as we have hitherto done, north side of the Juniata. Here also the people had begun to build a house of worship, but left it unfinished; probably for the same reason as the former. Lodged at Captain Patterson's, where we remained on the 23rd. Here we agreed to separate for a season; Mr. Duffield to go into Path Valley, and I along the Juniata.

'*Monday 25th.*—Set out early from Captain Patterson's, accompanied by our interpreter and Levi Hicks.

'*Tuesday 26th.*—Preached to a number of people in the woods; but the rain forced us to retreat into a small house.

'*Wednesday 27th.*—Baptized a child this morning brought to my lodgings; and preached to a small audience eight miles further on, and baptized several children, and lodged at John McMichael's.

'Mr. Duffield rejoined me on Friday the 29th. In Path Valley, twenty-three miles in length and about three in breadth, he preached to a large congregation on the Sabbath, and also preached on several folllowing days.

'*Sabbath 31st.*—Preached at Bedford; I in the morning, Mr. Duffield in the afternoon, to a large audience. Preached also on Monday.

'*Tuesday, Sept. 2nd.*—Crossed the Allegheny mountain; met with Benjamin Sutton, who had also been a captive many years among the Indians. He had lived among the Choctaws on the Mississippi. Told a long story about a wild tribe of Indians.

'Arrived at Fort Pitt on the 5th, and were kindly and courteously treated by the officers of the garrison, who furnished us with blankets and other necessaries. By invitation I preached to the garrison, while Mr. Duffield preached to the people of the town.

'Mr. Gibson, a trader who speaks the Indian language, introduced us to an Indian called the White Mingoe, the head man of his town. He is one of the Six Nations, and lives upon the Allegheny river, four miles from Fort Pitt. We explained the design of our mission, and he agreed to meet us with his people next day. But he never went home to notify them of the meeting.

'*Tuesday 9th.*—Having obtained all the information respecting the Indians which we could, and having sought divine direction, we set off for Kigalinphega, an Indian town, at the distance of one hundred and thirty miles. This place was fixed on because it was central to the other Indian towns, and because the king or head man of the Delawares lived there, whom it was necessary to consult before we attempted any thing among his people; and also because we were informed that the Indians there were thinking something about religion. Mr. Gibson furnished us with a letter and string of wampum to introduce us. In the afternoon Mr. Duffield preached to an attentive audience. We trust that our preaching here has not been in vain.

'*Wednesday* 10th.—While we were much occupied in preparing for our journey, a person came to us under deep impressions, inquiring what he should do to be saved. I gave him a book, but he insisted on my writing something for him, with which I complied.

'Joseph, our interpreter, embraced every opportunity of conversing with the Indians here. He met with one who appeared to be a sober man, and expressed much satisfaction at our going out to teach the Indians. We heard that this man and about nineteen others had separated themselves from the other Indians, and worshipped God in some way by themselves.

'The commanding officer, who was disposed to do everything in his power to favour our design, gave us a letter and a string of wampum to the Indian chiefs. We crossed the Allegheny river in a canoe, and swam our horses by the side of it, and rode down the bank of the Ohio. In the night there fell a heavy rain, which wet us much.

'*Friday* 12th.—The morning dark and heavy, with small rain. Our clothes being wet last night made our condition very uncomfortable. After travelling twelve miles we came to the second Beaver river, which we crossed, and proceeded six miles further to the third Beaver river, where we encamped, having but poor food for our horses. Joseph, our interpreter, who went on before to hunt for us, returned without anything, so that we had poor living for ourselves as well as our horses. However, we had some bread, for which we had reason to be thankful.

'*Saturday* 13th.—A heavy rain from the northwest came upon us before we had travelled far, from which we sheltered ourselves around under the trees.

'*Sabbath* 14th.—We rested on the Sabbath, and supposing this to be the first Sabbath ever kept in this wilderness, we gave the place of our encampment the name of Sabbath-Ridge.

'A number of Indians who had been trading at Fort Pitt came up with us, and wondered why we did not travel that Sunday. They had about one hundred *gallons of rum* with them. We explained the matter to them as well as we could.

'The weather clearing up about three o'clock, p.m., we decamped and set out with the Indians. Our interpreter, who had gone out to procure something for our subsistence, returned late in the morning with a young deer on his back, which we immediately divided; giving three quarters to the three companies of Indians who travelled with us, and reserved one quarter for ourselves. This was a seasonable supply for them, as well as for us.

'*Tuesday 16th.*—Entered more freely into conversation with the Indians, our fellow-travellers, and found them more sociable and communicative than before. Their chief man, especially, became more friendly when he found that we were not Moravians, against whom he had taken up a prejudice. On this day after crossing several streams and extensive savannahs, we arrived at Tuskalawa before night. Our fellow-traveller, the chief, now became very friendly, and invited us to his house, where we were treated with great respect and kindness. He brought us some green corn, which we roasted, and some cucumbers, which we ate without salt or any other condiment. Having preserved a small portion of the venison from the last night, we made some soup and gave part to our host and his family. Having prayed with the family, our interpreter explaining the nature of the service, we proceeded on our journey, and our kind host sent a young man seven or eight miles to show us the way. As we passed through the town we saw a number of Indians in a state of intoxication from the rum which they had brought from Fort Pitt, and when in this condition they appeared very terrible, and behaved as mad men.

'*Thursday 18th.*—Aftr travelling twenty miles through swamps and marshy grounds, we reached the town, at which we arrived about 3 o'clock, p.m. At the first house which we entered lived a widow woman, who was a near relative of our interpreter. They had not seen each other for many years, nor did he know that she lived here. Their meeting was attended with an agreeable surprise to both of them, which we could not but consider a token for good. The woman invited us to tarry with her, which kind offer we gladly accepted. She soon prepared for us a meal by cooking some venison, and baking some cakes under the ashes, according to their custom.

'We now sent notice of our arrival to the king or head man of the Delaware nation. In the mean time, our landlady furnished us with a little hut for ourselves, and spread some skins for our bed, which was far better than what we had been lately used to have.

'*Friday* 19*th*.—The king sent us word that he was ready to receive us. We went, accordingly, to the Council House. This house is a long building, with two fires in it, at a proper distance, without any chimney or partition. The entrance is by two doors, one at each end. Over the door was drawn the figure of a turtle, which is the ensign of the tribe. On each door was cut or engraved the face of an old man, an emblem of the wisdom and gravity becoming those who are senators. On each side was a platform or bed, fifteen feet wide, extending the whole length of the house. This served for sitting as well as sleeping, and was raised a foot or so above the floor, and was covered with a handsome mat made of rushes; on the end of this bed the king had his seat.

'As soon as we entered, the king rose from his seat (nothing unusual) and took us by the hand, and gave thanks to the great Being above, the Creator and Preserver of all, that we had opportunity of seeing each other in the wilderness, and appeared truly glad on the occasion. We were then conducted to a seat near his majesty; the council being seated on each side of the room. After sitting silent awhile, according to their custom, I arose, and by Joseph, our interpreter, delivered my speech. It is an invariable rule with the Indians, when they receive an address or speech, not to return an immediate answer, but to take time to deliberate.

'In the speech which I delivered, we gave them an account of the design of the Synod in commissioning us to visit them, with the view of ascertaining whether they were disposed to receive the Christian religion, and to have some ministers sent among them.

'In the evening an Indian and his sister, both advanced in years, came to our house. They had been in New Jersey in the time of the revival of religion among the Indians there, and had received some good impressions from the preaching of the Rev. David Brainerd. They afterwards joined the Moravians, but seemed to have in a great measure lost their serious impressions, but requested us to talk to them on the subject of religion, which we did through our interpreter. We also prayed with them, and on taking leave they seemed much affected.

'*Saturday*, 20*th.*—Five of the principal men came to our hut, and after sitting an hour in silence, they returned our string of wampum, saying they could not understand it. We told them we were sorry they had not understood, and would again explain it, which we accordingly did, and offered to return again the wampum. But they refused to receive it, saying their great man, that is their king, could not understand it, when they pulled out a string of wampum, of two single threads and one double, and proceeded to speak on the single threads, one of which was white, the other black and white. They spoke as follows:

' "Our dear brethren, what you have said we are very well pleased with, as far as we understand it. But dear brothers, when Wm. Johnson spoke with us some time ago, and made a peace which is to be strong and for ever, he told us not to regard what others might say to us; that the many people round about might be speaking of a great many things; yet we must look upon all these things as when a dog sleeps and dreams of something, or something disturbs him, and he rises hastily, and gives a bark or two, but does not know any thing, or any reason why he barks. Just so the people around may be saying some one thing, and some another, but they are not to be regarded."

'Again, on the double string they said "George Croghan spake to us that none should be regarded but what William Johnson and he should say to us." They then brought out and showed a belt of wampum of friendship, which Sir William Johnson had given them. The belt, they told us, he held by one end and they by the other, and when they had any thing to say they must go along the path marked on the belt. To this they added that they believed there was a great God above, and desired to serve him in the best manner they could; that they thought of him on lying down and rising up, and hoped he would look upon them and do them good.

'In the afternoon they sent us a belt of wampum and a speech, the purport of which was to invite the Indians of New Jersey, now under the care of the Rev. John Brainerd, to come and settle at Quiahoga, a town seventy miles west of this place, where, they said, they might have good hunting, and might bring a minister with them; and where all who wished to attend on the religious instruction might come together.

'As the next day was the Sabbath, we requested to know whether they would give us a hearing, to which they gave their assent, and exhorted us not to be discouraged at the delay of receiving a full answer to our proposals, as they always took time to deliberate. Accordingly, one of their chief men went around and gave notice at every house that we would preach to them at the council-house; and another of their counsellors came to our hut to conduct us to the place of meeting. A considerable number, both of men and women, attended; and I preached to them from the parable of the prodigal son (Luke 15). Good attention was paid, and the women appeared really to lay to heart what they heard. After sermon we sat awhile with them, and asked if it would be agreeable that we should speak to them again in the afternoon; they said it would.

'About three o'clock the people collected again, and Mr. Duffield preached to them from 1 Cor. 15. 22, in which he gave a plain narrative of all being dead in Adam, and that all believers would be made alive in Christ. The people appeared to be much engaged, and well pleased with what they heard. Our interpreter remained with them some time after the sermon, and brought us word that the king and chief man were desirous that we should speak again to them on the morrow, with which we were rejoiced.

'In the evening of this day, which was observed by the Indians like a Sabbath, several came to our hut and heard us explain many things contained in the Bible. Among them was a young man named Neolin, who for some time past had been in the habit of speaking to the Indians, and reproving them for their wicked ways, and was the means of reforming a number of them. The answer of this young man, when we inquired what put him in this practice, partakes of the marvellous. He said that six years ago a man came and stood in his door, and told him that all who followed bad ways would, after death, go to a miserable place, but those who hated evil and did what was right and pleasing to God would be taken to a happy place. We were informed by a trader who knows this man that one of the means of reformation adopted by him was boiling bitter roots and causing people to drink the decoction, which acted as an emetic, in order to cleanse them from their sins.

'Mr. Gibson had informed us that they had, in one of their towns, a woman who had been taken prisoner; and he had written a letter to the king requesting him to cause her to be restored to her friends, which he readily promised that he would do.

'In the afternoon the king and four chief men of the council came and delivered a formal speech, in which they acknowledged the evil of drunkenness, to which they were addicted, but said the blame did not entirely belong to them, but to the white men, who brought rum and sold it to them. They also complained of the conduct of the whites in other respects.

'In the evening, an old Indian, who had been with us before, came to our house, and informed us that there were many here and in other places who were desirous of hearing the gospel, and said they intended to go to Quiahaga, and send for a minister to come and live among them to instruct them. This day was so much taken up in important conferences with the chief men that no opportunity of preaching was afforded.

'*Tuesday 22nd.*—This day the head-men met in council, where we attended, and I preached to them from Luke 14. 16. In my discourse, I showed that there were rich provisions made in the gospel for poor sinners—the nature of these provisions, and why they were compared to a marriage feast—how men made excuses for not complying with the invitations by the ministers—and how some, by the grace of God were made willing—and then concluded with an exhortation to them to accept the gracious invitation.

'A solemn awe appeared on the face of the assembly. All seemed attentive to the things which were spoken, and some seemed affected. The interpreter was so much affected at times that he could scarcely speak; and, indeed, I must own that my own heart was warmed with the truths I delivered, and with the effect they seemed to have on these poor benighted heathen. Blessed be God! Let all the praise be to him! We have reason to hope not one opportunity enjoyed here has been in vain, and we trust that the good impressions which have been made will be permanent. May the Lord grant that our hopes may not be disappointed!''

Before the brethren departed, they delivered a solemn and interesting speech to the chiefs, which is recorded in Mr. Beatty's journal. This they accompanied agreeably to the Indian custom with a string of wampum, which the Indians received with apparent cordiality. To one who had learned to read a little while among the English they gave a Bible; to a woman a small book, entitled, 'A Compassionate Address to the Christian world.'

From every appearance a door seemed to be opened to introduce the gospel among these poor heathen. But the missionaries had now to return home, and we do not find that others followed them to improve the opportunity of usefulness now afforded.

SOME OTHER
BANNER OF TRUTH TRUST
PUBLICATIONS

Thoughts on Religious Experience

ARCHIBALD ALEXANDER

The nature of spiritual experience is probably both the most interesting and the most difficult subject in Christian literature: interesting because it concerns human life in all observable stages from childhood to death, and embracing all the emotions and behaviour possible in a man regenerated by the Holy Spirit; difficult because the adequate treatment of the subject makes immense demands upon an author. To trace accurately such experiences as conversion, sanctification and backsliding, as they appear in human consciousness, presupposes a sound biblical theology as well as spirituality of mind and a pastoral knowledge broad enough to interpret all the varieties in type which occur.

Twenty years a pastor and preacher in a revival era, then forty years a Professor at Princeton Theological Seminary (commenced in 1812 when he was the sole instructor), Archibald Alexander brought to this volume the best wisdom of his life. From his own observations, and from case histories drawn from Christian biography, he follows his subject with the hand of a master. He was, in Dr Theodore Woolsey's words, 'The Shakespeare of the Christian heart'. Primarily concerned with what ought to be the impress made upon life by scriptural truths he has nothing of the vague devotionalism of the religious mystics. But within this biblical context a wide variety of experiences pass under review, along with a consideration of the practical problems involved in an understanding of the new-birth, Christian growth, spiritual conflict and kindred subjects.

This lucid and fascinating volume, almost alone in the field which it covers, is commended to all readers.

368 *pages* 21*s*

The Confession of Faith

A. A. HODGE

The Confession of Faith, drawn up at Westminster in 1646 by over a hundred leading Puritan divines, presents one of the finest concise statements of the Christian Faith. It is the purpose of the author in this book to analyse the chapters and sections of that Confession, to give proofs and illustrations of its teaching and to assist the learner and teacher by a series of questions appended to each chapter. The result is a fine handbook of Christian doctrine providing in simple language an exposition and explanation of all the leading doctrines of Scripture. Professor Patton, of Princeton, referred to this volume as 'a very useful book, full of clear thinking and compact statements. It reveals Hodge's strong convictions, his power of analysis and his ability to make sharp and discriminating definitions.'

A. A. Hodge, the eminent son and successor of Charles Hodge, was finely equipped for this work. After three years' missionary work in India, and fourteen years as a pastor, he spent the remainder of his life teaching systematic theology in the theological seminaries at Allegheny (1864–1877) and Princeton (1877–1886). In this sphere he proved himself one of the greatest teachers that America has ever produced. Patton wrote of him: 'His thought and learning were those of a genius and a saint, and he occupies a unique position among his peers. He held the Reformed theology as a sacred trust. He defended it with zeal, taught it with enthusiasm, and reflected it in his life.'

430 pages 15s

Other Titles

A Body of Divinity Thomas Watson: 328 *pp*, 15*s*

The Christian Ministry Charles Bridges: 408 *pp*, 25*s*

The Christian in Complete Armour William Gurnall: 1200 *pp*, 35*s*

George Whitefield's Journals: illus., 596 *pp*, 25*s*

The Interpretation of Prophecy Patrick Fairbairn: 546 *pp*, 25*s*

John G. Paton: Missionary to the New Hebrides: 528 *pp*, 21*s*

Lectures on Revivals William B. Sprague: 470 *pp*, 15*s*

A Narrative of Surprising Conversions
Jonathan Edwards: 256 *pp*, 15*s*

The Office and Work of the Holy Spirit
James Buchanan: 296 *pp*, 21*s*

Robert Murray M'Cheyne: Memoir and Remains
Andrew A. Bonar: 660 *pp*, 25*s*

Simon Peter Hugh Martin: 160 *pp*, 12*s* 6*d*

Spurgeon: The Early Years: illus, 570 *pp*, 25*s*

The Ten Commandments Thomas Watson: 240 *pp*, 15*s*

The Works of John Owen: 16 volumes, approx 600 pp per
volume, 25*s* each

For free illustrated catalogue write to
THE BANNER OF TRUTH TRUST
78b Chiltern Street, London, W1, England